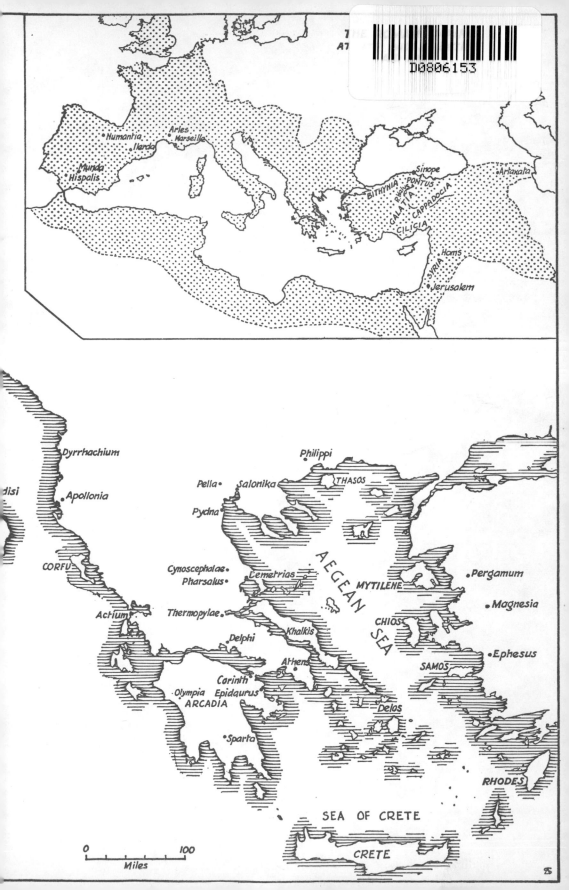

THE
AT...

D0806153

Numantia
Ilerda
Arles
Marseille
Munda
Hispalis

Sinope
BITHYNIA PONTUS
Rhine GALATIA CAPPADOCIA
CILICIA
Artaxata

Homs
SYRIA
Jerusalem

Dyrrhachium
Philippi
Pella
Salonika
THASOS
...disi
Apollonia
Pydna

CORFU
Cynoscephalae
Pharsalus
Demetrias
Pergamum
MYTILENE

AEGEAN SEA

Actium
Thermopylae
CHIOS
Magnesia

Delphi
Khalkis
Athens
SAMOS
Ephesus

Corinth
Olympia Epidaurus
ARCADIA
Delos

Sparta

RHODES

SEA OF CRETE

CRETE

0   100
Miles

Other Books by Stewart Perowne

THE ONE REMAINS

THE LIFE AND TIMES OF HEROD THE GREAT

THE LATER HERODS

HADRIAN

CAESARS AND SAINTS

THE END OF THE ROMAN WORLD

THE PILGRIM'S COMPANION IN ATHENS

THE PILGRIM'S COMPANION IN JERUSALEM

THE PILGRIM'S COMPANION IN ROME

JERUSALEM

DEATH OF THE
ROMAN REPUBLIC

DEATH OF THE ROMAN REPUBLIC

From 146 B.C. to the

Birth of the Roman Empire

STEWART PEROWNE

HODDER AND STOUGHTON

First printed in Great Britain 1969

SBN 340 10823 1

Reproduced from the U.S. edition by arrangement with
Doubleday & Company Inc.

Printed in Great Britain for Hodder and Stoughton Limited,
St. Paul's House, Warwick Lane, London, E.C.4.
by Compton Printing Limited, London and Aylesbury

To

ALEXANDER CAMERON SEDGWICK

and

fellow-members

of the

Phoenix-SK Club

CONTENTS

"Power tends to corrupt, and absolute power corrupts absolutely. Great men are almost always bad men."

Lord Acton (1887)

INTRODUCTION

"And this issue embraces more than the fate of these United States. It presents to the whole family of man the question whether a constitutional republic or democracy—a government of the people by the same people—can or cannot maintain its territorial integrity against its own domestic foes. It presents the question whether discontented individuals, too few in numbers to control administration according to organic law in any case, can always, upon the pretences made in this case, or arbitrarily without any pretence, break up their government, and thus practically put an end to free government upon the earth. It forces us to ask: 'Is there, in all republics, this inherent and fatal weakness?' 'Must a government, of necessity, be too strong for the liberties of its own people, or too weak to maintain its own existence?'"

LINCOLN, poised as it were upon a pinnacle of time, was able to survey the whole panorama of history. Here in this famous message to Congress of the 4th July 1861 he foresaw with precise and prophetic vision what the real *casus belli* of the devastating war then beginning actually was, namely the eternal dilemma, the everlasting knife-edge on which the balance of discipline and freedom must find its equilibrium. It was with the fate of the United States that Lincoln was practically concerned, the preservation of the greatest democratic republic that history had yet known or, a century later, has yet witnessed; but, as he notes at the outset of the passage cited above, the issue "embraces more than the fate of these United States." In our own day and generation it has embraced the fate of more than a score of newborn nations in Asia, Africa and America itself, the destinies of millions of human beings. In how many of them, already, has a government been proved to "be too strong for the liberties of its own people," in how many more "too weak to maintain its own existence"? With all his analytical prescience Lincoln could hardly have envisaged that his misgivings as to the natural stability of human politics would be so tragically, so widely, vindicated within a century, nor that his own countrymen would be so vitally involved in countries other than their own in the attempt to establish, or re-establish and maintain "administration according to organic law." To seek, therefore, for precedents and parallels in such a case may be rewarding, because the eclipse of a democratic republic is an eclipse which chills each one of us. The dissolution of an empire does not. An empire, we feel, is an essay in pride, and pride, as we all know, goeth before a fall. This feeling, though natural is also fallacious; because when an empire perishes a great deal perishes with it, including nearly always political stability over a wide area. It is also true, if regrettable, that a republic can be just as aggressive and overbearing as an empire, and in past history has often proved to be so. If, therefore, we can find in past history an instance of a genial empire, or of a rapacious republic, we may well take pleasure and find profit in the study of it. It so happens that the grand examples of both had one and the same origin—Rome.

The very name Rome still strikes upon our ears like a knell, a passing-bell tolling for one of time's noblest victims. It is from Rome that we have inherited much of our civilization, our law, even more our respect for it, our administrative ideals, our belief in the ordered amenities of life. Much of this treasure has been transmitted to us, enriched by spiritual values, by the Church of which Rome became, and still is, the hearth and heart; all of it was preserved for us by the empire before which for so long time seemed to stand still in respect. But all of this great patrimony had its rise in the Roman republic, the model for so many later ones—the very word republic is Latin, *res publica*, the common business. The Roman republic raised itself to heights of dominion that no later republic, not even the Venetian, was ever to equal until the birth of the United States. It became the mistress of East and West, of the cities of Greece, the kingdoms of Asia Minor, of the Levant, of the Holy City of Jerusalem, of the fabled and numinous land of Egypt, of the opulence of Carthage, of the ranches and mines of Spain, of the fields of France. Its eagles glistened beneath the suns of Mesopotamia, its standards streamed amid the mists of Germany and Britain. The satrapies of Cyrus and Alexander became its provinces: Roman consuls and praetors administered what had been the appanages of kings and pharaohs. Rome was unprecedented, Rome was supreme. Her republic had subdued and conquered all her enemies—except one, herself. And so the republic perished. That alone would command our sympathy and our attention—this suicide of a state. But there are three other reasons why the death of the Roman republic may call us back to mourn, once again, the passing of such splendour.

The first is the most remarkable. Rome did not die with the republic. On the contrary, from its ashes arose the Roman empire, an institution which in one form or another was to endure for more than a millennium and would be, as mentioned above, one of the golden links in the chain which unites present with past. This mere fact is a tribute to the unique viability of Rome herself, unique and unprecedented. Assyria, Babylon, Egypt, each one of these great powers had, in the end, found a doom which proved irrevocable. They were overthrown and for ever ceased to be. Persia may seem to have maintained its continuity, but the gap between the defeat of Darius by Alexander and the revival of power under the Parthians had in fact broken it. The Persia of the Arsacids was wholly different, externally and internally, from that of the Achaemenids: it was anything but a world power. With Rome, alone, there was neither end nor change. The empire indeed was scrupulous in maintaining all the outward forms of the republic, as the polity still continued to be called: the consuls were still elected, the Senate still deliberated, and would do so for centuries to come. (To this day the college of cardinals is known in canon law as the senate of the Roman pontiff; and the Pope still retains one Roman republican title, namely pontifex maximus.) So tough was the Roman republican fibre, so lively the germs of its being.

The second reason for the interest of the period is that it is so copiously documented. All too often, in dealing with the world of Greece and Rome, we are tantalized by our lack of source-material. For the second century A.D., for instance, which saw the apogee of material felicity throughout the empire, an age of peace, unity and prosperity such as Europe had never known before nor has ever enjoyed since, we are almost wholly dependent on two narratives, one written two centuries later in the form of biographies, the other a mere epitome made in the ninth century. But for the last hundred years of the republic we possess a really copious literature—histories, biographies, memoirs, poetry, letters. Such is their profusion that no single period of history is better illustrated, more strongly illuminated, before the invention of printing.

The third reason is the most telling, the most human, and therefore in the long run the most compelling. It consists in the *personae* who acted out the drama and made the age. It is no wonder that Shakespeare chose many of them to animate his most vivid and moving historical plays. What a pageant they are. There is old Cato, there are the Gracchi, there is Cornelia, their mother—for in this scintillating company the women shine as brightly as the men. There are the war-lords Marius and Sulla, the tycoon Crassus, the later great generals Pompey and Julius Caesar, Lucullus the epicure, Catiline the gangster, Milo and Clodius the thugs, Antony, Cleopatra, Octavia, Brutus, Cassius and the last republican, Cicero. Gradually the stage is darkened, the characters disappear one by one, as act succeeds act; treachery is heaped on treachery, and vengeance demands vengeance. Pharsalus, Philippi, Actium, three battles fought on Greek soil and sea for the dominion of Rome, leave at last as sole victor the heir, great-nephew and adopted son of Julius Caesar, Octavian, soon to be hailed as Augustus and first emperor of Rome.

Such is the story, moving to its inevitable end with all the pomp, all the poignancy of a Greek tragedy. For us it has a contemporary relevance; but it possesses more than that, because the last days and death of the Roman republic demonstrate as few other periods do how great and how little men can be, for what unlawful rewards they are tempted to strive and to what irrevocable disaster they may be brought by the absolute corruption of absolute power.

CHAPTER I

THE CHILD OF DESTINY

THE end of the Roman republic is more vivid, more a reality to our eyes and minds than almost all other epochs of antiquity because, as noted in the Introduction, it is so abundantly documented; but even were this not the case it would still capture our imagination more than the historic stages which preceded it. Ends always do attract more than beginnings. Who does not know at least the outlines of the downfall of the dominions of, say, Persia, Babylon, Constantinople or Vienna, yet how few could describe their origins? The reason is simple: for every man, his birth is behind him, done and done with, but before him, inevitably, lies death; and so it is with the death of states and of institutions that he has this inborn sympathy. Nevertheless, putting natural sentiment aside, it is impossible to comprehend the final stages of anything without some grasp of what preceded them or we shall place ourselves among those who, in the words of G. B. Shaw, claim to know the X-Y-Z of matters of which they have never studied the A-B-C.

The origins of Rome are obscure. We have to rely on tradition helped and checked, as tradition increasingly is both supported and corrected, by archaeology. The Romans themselves had a perfectly clear picture of their origins—not only their poets, such as Virgil, Propertius, Tibullus and Ovid, but their historians, Livy, Dionysius and Plutarch, all agreed about it. Their primitive city arose on the Palatine hill and was founded during the second half of the eighth century B.C. The actual year fluctuates between 754 and 748; 753 is the conventionally accepted date. The population, consisting of shepherds, was predominantly Latin with an admixture of aliens such as Sabines, Etruscans and others. The eponymous founder of the city was Romulus, the suffix -ulus being Etruscan; it denotes a founder. As the foundation-story

grew it was embellished, as such stories tend to be. Romulus falls
out with his brother Remus; Romulus is a fighter; his successor,
Numa, a man of peace and piety. This is a Roman adaptation
of a very ancient Indo-European myth. The two brothers are
Cain and Abel, or Esau and Jacob; Romulus and Numa are
Varuna and Mitra, or Uranus and Zeus.

Alongside the Romulus story—and other embroideries, · included among which are a divine paternity and the famous she-
wolf wet nurse—another legend later became current that Aeneas,
fleeing from Troy after its destruction by the Greeks, found his
way to Italy and so to Rome where he was entertained by
Evander in a hut on the Palatine. This legend first appears at
the end of the sixth century and is of Greek, not Roman, origin.
But the Romans adopted it and it forms the theme of Virgil's
great epic. So here we have, in these twin legends, a striking
example of a typically Roman trait—their love of simplicity combined with forcefulness (Romulus) and their love of grandeur
(Aeneas).

Archaeologically, there are, it is true, a few traces of Chalco-
lithic and Bronze Age habitation in Rome, mostly on what is now
the Esquiline hill on the other, eastern, side of the Forum from
the Palatine; but it is only in the middle of the eighth century
B.C., at the beginning of the Iron Age, that any extensive settlement comes to light; and then on the two ridges of the Palatine.
Below, in the Forum, was a cemetery in which both cremation
and inhumation were practised. The inhabitants appear to have
been shepherds and swineherds. So here, at the outset, archaeology confirms tradition. Romulus may well have existed: the fact
that Cyrus was later said to have been suckled by a bitch is no
proof that he never lived. The Palatine is certainly the spot
where we should expect to find a settlement because it is near
the Tiber and isolated by steep slopes on every side except the
east, where it is connected with the Esquiline by a narrow shoulder which could easily be blocked. It is, in fact, the classic site
for a strong-point—the abruptly-sided knoll, connected with the
massif by a single, defensible ridge—which was to remain the
accepted pattern down to the days of the Crusades. The name

Forum comes from the latin word *foras,* meaning "outside." The area was low-lying and swampy; no place for the living, so let it be assigned to the dead; but gradually the hills on the other side of it, the Esquiline and the Quirinal, became the sites of villages and it was only natural that they should use the intervening space as a market for the exchange of goods and as a rendezvous for the exchange of ideas. It was to become the most famous meeting-place in the world, and in all history. These later settlers appear to have been of a different race from those on the Palatine, which accounts for the different burial customs co-existing in the Forum cemetery. They were probably Sabines and men of Umbria. But the two communities gradually became one and co-operated about the end of the eighth century in the draining of the Forum and the building of a permanent market-place. Thus we see that the unbiased findings of archaeology support Roman tradition.

At this period the "Romans," as they were afterwards to become, were simply primitive villagers. The lords of the land were the Etruscans. The Etruscans are still a mystery. They were highly civilized; we have abundant remains of their art and artifacts, of their tombs, their bronzes, their sculpture, their pottery and paintings. But we do not know where they came from, nor can we yet read their language. It is not of the Indo-European family. All we know is that many Latin words are of Etruscan origin, which means that some English ones—*person* is the commonest—are, too.

While the Etruscans were still ruling, the new race was being formed. One day it would supplant the Etruscans, just as one day the conquered English were to assimilate and rule the superior Normans. With two other peoples the Romans would have to deal, for both were already their neighbours—the Greeks and the Carthaginians. The Greeks had founded numbers of colonies in southern Italy and Sicily, each one a centre of culture and amenity such as Rome was not to know for some time, while the Carthaginians not only controlled the sea-ways of the western Mediterranean, but they too had established themselves in Sicily.

For two and a half centuries Rome was to be ruled by kings, Etruscan kings towards the latter part of the era. Their oppression finally became too much for the Romans, who expelled the last Tarquin in or about the year 509 B.C. By that time, Rome had established her power in Latium, having become head of the Latin League after destroying Alba; and in alliance with the Latins she founded Latin colonies, or settlements, in which Romans and Latins lived together with the Latins enjoying slightly curtailed rights. The Sabines, too, were brought through warfare into league with Rome. Veii, the Volscians and the Gabii—these also were drawn within the Roman ambit. And strangers had settled in Rome itself where they constituted a new class, the *plebs* or people. They had no say in the government, but by the constitution of Servius Tullius, the Latin king who ruled between the last two Etruscan Tarquins, the plebs' lot was eased, when entry into the army was based on landed property instead of citizen birth and plebeians were allowed to vote for office-holders, but not to hold office themselves.

When the last king was expelled Rome had to rid herself of more than a monarch. Henceforth she was to be ruled by Romans, not foreigners; but the dispossessed Etruscans fought back. The Romans lost their footholds north of the Tiber, perhaps even in Rome itself. Tarquin rallied thirty Latin towns for a final onslaught. The two consuls who had succeeded the sole king surrendered their newly-won rights to a single commander, a dictator as he was called. When it came to the push the Romans would always be practical rather than theoretical and thus early they showed it. The victory of Lake Regillus in 496 was their reward and within three years a new Latin League had come into being, based on the equality of Roman and Latin. Rome's next foes were the hill-tribes who lived beyond the Latins. In the wars against them, which occupied the next fifty years, the brunt of the fighting fell to the Latins, but the Romans took good care to claim their share of the advantages. "Thus," in Myres' words, "Rome grew steadily and almost unconsciously at the expense of her kinsfolk and allies." With the capture of Veii in 396, after a ten years' siege, Etruscan power was crippled.

Meanwhile, the internal polity of Rome was being developed. The class struggle, which had been mitigated by Tullius' concessions, came to a head early under the republic. The situation is lucidly summarized by Myres. The claims of the plebeians were as follows:

1. *The right to full equality of citizenship with patricians;* a demand first formulated in 509, but only fully conceded by the Licinian Laws of 367.

2. *The right to be secured against personal enslavement for debt;* first claimed in 495, and finally conceded in 367.

3. *The right to manage their own affairs and to appoint independent officers of their own;* first claimed in 493 and conceded as early as 471.

4. *The right to a fair share of conquered territory;* repeatedly contested from 493 onwards. The importance of this claim in early times has probably been greatly exaggerated by later writers in order to provide historical precedents for the agrarian legislation of the Gracchi. But there can be little doubt that the question of the mode of distribution arose from the first moment when there was conquered territory to divide; for the plebeians fought in Rome's battles, and might justly claim to share in the fruits of her victories.

5. *The right to know the laws and rules of court;* first claimed in 462 and conceded in principle in 450, but not finally assured till 304.

The salient fact in the foregoing tabulation is the obstinacy of the patricians in yielding equality of human rights to their plebeian fellow-citizens. It is this very trait which was to precipitate the ultimate class-struggle in the days of the Gracchi, and that in its turn heralded the final collapse of the republican régime. Only one of the demands was granted almost at once, and that almost scornfully, namely that the plebeians might manage their own affairs; but the right that went with it, that of electing annually two of their own order as the recognized champions of their rights against the arbitrary power of the magistrates, was, again, to have a decisive influence in the days of the Gracchi. These officers were known as tribunes, perhaps

because they were chosen by local "tribes." Originally there were
two of them, like the consuls, then four; and by the middle of the
fifth century their number had increased to ten.

The powers of the tribunes were peculiar. They were not
magistrates, they could not hold the *imperium*, or "command";
but they enjoyed the powers of (a) *auxilium*, or "help," that is
of protecting a citizen from a magistrate, (b) *intercessio*, "coming between," or vetoing a magisterial decree, a legislative bill
or decision of the Senate. They presided over the assembled
plebs and could put to them bills which, if accepted, became
plebiscita, binding originally on the plebs only. They might also
coerce and punish offenders against the plebs subject to an appeal
to that body. During their year of office their persons were
sacrosanct, but they might not leave the city for a whole day (except during the Feriae Latinae, when the people assembled on
the Alban Mount to the south of Rome). Their power did not
extend to more than a mile beyond the city gates.

At the same time as the institution of the tribunate the
plebeians were allowed to appoint from among themselves two
aediles, to supervise public works, weights and measures and
watchmen. They thus obtained some control over the economic
affairs which were principally their own concern.

To us, it must seem strange that the patricians should have
been so chary of conceding basic rights to their fellow-citizens,
and that such elaborate and involved machinery should have
been contrived to grant so little. Even these concessions were
only wrung from the patricians by what is known as the "first
secession" when, in the year 494, the plebeians—who, returning
from a war in which they had helped to overcome the Volscians,
felt themselves ill-treated by the Senate—withdrew to a hill called
the Sacred Mount, at the confluence of the Tiber and the Anio,
some three miles from Rome. They said they were going to found
their own city and were only induced to come back by Menenius
Agrippa, who recited to them the parable of the "Belly and the
Limbs," each unable, like patrician and plebeian, to exist without
the other.

Much had been gained; but much more remained to be fought

for even as regards personal, as distinct from political, rights. One basic right had indeed been secured for all the citizens, plebeian no less than patrician, at the very beginning of the post-monarchic era. Valerius Publicola, one of the first consuls, had carried a proposal that no consul might put a Roman citizen to death without allowing him to plead his cause before the Comitia Centuriata. The law, which unfortunately carried no sanction, had frequently to be re-enacted; and we shall encounter it when we come to discuss a crisis in the career of Cicero. But the law of debt remained unaltered. The plebeians had no share in the newly-acquired territories, nor might their newly-created officials hold any of the regular magistracies. Nor did the ordinary Roman even know what the law was: in practice, it was what the patricians said it was.

In 462 a tribune proposed that, following the example of many a Greek state, a commission of five plebeians be appointed to define the powers of the magistrates and publish a generally applicable code of law. For years the patricians resisted even this request: only in the year 454 were three commissioners appointed to visit Greece and to copy the famous laws of Solon in Athens, and to acquaint themselves with the customs, institutions and laws of other states—or so the tradition, handed on by Livy, who even gives the names of the commissioners, declares. It may have been adorned in later times to give a Greek ancestry to Roman law; but at least the commission produced results. When they came back after two years' absence a new commission of ten was appointed to draw up a code of law, which resulted in the "Twelve Tables," "the fountainhead of all law, public and private" in Rome, as Livy calls them. The ten commissioners, however, were loath to lay down their powers. They behaved just like the Greek oligarchs and under the tyranny of these very lawgivers no man's life or property was secure, and many leading citizens left the city. Once again, in 450, the plebs seceded, this time perhaps only as far as the Aventine. The commissioners resigned. In the following year, by what was really an understanding between the two orders, though known as the Valerio-Horatian laws, after the two consuls for the year, the following provisions were promulgated:

1. *The right of every Roman citizen to appeal to the people against the capital sentence of a magistrate within the city.*

2. *The "plebiscita" or resolutions of the plebeian council were given the same force as "laws" passed in the Comitia Centuriata.*

3. *The sanctity of the persons of tribunes and other plebeian officials was re-affirmed as a principle of public law.*

Four years later marriage between patricians and plebeians, forbidden by the Twelve Tables, was legalized by the Lex Canuleia, so-called for the tribune Canuleius who had introduced the relevant *plebiscitum*. This was an outstanding victory of the plebeians which, in fact, they had achieved only after yet a third secession, this time to the Janiculum beyond the Tiber. Another point had been raised during this "walk-out." Canuleius had proposed that plebeians should be eligible for the consulship; but this was too much for the patricians. A compromise was reached whereby the consulship was "saved from pollution" as the patricians put it, by the appointment of military tribunes, varying from two to eight in number, who should exercise the powers of the consuls; but they might not celebrate a triumph, and so were accepted as being inferior to consuls in status and prestige. The first military tribunes were elected in 444, but it was not until 400 that even one of them was a plebeian. With the far-sightedness of their kind the canny patricians saw that in the end they would have to yield over the consulship and so they contrived to have removed from consular jurisdiction, and thus to retain in their own hands, one of the functions which they regarded as vital. Hitherto the consuls had been responsible for the *census,* that is, the roll of the citizens, according to their tribes, wealth and dwelling-places. Once every five years the list was revised and a solemn rite of purification was performed. This was called *lustrum,* whence the word "lustre," meaning a period of five years. In 445 this venerable office was confided to special censors who, like the consuls, were to be two in number and always patricians.

If the censorship, why not the treasury too? It was a fine no-tion, but here the patricians overreached themselves. Ever since the beginning of the republic the consuls had appointed two quaestors or "examiners" to collect the revenue and to keep the accounts. Just before the reforms of Canuleius the appointment had been transferred from the consuls to the Comitia Tributa, and they had been empowered to supervise all military expenditure. In the year 421 it was proposed to add two more quaestors for urban finance, and to commit all financial business to the enlarged board of four. So successful were the plebeians in urging their own claims that they succeeded in being made eligible not only for the two original quaestorships but also for the two new ones which the patricians had particularly wanted to keep in their own hands. In 406 three out of the four were plebeians. By winning this right the plebeians had done far more than assure their hold on finance and on legal proceedings which concerned it, considerable as that advantage was: it enabled plebeians to enter the Senate, because it became the custom and then the rule to fill vacancies in the Senate from among the ex-quaestors. In the year 400 a plebeian, the first to do so, took his seat in that august body. Having attained thus much, after so long a struggle, the plebeians naturally felt more than ever entitled to complete equality and more than ever resented the lack of it. Yet during the years succeeding the laws of Canuleius the demand for equal rights lost impetus. The principal reason is that Rome was engaged in the wars mentioned above. In those days wars were not only apt to unite politically, as they still are, but also to enrich economically and financially, as they have long since ceased to do. In campaigns such as that against Veii plebeian warriors, no less than patrician, found scope for leadership and loot and the acquisition of land, the *summum bonum* of a community which was nourished solely by agriculture. Political grievances, if not forgotten, were mollified by material gains. The patricians still retained most of their privileges, and all their pomp. A final show-down was inevitable; but it was postponed by an external disaster of the first magnitude which not only "froze" internal political development, but for some years arrested Rome's march to the hegemony of Italy.

In the year 391 a horde of Gauls under their leader Brennus swept down into Italy, hungry for land, as they themselves declared. On 18th July—a day for ever after kept as "black" by the Romans—they utterly defeated a Roman army on the bank of the river Allia, a tributary of the Tiber. The Gauls then occupied the defenceless city (its sole bulwark was a turf rampart and a ditch), looted it and burned it. Only the Capitol held out and a night attack on it was thwarted by the sacred geese of Juno. "The gods slept, but the geese stayed awake," as St. Augustine was to put it eight hundred years later, when once again Rome had fallen to the northern invaders. On this earlier occasion, after a siege of seven months, a shameful composition was made. The city, as Livy says, which had been victorious in war for four and a half centuries, and was destined to be the mistress of the world, was sold for a thousand pounds of gold. As the bullion was being weighed out, the Romans complained that the balance was not fairly set; whereupon Brennus contemptuously threw his sword into one of the scales, crying "Vae victis, woe to the vanquished!" He then made off to the north, taking his tribesmen with him.

Rome was devastated: it had for all intents and purposes ceased to exist. So much so that some of the surviving citizens seriously suggested abandoning the site altogether and moving to Veii. But Roman resolution won the day. The city was rebuilt, albeit on a haphazard plan, like London after the fire of 1666, and was surrounded with a wall, parts of which still survive near the railway station. This resolution, this toughness, was in fact the outstanding virtue of the Romans: again and again it was to be their sovereign asset. Their great laureate, Virgil, makes the Sibyl, the prophetess of Cumae, when addressing Aeneas, at that time a fugitive, say to him, "Yield you not to ill fortune, but go against it with more daring." This is a Stoic maxim, and the reason for the Stoic philosophy becoming almost the established religion of Rome's ruling class is precisely because it chimed with the instinctive "firmitude" of the Romans. Thus it happened that the real growth of Rome, its emergence as a power from being just one of many little city-states, is to be reckoned from this very disaster.

During the century which followed the incursion of the Gauls Rome was to fight decisive wars against the Latins and the Samnites and was—it was a new departure—to treat with states outside Italy as an equal. First it was against the Samnites, the warlike highlanders to the south, that Rome had to contend. The First Samnite War lasted only two years, from 343 to 341, and ended in a Roman victory. Meanwhile the discontent of the Latins had been growing. They did much of the fighting but Rome took all the winnings. And in 348 Rome had made a treaty with a foreign power, her first: it was with Carthage, the greatest maritime state of the age, and by it Carthage had recognized Rome as the ruler of all Latium. This was too much for the Latins, who now demanded that one consul should be Latin. Rome's reply was swift and brutal. In the two years 340–38 the Latins were for ever humbled. The Latin League was dissolved and the plantation of colonies in Latium ensured that no revolt should occur in the future. The Samnites took longer to tame. The Second Samnite War lasted twenty-three years and during it Rome, after early successes, suffered a crushing disaster at the Caudine Forks, where the Samnites entrapped both consuls and their armies. But again, as after the Gaulish havoc, Roman resolution triumphed. The Senate repudiated the peace which had been extorted by the Samnites, fought doggedly back, and despite Etruscan adhesion to the Samnite cause, succeeded in detaching or beating the Samnite confederates one by one, and finally entered the Samnite capital, Bovianum, in 304. Four years later the Samnites, seeing the Romans yet again occupied with the restless Etruscans, returned to the attack. They sought to frame a general league of all those who were dissatisfied with Rome's continuing aggrandizement. Even the Gauls from beyond the Apennines were invited to join the confederacy. But Rome was ready. Business was suspended; eight legions took the field. The Etruscans and Umbrians retired to defend their own country. The Gauls turned on the Etruscans. The Romans were now able to concentrate on the Samnites. Again they took, and this time sacked, the capital, and executed the general who had defeated their army at the Caudine Forks. (Chivalry was unknown to the Romans.) The league of the Samnites with Rome was renewed; but the hill country remained disaffected, and a source of anxiety to Rome until Sulla scorched its earth more than two hundred years later.

So far the interests and activities of Rome had been confined to the Italian peninsula: now, by her penetration of the Samnite country and her dominion over Lucania and Apulia, she was to come into contact with the cities of what is called Magna Graecia, or the Greek cities in southern Italy and Sicily, Greek cities as old as or older than Rome, richly cultivated, the heirs of the most humane and most highly developed civilization the world had yet seen. Through them, she would become involved in the politics and destinies of mainland Greece, of the Greek kingdoms in Syria and Egypt, above all with Carthage herself. If Rome was to be, in all Italy, the one state destined to deal with these august, venerable and powerful states, clearly she was no longer the little midland town whose citizens seemed to spend their days squabbling among themselves or with their neighbours. But recently Rome had been the child of destiny: now Rome had come of age.

CHAPTER II

THE EMPIRE STATE

OF ALL the Greek states of Magna Graecia the city of Tarentum regarded herself as the Champion and Protector. She was a colony of Sparta, with whom she maintained close ties, and by her geographical position enjoyed great commercial advantages. She alone had never fallen victim to Sabellian, that is, Italic, raiders from the north. In the year 338, when Rome was busy with the Latin War, Tarentum had called on king Archidamus of Sparta for help, but he fell, almost at once, in a fight against the Lucanians. Before he died he had shown that he appreciated the "special position" of Rome by making a military alliance with her, so as to threaten the Samnites from north and south alike. He was the first Greek to realize the importance of Rome. Four years later the king of Epirus, the part of Greece nearest to Italy, who was called Alexander and who was the uncle of Alexander the Great, tried to organize the Greek towns and their Lucanian neighbours into a single confederacy. He might have succeeded, but his Italian allies suspected his motives and he was assassinated in 331.

Tarentum, spoiled by affluence, jealous as she was of the upstart on the Tiber, had tried to counteract the northern threat by diplomacy. It was to her interest to play off Rome and the Samnites against each other in order to preserve a balance between them, and to that end she had offered arbitration during the Second Samnite War. Rome's final success had quite upset the Tarentines' calculations. Rome was undisputed mistress of central Italy; she was the ally of the Lucanians, the ruler of Apulia. She, too, had planted colonies at Luceria and Venusia, the latter within a hundred miles of Tarentum itself. She had even become the protectress of the Greek cities in Campania, including Neapolis, or Naples, in 328. In 273 Poseidonium, or

Paestum, whose Doric temples still proclaim its Greek origin and entity, would become the site of a Latin colony. Yet another king of Sparta, Cleonymus, was called in to aid the Tarentines, who were by this time, like Ophelia, incapable of their own distress. In a battle with the Lucanians he actually met Roman soldiers. After this campaign Tarentum saw her danger only too plainly. There was Rome, already a growing commercial centre, with a great road, the Appian Way, reaching first to Capua and then to Venusia, with colonies increasing in Campania, and with a fleet to guard her shores and, perhaps, encroach on those of others. The Tarentines perforce came to terms with Rome. The treaty stipulated that no Roman ship might pass east of the Lacinian promontory, which forms the western extremity of the "instep" of Italy.

The Third Samnite War, far from favouring Tarentum, only encouraged the rapacious Lucanians to step up their raids. Once again Tarentum looked for help from abroad, this time from Syracuse, whose ruler had united the Sicilian Greeks under his aegis. He saw his way to absorbing the Greeks of southern Italy as well; but all came to naught on his death in 289. The Lucanian raids continued; and so in 283 the harassed Greeks sought the protection no longer of effete Tarentum, but of rising Rome. At once Roman garrisons moved into the key towns, including Rhegium, the gateway to Sicily, and Thurii where the tomb and epitaph of Herodotus of Halicarnassus, "the father of history," were proudly displayed. Why did the Greeks appeal to Rome, who was still in the eyes of many of them a "barbarian"? Two reasons may be put forward. The first is that two years earlier, in 285, the Romans had completely routed another Gallic invasion, overcoming the very tribe that had humiliated Rome a century before. Yet another Gallic tribe tried conclusions with the southerners, and met with the same fate. The Etruscans, who had joined the invaders, were compelled to surrender in 280 so that Rome, in Tenney Frank's words, "was acknowledged arbiter of the whole region as far as the upper Apennines and the Rubicon." If Rome could thus secure her northern marches against these vigorous invaders who had occupied Rome itself only a hundred years earlier, was it likely that the soft and civilized Greeks of the south would be able to withstand her? The second reason was that in coming to terms with Naples Rome had shown that she could be generous and that she did appreciate the spirit of Hellas and was ready to protect it. The Tarentines did not see things in this light at all: they were disgusted that they, the avowed protectors of the Greeks, had by those very Greeks been spurned in favour of Rome. They sought a pretext for a breach with Rome. When some of the Roman ships stationed at Thurii appeared off Tarentum, the Tarentines simply sank them, claiming that the ships had infringed the treaty of 302 (if, indeed, it was not made earlier, as some good scholars hold). A Roman embassy, sent to demand reparation, was treated with indecent contumely, and Rome declared war on Tarentum. The Tarentines found ready allies in the Lucanians and Samnites and their neighbours the Messapii, but the Italiote Greeks remained passive. The Romans won the first round, whereupon the Tarentines called in yet another mainlander, this time Pyrrhus, king of Epirus.

The advent of Pyrrhus was to have consequences out of all proportion to the purely military results of his campaigns, which were nugatory. For the first time Rome found herself arrayed against a Greek army, that is a host trained on the principles which had made Alexander invincible.

Pyrrhus, with his twenty thousand men and his elephants, may well have hoped to found an empire in the West to match that of Alexander in the East. His first two encounters with the Romans resulted in victory for the invader. He nevertheless suffered heavy losses and was forced to admit that these barbarians—for such the Greeks accounted all non-Hellenes—"did not fight like barbarians." He had also to concede that a few more such victories, so costly were they, would ruin him, whence comes our term "Pyrrhic victory." Pyrrhus, anxious to return home where domestic politics were causing anxiety, made overtures for peace. The Senate, who must have been disquieted, to say the least, by the results of their excurisons into foreign affairs, were ready to accept a curtailment of their authority in south Italy. But once again it was Roman resolution that carried the day; this time in the person of the veteran Appius Claudius, the man who as censor in 312 had admitted Latins and even the sons of freedmen into the Senate, had brought pure water into the city by means of an aqueduct and had built the great south road which bears his name to this day—the first great Roman, in fact, of whom we have more than a legendary picture.

Appius Claudius was now infirm and blind; but he had himself led into the Senate and there delivered a stinging oration which was still circulating in Cicero's day. He began by saying that he had often found his blindness a handicap but that now he wished he were deaf as well, having heard the humiliating proposals of his colleagues. They were shamed into silence, and the war continued. Pyrrhus was in a quandary. He had found that although after his first victory the Greeks had rallied to him when he made a raid on Latium, the Latins remained steadfast to Rome, so surely had she built her political structure. He could not go home now that his terms had been refused, leaving his protégés still vulnerable to Roman vengeance. He therefore in 278 crossed into Sicily, having been invited there by the Sicilian Greeks, who feared Carthaginian encroachment. The Romans won over the Greek cities of the south and compelled the Lucanians and Samnites to submit once more. Three years later, having won no lasting advantage in Sicily, Pyrrhus returned to Italy. He attempted to reinstate himself, but was beaten by a Roman general and forced back on Tarentum. Next year he sailed for home, and the Romans soon drove his Epirote garrisons out of Italy and planted more colonies in the "liberated" territories. By 272 Tarentum itself, together with the whole of southern Italy, had submitted to Rome.

In the preceding year the Greek king of Egypt, Ptolemy Philadelphus, had sought an alliance with the new power. Ptolemy was a man of wide culture, the founder of the great university and library at Alexandria, his capital, and the builder of its famous lighthouse. In accordance with Egyptian custom he married his sister, who thus became known as *philadelphos*, brother-lover, a title afterwards bestowed on him as well. It is in commemoration of this union that so many Philadelphias were founded up and down the Levant. If so important and gifted a sovereign sought the favour of Rome, it did indeed mean that Rome, as an international power, had "arrived." Pyrrhus had realized this too. As he was leaving Italy he said to a companion: "What a wrestling-school we are leaving for the Romans and the Carthaginians." It is to that famous rivalry that we must now turn our attention. But before doing so let us note that out of the spoils of the southern campaign Rome was furnished with a second aqueduct, the Anio vetus, which brought water from near Tivoli. This is not just a picturesque detail: it shows that, as already emphasized, wars did pay in ancient times. It is also proof of the growth of Rome and of its hold on the surrounding region.

Yes, Rome had now passed the first, formative period of her destiny. She was a great power. She ruled Italy from the Arno to the strait of Messina. Indeed the name Italia, by which the Greeks had for centuries known the southern part of the peninsula, gradually comes into use by the Romans themselves to denote the whole of it. The next stage would be, as Pyrrhus had foreseen, the clash with Carthage. But before describing it, however briefly, it will be well to know how well Rome, which had so recently been but one city-state among many, was equipped to cope with wider responsibilities. Cineas, Pyrrhus' ambassador, had described the Senate as "an assembly of kings." How far did they live up to this description, and what other magistrates or assemblies controlled the affairs of Rome?

We have already seen that the increase of business had led to an increase of officers charged with its conduct. The consuls remained two in number and took it in turn, month by month, to transact routine affairs. Being in theory substitutes for the former king, the consuls sat on a *sella curulis,* or throne, of Etruscan pattern. This right was enjoyed also by the praetors and the curule aediles. The consuls summoned and presided over the Senate and the popular assemblies. They could try cases. They raised the legions, and their command of them in the field was unfettered. Ever since 326 a consul on active service might be continued in his command, even after his year of office had expired. He was then said to be acting *pro consule*. He retained his supreme powers as long as he was on active service, but automatically resigned them when he re-entered Rome. Later on, in 180, it was ruled that consuls must be at least forty-three years old, and must have served as praetors. The praetors were primarily legal officers. Originally there was but one, then in 246 a second was added called the "foreign" praetor, because he dealt with cases concerning foreigners, and the original praetor was called the "urban" praetor. The praetor was the chief interpreter of the law, and at the beginning of his year of office published his edict, as a guide to his intended construction of it. By the first century, with the increase of oversea commitments, the number of praetors had risen to six. After the year 179, the lower age limit for a praetor was forty, and a candidate must have been at least a quaestor.

The quaestors and aediles have already been mentioned. A man might become an aedile at thirty-one. The office was not a required stepping-stone towards the others, but after 364 the aediles superintended the stage plays of the capital, and after 264 the vile exhibitions of the arena where gladiators fought each other to the death, and later the so-called "hunts," which were simply *battues* of rare and beautiful beasts collected at vast expense from all parts of the known world. This love of killing for its own sake degraded Rome throughout its whole history; even though the slaughter of man by man was prohibited by the first Christian emperor, Constantine, in A.D. 325, it continued into the fifth century. St. Augustine was candid enough to admit the fascination it could exercise. From the time of the First Punic War, aediles were expected to provide these "shows" chiefly or wholly from their own resources, and so the aedileship became a useful if costly means of currying favour with the mob.

The quaestors, like the praetors, increased in number with the provinces, until by the time of Sulla there were twenty, and in the days of Julius Caesar, forty. Four special quaestors were appointed in 267 to look after the fleet. The curious role of the tribunes has already been explained. Before the Second Punic

War they had acquired the right to sit, but not to vote, in the Senate. The chief magistracies were endued with *potestas*, that is authority adequate for the discharge of their duties; but only consuls, praetors and the dictator possessed *imperium*, the right to command an army, this right being extended, as shown above, to those who acted *pro consule* or *pro praetore*, whence the later terms proconsul and propraetor. The fact that the censor was in addition to his other duties charged with the administration of tax-farming, state domains and major roads, bridges and aqueducts, gave the office great power and prestige.

Such was, at any rate after the passing of the Lex Villia of 180, and in principle before it, the *cursus honorum*, or ladder of office of the Roman republic. It may be useful to summarize it before we pass on to the very complicated question of the legislative assemblies.

1. The prerequisite for all office-holding was ten years service in the army.

2. An interval of two years must elapse between the holding of any two offices.

3. The minimum ages for various offices were:
   for quaestor, 28;
   aedile, 31;
   praetor, 34—later 40;
   consul, 37—later 43.

4. To qualify for election as consul, a man must have held the office of praetor and, similarly, to become a praetor he must first have been a quaestor. According to the rules, that is: but it must be admitted that as time went by, the rules, both as regards age and qualification, were not seldom waived.

When we come to the assemblies the difficulty of sorting them out is complicated by the fact that there were, from first to last, no less than five.

(a) The *Concilium Plebis*, the people's council, has already been mentioned. After 287 its plebiscites were binding on all alike.

(b) The *Comitia Curiata* was no more than a survival from the days of the kings. It consisted of the members of the thirty *curiae* or parishes into which the patricians were divided. In republican times it met only to confer the *imperium* on 'consuls and praetors, being in practice a mere quorum of the consul's own retinue. It also acted in cases of adoption.

(c) The *Comitia Centuriata* was an assembly held not in a building, but in the Campus Martius, to which the people were summoned by "classes" and "centuries," based on property qualifications. Wealth had the preponderance of votes. Each century had one vote, so that a class had as many votes as it contained centuries; but the richest class had as many centuries as the rest put together, and so could always outvote them. This assembly had four main functions.

(i) It elected the consuls, praetors and censors and for a long time decided on peace and war, though this office was later assumed by the Senate. (ii) It had legislative rights, subject to approval by the Senate. (iii) It could hear appeals from the sentence of a consul. (iv) It tried all offences against the state, and no case involving the life of a citizen could be decided by any other court.

(d) The *Comitia Tributa* grew out of the informal *concilia plebis* held at first by the tribunes. After the Valerio-Horatian laws of 449, this assembly was summoned by consuls and praetors as well as by tribunes, and was openly recognized as a constitutional body for electing the tribunes, quaestors, aediles and minor officials. It could also initiate certain legislation. As already noted, the Lex Hortensia of 287 made the plebiscites binding on the whole community. In fact, most of the laws known to us are of this category. The Comitia Tributa might assemble within the city or outside it, but not more than a thousand paces from it, because the power of the tribunes did not extend farther. It was determined by lot which of the thirty-five tribes should vote first, the one selected being known as the "prerogative tribe."

(e) Finally we come to the *Senate*. Under the kings the Senate was a purely advisory body of elders. It possessed neither initiative nor active powers, nor was its advice binding. Its members were the king's nominees. In the same way, under the republic the Senate remained *in theory* an advisory body without any power of enforcing its opinions; and it was only at the invitation of the presiding magistrate that it could express one. This is called a *senatus consultum,* on which a magistrate could act or not, as he saw fit. *In practice* the Senate gradually arrogated to itself the whole administration of the state. Steadily, and almost unnoticed, it encroached upon the powers not only of the magistrates, but of the people as well. During its best days, that is during the great wars which we shall shortly be discussing, it is no exaggeration to say that the Senate was the best representative of Rome, and the true source of its greatness.

Why did this occur, this assumption of government by what was in origin a purely advisory body? Three main reasons may be given.

First, the Senate was the only body in which debate was possible. The popular assemblies, meeting in the open air, at the beck and call of a magistrate, with no regular program, no agenda— how could they assume responsibility, any one of them, for the planned conduct of war and peace? The Senate alone possessed continuity: it met in its *curia* or in some convenient temple, and there it could discuss matters at its leisure, and come to reasoned decisions. It thus became the rule that the Senate should prepare bills for the Comitia, and discuss all questions of foreign policy and diplomatic relations; and these came to be regarded as the special province of the Senate, though they were in fact usurped functions. The second reason is that the collegiate principle of all Rome's regular magistracies left the state without a head: as long as the Senate could act as such, and made good its claim, the *fait accompli* was accepted by all classes. When, in the last years of the republic, it failed to do so, then it was that the rule of one man, supported by the army, supplanted it. But until the advent of those dire days, it was the Senate that was the crowning glory of the Roman state.

Finally, whereas the magistrates were only annual, the Senate was permanent, and it consisted almost entirely of ex-magistrates. It follows that hardly any "new departure," any radically fresh policy, could be inaugurated, much less carried through, by magistrates with so short a term of office. It was natural that even the consuls should turn to the Senate for counsel, because the Senate was the repository of the accumulated wisdom of the state. So it came about that the Senate took control of the finances, directed what troops should be raised and whither they should be sent, through the aediles and censors gave out state contracts and thus became the chief employer of labour, framed bills for the Comitia Centuriata, and gave to the votes of that assembly the final validity of its sanction. The provinces, when they came into being, were managed wholly by the Senate. Finally, a *senatus consultum,* if assented to by tribunes, who seldom refused, was to all intents and purposes a law.

The Senate at this period and down to the days of Sulla numbered three hundred. It was in the hands of these men that the destiny of Rome resided; and it was this "assembly of kings," as Cineas had called them, that was now to launch Rome upon its imperial mission; for by its defeat of Pyrrhus, its unification of Italy and its first links with Greece and Egypt, its contacts above all with Carthage, Rome had already become the empire state.

CHAPTER III

POWER AND POLICY

T HE prophecy of Pyrrhus was fulfilled within a decade: in 264 Rome and Carthage were at war, a war which was to change and determine the whole course of European history. As Aristotle pointed out, wars may spring from little things, but are not fought about little things. In this case, the "little thing" that precipitated the clash was no more than a dispute as to who should govern Messana, or Messina as it now is, in Sicily. The real *casus belli* was nothing less than the rivalry between Carthage and Rome for the mastery of the Mediterranean.

It so happened that a company of Lucanian mercenaries who had been employed by the ruler of Syracuse had, on his death in 289, seized Messana by treachery, and there set up a brigand state. Mamertines they called themselves, sons of Mamers, the Sabellian war-god. Fifteen years later the then king of Syracuse, Hiero II, decided to rid himself of these gangsters. He defeated them in the field, and was about to invest Messana when he was ordered to desist by the Carthaginians, who now possessed half of Sicily and had no desire to see Syracuse in control of the strait. They installed a garrison in Messana in order to "protect" it from Hiero. The Mamertines appealed to Rome.

Should Rome respond, should Rome have responded? The debate on this question which started in the Senate in 264 B.C. is still going on. On the issue whether Rome should intervene or not turned the whole future history of Rome, and so of Europe as well. At first the Senate was inclined to refuse. The Mamertines, even if of Italic origin, were thoroughly disreputable. Hiero of Syracuse had already shown himself to be friendly to Rome, and with the Carthaginians Rome had for long been in treaty relations. Besides, the Carthaginians had a fleet and Rome had

not. Equity and interest alike, therefore, forbade Roman inter-
ference in this dispute. That was the view of the Senate. But
Rome was now a democracy. The populace saw the war as a
profitable adventure. At this point it is well to cite a historian
with whom we shall have much to do later, the Greek Polybius,
who, a century after the events now under review, was to become our earliest extant source for Roman history. He saw rightly
that the clash between Rome and Carthage was one of the
great turning-points in human affairs, and so he starts his record
by telling us how it came about. Of the great debate which we
have now reached he writes as follows:

The Romans were long at a loss, the succour demanded being so
obviously unjustifiable . . . But fully aware as they were of this they
yet saw that the Carthaginians had not only reduced Libya to subjec-
tion, but a great part of Spain besides, and that they were also in possession of all the islands in the Sardinian and Tyrrhenian seas. They
were therefore in great apprehension that if they also became masters
of Sicily they would be most troublesome and dangerous neighbours,
hemming them in on all sides and threatening every part of Italy. That
they would soon be supreme in Sicily, if the Mamertines were not
helped, was evident; for once Messene had fallen into their hands,
they would shortly subdue Syracuse also, as they were absolute lords
of almost all the rest of Sicily. The Romans, foreseeing this and
viewing it as a necessity for themselves not to abandon Messene and
thus allow the Carthaginians as it were to build a bridge over to Italy,
debated the matter for long, and even at the end the Senate did not
sanction the proposal for the reason given above, considering that
the objection on the score of inconsistency was equal in weight to the
advantage to be derived from intervention. The commons however,
worn out as they were by the recent wars and in need of any and
every sort of restorative, listened readily to the consuls, who besides
giving the reasons above stated for the general advantageousness of
the war, pointed out the great benefit in the way of plunder which
each and every one would evidently derive from it. They were, therefore, in favour of consenting, and when the measure had been passed
by the people, they appointed to the command one of the consuls,
Appius Claudius, who was ordered to cross to Messene.

This passage has been quoted at length because it is far more than a brief chronicle of a minor event. The crossing of the strait of Messina by Appius Claudius—what relation he was to his great namesake we do not know—in 264 was to have a greater influence on the destinies of Rome than the crossing of the Rubicon by Julius Caesar in 49. There across that narrow strait—it is less than two miles wide and is to-day spanned by a power-cable—lay a rich and cultivated island, the home of Hellenic culture, of ancient wealth, of urban amenity such as Rome could only dream of. Beyond it, too, lay the prospect of dominion, of new lands to own and exploit, new populations to tax, new prisoners to enslave. On the day that Appius Claudius crossed the strait of Messina, he founded the Roman empire.

As to the motives of Roman imperialism, as mentioned above, the debate is still going on. Was it fear of aggression? Was it commercial rivalry, was it lust for wealth, was it idealism, or was it just love of power? All these causes have been put forward by different scholars of different races at different times. In fact, the argument is largely irrelevant. The motives of mankind are nearly always mixed, and that applies to states no less than to individuals. Our own age is able to recognize this better than preceding ones. In the past a large part of the globe was ruled by imperial powers who naturally regarded themselves as the best possible rulers, actuated by the best possible motives, even if other imperial powers were admittedly greedy, cruel or hypocritical. A great deal of contemporary thinking and feeling tended therefore to be thrown back onto Rome. The Romans would be blamed for doing what their virtuous modern successors were so careful not to do.

Now the empires have gone, and so we can review them dispassionately: our own national feelings, our patriotism, our policy are no longer engaged. A Frenchman, an Englishman, a Dutchman, looking back over the history of his country in its imperial days, sees that often a territory was occupied not seldom reluctantly, to keep some other power out. Other colonies started as trading posts. Others again were deemed vital to communications. As time went by imperialism became a creed. It produced arrogance beyond a doubt; but it also produced a genuine and lofty idealism: the memory of a Lyautey or a Cromer will long be green. So it was with the Romans. They, too, would have colonial governors of integrity and high standards, men like Cicero, for instance, or the younger Pliny. They would also breed scoundrels. In the end it was the scoundrels who won. That is the Roman tragedy. Our own century was to know, and to adopt, the philosophy of a Woodrow Wilson, who saw and induced mankind to see that the day of empires was over, and that if "no man is good enough to rule another man without that other man's consent," very few are good enough to rule him even with that consent. And so a new conception of human relationships has come into being. No such reformation moved the Romans. It was a Roman historian, Sallust, who first declared that the besetting sin of Rome was *libido dominandi*, the lust of domination. Four centuries later St. Augustine often reiterated the charge.

When Appius Claudius landed in Sicily he can hardly have seen that what looked like being a brief and profitable expedition was to land Rome in a war which would last for twenty-four years, to be followed after a restless interval of twenty-three years by another, far more devastating, lasting seventeen years, and finally by yet a third, half a century later, which after a three-year contest would result in the destruction of Carthage. It would also result in Rome's becoming mistress of Greece, and of many other lands besides. For this First Punic War, as it is known, brought about a wholly new political conception in inter-state relations; it also made Rome into a maritime power. It is not necessary to describe the war in detail. As Polybius himself says of it, it "dragged on like a boxing-match, in which swift blows are struck and parried, but no plan or policy is intelligible to the bystanders." Hiero soon came to terms with the invaders, and remained a loyal ally and friend of Rome for the rest of his long life. With Carthage it was utterly different. Each side realized what was at stake, and that there could be no compromise.

Rome also realized at the outset that to defeat Carthage, the great maritime power, she too must have a fleet, which so long as her activities were confined to Italy had not been necessary.

With typical Roman resolution she set about creating one. A captured trireme is said to have been the model for her warships, and her sailors to have been trained to handle the oar by practising in scaffolding erected on land. These may be later embellishments; the fact is that Rome did succeed in building a fleet, and that she did prove herself more than a match for the seafaring Carthaginians, her success being due in part to the adoption of a new and improved mechanical grapple. The Romans even invaded Africa, and Carthage sued for peace; but the Roman terms were so harsh that the Carthaginians preferred to fight on. In the end, after the tide of war had washed back and forth more than once, the Romans won "the last battle," a naval engagement off the western tip of Sicily, and Carthage surrendered. By the terms of the peace, she agreed to return all Roman prisoners and deserters, without ransom, and to pay an indemnity ot thirty-two hundred talents, something like five million dollars, in ten years. Most important of all, she surrendered all her holdings in Sicily to Rome. This meant that Rome, almost unwittingly, had acquired the first province in what was to be the Roman empire; it also meant that she would have to rule it. This would be an innovation, for although Rome was mistress of Italy, she did not govern it directly.

The citizens were now nearly three hundred thousand in number, apportioned to thirty-five tribes. Not all of them yet enjoyed the suffrage, though this was being rapidly extended. Many citizens, too, lived in the colonies, those little Romes from Rome, which the mother-city had scattered all over the peninsula: they would vote only if they happened to be in Rome. The tribes were supposed to cover Latium, Etruria as far north as Veii, much of Campania, the hill-men Hernici, Aequi and Sabines, and the Picentine country on the Adriatic coast. All the communities within this area or beyond it who enjoyed full citizenship, or the limited privileges of commerce and intermarriage without being eligible to vote or to compete for honours, were known collectively as *municipia*. Their constitutions were modelled on that of Rome, with two annually-elected praetors, auxiliary magistrates where necessary, a senate or town-council and a popular assembly on the lines of the Comitia at Rome. The rest of the population, and a few ancient towns in Latium, like Praeneste and Tibur, were classed as "allies," with two grades of privilege; the upper being permitted, after holding office in their own towns, to become Roman citizens; the lower having no access to citizenship, but being bound to supply troops, or ships and marines, when required. As in the case of the "protected" states of later empires, their foreign relations were wholly in the hands of Rome. The colonies, too, had the same grading. In them, as in the municipia, justice was administered by a *praefectus* appointed by the urban praetor at Rome.

This whole conception of dominance (for such it was) is remarkably liberal, seen in the context of its time. Besides being typically Roman in its practical empiricism it undoubtedly reflects much older Greek ideals of the city-state. Aristotle himself, in his *Politics*, defines the state as a "partnership," and such basically the Roman concept was, although Rome was always and unchallengeably to be the senior and ruling partner.

Carthage had known no such civilized scheme. The Carthaginians were Semites, Phoenician colonists from Tyre, who in the ninth century B.C. had founded their "New City" Kirjath-Hadeshath, known to the Greeks as Carchedon and to the Romans as Carthago. The Greeks called the whole Phoenician race *Phoinikes*, which the Romans adapted as *Poeni*, whence the adjective Punic. "The business of Carthage was business." They had no culture, and no gift for conciliating other races. They were brutal to the point of savagery. They expanded their sway by the employment of an army of mercenaries. The north African littoral, from the gulf of Syrtis to what is now Morocco, two-thirds of Sicily, all were subject to Carthage. She had footholds in Sardinia and Corsica. All her possessions were treated simply as "plantations," estates whose one function was to produce money. When by the treaty of 241 B.C. Rome acquired the whole of Carthaginian Sicily, the old federal system could clearly not be applied to so great, so distant a region, and one in which no indigenous government existed. So Sicily became a separate department, or *provincia*, for that is what the word originally meant. The conquered territory either paid tithe, in kind, or was added to the state domain, to be let out to Roman capitalists, whose vast ranches, worked by slave labour, generated economic disorder and social chaos. The future of Sicily was ruinously mortgaged; but this occupation of Sicily was also the beginning of Rome's moral and political decline; for not only the rich were demoralized by it: the supply of tributary corn was the first instalment in the demoralization of the Roman plebs. Carthage, enfeebled as she was, soon had a rebellion of her mercenaries to cope with, and could only acquiesce when the Roman appetite, growing on what it fed on, occupied Sardinia and Corsica. "Manifest destiny" was now at work. It was clear that the struggle with Carthage had only been suspended: it was resumed after twenty-three years of preparation during which Rome, in the pursuit of "security," had made her first military contacts with mainland Greece, in subduing the pirate stronghold of Illyria. She also had to repel another Gallic inroad, during which the invaders reached Clusium, only three days march from Rome. More important, for the purposes of this study, was the domestic unrest which was the sequel of the war with Carthage. The rich and privileged had grown richer; but the poor had become, as is their custom in war-time, even poorer. Business had been curtailed, money was scarce. "Veterans," demoralized by years of violence and adventure, crowded into Rome, with resentment as their sole asset. The Senate did nothing to relieve them—what concern was it of theirs? Thus it was that a tribune, called Flaminius, intervened with a proposal that the lands confiscated from the Senones and Piceni, which were now state domain, should be distributed among the poorer citizens. The opulent nobles, who were exploiting the land by the same methods as they used in Sicily, naturally threw out what they regarded as a revolutionary bill. Flaminius thereupon put it to the Concilium Plebis, and declared it law. Law it undoubtedly was, but even by this time it was not in accordance with constitutional usage; and later critics were to regard Flaminius as the forerunner of the Gracchi. It was the arrival of these new colonists which provoked the Gallic inroad mentioned above; but in the end Rome triumphed once again. Her northern frontier was advanced from the Rubicon to the Po; Mediolanum and Comum (Milan and Como) were captured, and yet a third *provincia,* Cisalpine Gaul,* was added to the nascent empire.

Meanwhile Carthage had not been idle. Her great general Hamilcar Barca (whose name means lightning), who had shown his mettle in the first war with Rome, had been consolidating himself in Spain. Spain was rich in minerals, and in men; it also brought Carthage a stage nearer to Rome—and revenge, for that is what Hamilcar had sworn, and had made his son Hannibal swear, to pursue and to consummate.

The Second Punic War is one of the most famous struggles in all history: the contest of one man against a nation as it has been called, for it was Hannibal alone, not Carthage, who conducted and animated it. In the year 219, at the age of twenty-eight, he laid siege to a Roman outpost in Spain, Saguntum, and captured it. The next sixteen years saw the war carried over the Alps into Italy, disastrous defeats of the Romans at the Trasimene Lake and at Cannae, revolts among the "allies," the loss of Tarentum, and then in 208, the victory of the Metaurus, which the Victorian scholar Creasy justly included among his fifteen decisive battles of history. Rome was saved. Meanwhile the war had spread, as wars do. Spain had witnessed a final Roman victory, Sicily the opposition and capture of Syracuse. Finally young Publius Scipio—he was only twenty-four—scion of a famous family whose father and uncle had both fallen in the Spanish campaigns, volunteered to restore the fortunes of Rome. He did. He reconquered Spain, crossed to Africa and on the 19th October of the year 202 administered the *coup de grâce* at Zama, some five days' march from Carthage.

The results of this second war were more far-reaching, more corrosive of the Roman character, even than the first. If we were searching for a prototype of a "modern war," a war, that is, which causes only harm at home and abroad, we have it in the Second Punic War.

Two new provinces were created in Spain, held by four legions. Thus a standing army came into existence, and permanent mili-

* See note at end of book.

tary service to feed it. The successful general and his troops were henceforth a menace to stability. This in itself was to have consequences fraught with peril to the Roman polity. The Syracusan kingdom was merged in the province of Sicily. Numidia in north Africa was made into a dependent kingdom in order to threaten and annoy Carthage. This innovation, too, was a prototype: as Tacitus was to put it, "Rome made even kings the instruments of servitude." Carthage was left degraded and helpless, bereft of army, navy or self-respect. Rome was mistress of the Mediterranean at last.

In Italy itself the consequences were no less ominous.

First, the war had been marked by the destruction of the Gauls and the harsh treatment meted out to the revolting "allies": more and more Rome was becoming estranged from her Italian neighbours, more and more regarding herself as the sovereign and them as subordinates. Loyal services were hardly acknowledged.

Secondly, the power of the Senate, owing to the necessary prolongation of military commands which were in its gift, and its control of finance and foreign policy, both increased and encroached on the powers of the magistrates and Comitia.

Thirdly, the depopulation of Italy had begun. The old yeoman farmer was yielding to the big capitalist rancher, with his sheep-runs and his slave labour. With the decline of cultivation came a rising demand for imported corn, and the influx into the towns of paupers whom it was imperative to feed and to amuse, lest they rise in rebellion. "Bread and circuses" was now an unwritten clause in the constitution.

Thus of every one of the ills which later threatened and finally ruined the republic the germs were already planted in the body politic, even though its innate robustness might conceal the effects for some time to come.

In 202 Rome was only less exhausted than her defeated rival. Surely now she should do all she could to maintain peace at home and abroad. But in fact the internal deterioration would be accelerated, while overseas Rome was to increase her dominions.

Even during the Second Punic War Rome had, as we have seen, been engaged in Illyria. We must now examine the Greek scene rather more closely. When Alexander the Great died in 323 at the age of thirty-two, his marshals grabbed what they could of his vast empire. In the end there were three survivors.

Lysimachus held Macedon itself, with a certain governance of the city-states of Hellas. Seleucus, from his capital of Seleucia on the Euphrates, ruled the whole of the old Persian empire in Asia, except for the southern part of the Levant and part of the littoral of Asia Minor. Ptolemy Lagos, the ablest of the three, established himself in Egypt, making his capital Alexander's own foundation, Alexandria, to which he succeeded in hijacking Alexander's corpse. By its possession of Cyprus and Lebanon, Egypt had a monopoly of good ship-timber, and so was able to become a maritime power. Besides the coastlands of Judaea and Phoenicia, Cyprus and Cyrenaica, Ptolemy ruled Samos, Thasos and Ephesus in the Aegean, together with other towns in the islands and on the coast of Thrace. The Ptolemies were constantly at odds with the Seleucids, to whom after 198 they were forced to resign all their Syrian provinces. But Alexandria easily retained its hegemony in the world of commerce, science and the arts. Nor had the Syrian kingdom survived intact. The Parthian Arsacids reclaimed the greater part of what had been Persia, and Antioch on the Orontes now became the Seleucid capital, which as a centre of Hellenic culture was to rival Alexandria itself. In Asia Minor, a Gallic invasion at the time of Rome's war with Pyrrhus had disrupted the Seleucid domain, and had brought into being Celtic states in the heart of the country. A merchant prince called Attalus seized the opportunity to throw off his allegiance to Antioch and to found at Pergamum a kingdom which was to play a considerable part in Roman history. Of the few Greek states that contrived to remain independent, the most important was the island of Rhodes. Athens and Sparta were still nominally independent, but Macedonian garrisons in three fortresses known as the "Fetters of Greece"—Demetrias in southern Thessaly, Chalkis in Euboea and Corinth—deprived them of any real initiative. The smaller states of western Greece organized themselves into two leagues, one in Aetolia and the other in Achaia. The Aetolian League had been forced to come to terms with Macedon in 217, and some of its members then took to piracy.

Piracy in antiquity, and indeed up to a century or so ago, was by no means the rare phenomenon it now is. On the contrary, it was a recognized calling, which always came to the fore in disturbed conditions; and we shall meet it again more than once. It was these Illyrian buccaneers that Rome, in alliance with the two leagues, had chastised in 230–28, thereby earning the gratitude of Greece. Rome had admitted Corcyra (Corfu) and two other states on the coast to alliance with her, and had placed them under prefects directly responsible to the consuls, just as she had done before in Campania. But Rome had no desire for conquest in the East—she had yet to settle the score with Carthage—and sent envoys to the leading Greek cities to explain her policy. The citizens were delighted. They were saved from the ravages of the pirates and, equally important, here was a new power to counterbalance the hated and domineering Macedon. Corinth admitted the Roman ambassadors to the Isthmian Games, Athens gave them the freedom of the city and allowed them to be initiated into the Eleusinian Mysteries. A second Illyrian war was provoked in 221 by a double-crossing rogue called Demetrius, who thought that the Romans were too busy fighting the Gauls to oppose his schemes of expansion. Demetrius was crushed; Roman influence re-established. The most important and most baneful result of this little war was that it forced Demetrius to fly to the court of Philip V of Macedon, and to instil into the mind of this young and ardent prince a hatred of Rome of which the fatal results will be described in the next chapter.

CHAPTER IV

ROME AND GREECE

HITHERTO, the contacts between Rome and Greece, the new with the old, had been sporadic and superficial—a legal commission, the repulse of Pyrrhus, a punitive expedition in Illyria followed by a second, together with what may be called Hellas at second hand, the colonies of Magna Graecia—that was the sum of Roman involvement in the Greek world. A wholly new stage was now to be reached in their mutual relations. A development which, starting with the "liberation" of Greece from its Macedonian overlords, would lead first to the total subjugation of Greece by Rome, and then, in the famous words of Horace, to the "capture of the uncouth conqueror by captive Greece." Both Greece and Rome were to be transformed in the process; Greece into a subordinate geographical region, a status it would not shed until the beginning of the nineteenth century; Rome into an empire without an emperor, until in the first century B.C. he inevitably arrived, and the Roman republic was extinguished. This may seem paradoxical, that a Rome increasingly imbued with the spirit of Hellas should swerve from the path of republican democracy, the ideal we owe to Greece; but in fact it is not. It is true that the Greeks wrote a great deal about politics, but it is also true that in practice they showed themselves inept politicians. The best of them realized this: they could combine, heroically, as one of them put it, when it was a question of repulsing the Persians, but crystallized into factions as soon as the threat was removed. Thucydides confesses that even in its heyday the government of Athens, although it was called a democracy, was in reality the rule of one man, Pericles. Aristotle, in his *Politics*, admits that democracy is rare, and that in his day it had become customary for states to submit to the power of oligarchs, despots or the mob. Demosthenes devoted the finest oratorical powers to defending, advocating and trying to resuscitate a democratic polity which had in fact already gone down before Macedonian absolutism. He died an exile and a suicide. So far as Greece itself is concerned Alexander the Great and his brilliant father before him simply gave recognized form to a condition which had long existed: they imposed absolute rule on those who could not rule themselves. Rome, in her turn, would do exactly the same. But first she had to reckon with the last successors of Alexander, the rulers of Macedon, Syria and Egypt. Of these, the Egyptian Ptolemies had already ceased to count. As early as 273 Egypt had made a treaty with Rome. During the Second Punic War, when Hannibal had destroyed Rome's grain supply, Egypt was able to feed her ally, who now exercised a *de facto* protectorate over her.

Philip V of Macedon had come to the throne at the age of seventeen and he was only twenty-one when in the year 217 he learned of the defeat of the Romans by Hannibal at the battle of Lake Trasimene. He had been studiously indoctrinated with his own destiny and virtues, and with a dislike of Rome, by Demetrius, and now felt that there really was an opportunity to do what his great ancestor had been prevented by death from doing, namely to build a Macedonian empire in the West; but by the time Philip had quelled an Illyrian dissident in the following year, Hannibal had won the battle of Cannae, and it was clear that he would be in no mood to share the spoils with any partner. Nevertheless, with a view to picking up what he could from the debris of Rome, the young jackal opened negotiations with Hannibal. The old fox had no intention of admitting a possible rival into Italy if he could help it, but glad enough to have him create a diversion, he made an alliance which promised Philip a free hand against Rome in Illyricum, in return for which Philip was to help Hannibal "in whatever way the signatories might determine." For a time Rome, hard pressed as she was by Hannibal, was yet able to mobilize enough forces of her own, supported by the Aetolian League, Attalus of Pergamum, Athens and Sparta, to keep Philip occupied in self-defence; but with the arrival in Italy of Hasdrubal in 207 with reinforcements for Hanni-

bal, Rome had to concentrate wholly on survival. She was compelled to allow Philip to overrun a large part of Illyricum. In
205 Rome made a disadvantageous peace with Philip, accepting
the *fait accompli*. It was humiliating, but Rome had made useful
friends among the Greeks.

Foolhardy Philip was unable to let well alone. In this very year,
205, the reigning Ptolemy died, leaving his kingdom to an infant
son. What an opportunity! Philip proposed to Antiochus III of
Syria, who called himself "the Great," that they should combine
to despoil Egypt. Antiochus was to have Cyprus, southern Syria
and Palestine, and Egypt, too, if he could get it. Philip was to
have the fertile and populous "Green Mountain" of Cyrenaica, as
well as Egypt's maritime holdings in the Aegean.

The Egyptians appealed to Rome.

What was Rome to do? Philip was being as crudely provocative
as he could. A corps of four thousand Macedonian "volunteers"
had fought for Carthage at Zama. Philip, despite spirited and
sometimes successful opposition on the part of Rhodes and Attalus, was wreaking havoc in the Aegean. Antiochus was steadily
eroding the Levantine appanages of Egypt, Rome's ally and
protégé. Yet Rome had every reason for wanting to avoid war.
Rome was worn out, for one thing, after the life and death struggle
with Hannibal. For another, according to the hallowed precedent
of what was known as the fetial institution, it was considered
unjust for Rome to go to war except in self-defence. This
sanction, which dated traditionally from the days of the kings,
still commanded respect. Even when the appeal of Egypt was
reinforced by those of the Aeolians and the Athenians, Rome
hesitated. In fact, the people first of all voted down the motion
to declare war. They had suffered too heavily in the war just
ended to want to embark on another. The loss of life had been
terrible. The countryside was devastated; taxation crushing. The
Carthaginian indemnity came in such small instalments that it
could barely pay for a single legion. Only when it was put to
the people that unless they resisted Philip he would do unto
them even as Hannibal had done would they agree to declare
war. Throughout its course, Livy tells us, the populace was op-

posed to it. So much so that at the very outset of what was to be her career as an imperial power bent on conquest whether she willed it or not, Rome took a fatal step towards the stifling of true republican equality. The citizens were war-weary: they were allowed to go home. Only volunteers, rootless and restless veterans mostly, were to fight against Philip; whereas the allies were retained with the colours, and assigned to garrison duty not only in Italy but in the provinces as well. Thus, in the words of Myres, the "fatal step was taken to divorce the voting-force from the fighting force of the State; to replace the old levies of yeomen by bodies of professional adventurers; and to establish new and invidious distinctions between the citizens and the Italian allies."

The present study is not a military history, nor will it be necessary to describe the campaign in detail, particularly as it was the political outcome of the campaign which was to mark a watershed in Roman foreign policy. But two points may be made. Ever since the perfecting of the phalanx by Philip II of Macedon, Alexander's father, in the middle of the fourth century, this formation had been unbeatable and unbeaten. It depended for its effect on a scientific blending of infantry and cavalry, on an improved pike and, not least, on great reserves of man-power. A century and a half later, it had declined in effectiveness, but was still formidable. It was now to meet the legion, and the legion was to prove its superior. Secondly, the results of this campaign were to have, as will be shown, a direct effect upon the deterioration of the Roman political character.

The first two Roman commanders achieved nothing at all. But in 199 a young man not yet thirty, called Titus Flamininus, defying the age limit and the custom that required a man to serve as quaestor and praetor before aspiring to the consulship, put himself forward as a candidate for it. The tribunes said it was shocking to flout legality in this way—he had not even been an aedile or a tribune. But (and here comes the fatal precedent) Flamininus was a popular soldier, who had not only done well in the Second Punic War, both in the field and as military governor of Tarentum, but had also been the director-founder of two new colonies for veterans. So the Senate put the issue to the Comitia, by whom, backed by his colonists, Flamininus was duly elected.

Not only was Flamininus an enterprising and able soldier, he was also an ardent philhellene, one of the first of a new breed of Roman. It was his ambition, and he was a very ambitious man, to shine as the liberator of Greece. And as such he was to shine. He both outmanoeuvred his military opponents and captivated the Greek civilians. Plutarch, after quoting Pyrrhus' remark about the unbarbarian discipline of "barbarian" Rome, and saying that men now applied it to Flamininus, goes on: "For they had heard the Macedonians say that a commander of a 'barbarian' host was coming against them, who subdued and enslaved everywhere by force of arms; and that when they met a man who was young in years, humane in aspect, *a Greek in voice and language,* and a lover of genuine honour, they were wonderfully charmed, and when they returned to their cities, they filled them with kindly feelings towards him and the belief that in him they had a champion of their liberties."

Philip was now anxious to make peace. His allies had fallen away, the Roman fleet threatened the Peloponnese, and Antiochus showed no sign of wishing to help him. Flamininus granted him a truce of two months with permission to send a deputation to Rome; but Flamininus arranged with his supporters in Rome to ensure that the terms approved by the Senate should be little short of unconditional surrender, namely the evacuation of all Greece and the abandonment of the "Fetters." Philip decided to fight on. Flamininus had also contrived to have his command extended *pro consule,* being determined that no one should share with him the honour and glory which now beckoned to him. Early in 197, after literally talking his way into a hostile Thebes, the Roman advanced into Thessaly, and there compelled Philip to give battle on broken and hilly ground, the least favourable, that is, to the phalanx. After an initial success, Philip was routed. The battle took its name from two neighbouring hills, the "Dogs' heads" or Cynoscephalae. A French scholar has called Cynoscephalae "the Jena of Macedon." The descendants of the soldiers of Alexander had given way at first shock before the "unknown quantity" of the Roman army. Greece learned with stupefaction that the phalanx had found its master. Philip was now compelled to accept much the same terms as he had formerly rejected. He surrendered all his possessions in Greece, Illyria, Thrace and Asia Minor, handed over his fleet, and reduced his army to a mere five thousand men. An indemnity of one thousand talents was to be paid half in cash down and the rest in ten yearly instalments. On these conditions Philip became, like beaten Carthage, the "friend and ally" of Rome.

A free Greece! That was the ideal, and surely now it would be realized. At the Isthmian Games, held on the isthmus of Corinth the following year, Flamininus solemnly proclaimed the freedom of the Greeks. At first, people could hardly believe their ears: they asked to have the proclamation read over again. So once more, to a now hushed audience, the good news was announced. The applause was so loud that it reached the sea, and some even said that it made the birds fall from the sky. Flamininus the Liberator—he was hailed and caressed as such by one and all.

Or so it seemed, but already it was becoming clear that it is one thing to confer freedom, and another to use it—a lesson that later liberators have often had to learn. Flamininus had slighted the Aetolians, and had underrated their part in his victory. They soon made mischief: what the Greeks had got now, they said, might be a smoother shackle than they had before, but it was a heavier one. The Thebans, perpetually jealous of Athens, were disgruntled because three islands were now restored to her. Nabis, the pirate-king of Sparta, actually defied the Romans for another two years. In 194 Flamininus considered that his work was done. He withdrew his garrisons from the "Fetters." At a farewell assembly in Corinth, he exhorted the Greeks "to use their freedom wisely." He returned to Rome to celebrate a triumph, of which the most attractive feature was a contingent of twelve hundred Romans who, having been taken prisoner during the war against Hannibal, had been sold as slaves to Greek masters. These the Greeks now voluntarily ransomed, at something like $150 a head, and sent them home to their families. All too soon this euphoria was dissipated by Greek intrigue and folly. It is in this context that Plutarch, himself an upright and patriotic Hellene, makes the following comment: except for the great actions on land and sea against the Persians, "Greece has fought all her battles to bring servitude upon herself, and every one of her trophies stands as a memorial of her own calamity and disgrace, since she owed her overthrow chiefly to the baseness and contentiousness of her leaders." This is only too true. No sooner had the Romans retired than the Aetolians, with unbelievable folly, started to intrigue with Antiochus. The Seleucid king, knowing that Rome's hands were full not only in Greece but in Cisalpine Gaul and Spain as well, pounced upon Egypt, and wrested Palestine from the Ptolemies. Rome protested but could do no more. In 195, Antiochus attacked Cyprus, a dependency of Egypt, and rich then as now in timber and minerals. Rhodes, Pergamum and the smaller Aegean states appealed to Rome.

Then came the news that Hannibal himself was at Antiochus' court. When Antiochus, against Hannibal's advice, decided to make common cause with the Aetolians, and to invade Greece, Rome was forced into action. At Thermopylae in 191 the Aetolians were scattered, the invaders routed and Antiochus driven back into Asia. His navy was defeated. Philip remained loyal to Rome, and chastised the Aetolians still further. Then, in 190, came the final victory of Magnesia, near Ephesus. Antiochus was forced to recede into Syria, surrendering all his possessions west of the Taurus mountains and the river Halys—the traditional boundary of the Persian realm. Fifteen thousand talents was the enormous sum of the war indemnity—some twenty thousand dollars. He was also to hand over Hannibal, but the old enemy escaped.

Thus Rome, hardly free, as she thought, of the burdens of Greece, was laden with those of Asia. Matters soon got out of hand. Rome rewarded her friends, such as Eumenes of Pergamum and the Rhodians, with accessions of territory, and all other Greek states were declared independent. The Scipios (for it was to the great hero of Zama and his brother that the campaign had been entrusted) went home loaded with booty, whereupon their successor, the new consul called Vulso, went off on a *razzia* of his own, looting and desolating in Galatia. This campaign, if such it can be called, did, it is true, recover an enormous amount of spoil which the Galatians had stolen from peaceable victims. But it was a flagrant disregard of orders and the first time that a disciplined Roman army had been employed primarily in the accumulation of plunder. Unfortunately, it was not the last. The Senate acquiesced in Vulso's insubordination, and he even celebrated a triumph, over Rome and her discipline as much as over the lawless Galatians.

With the suicide of Hannibal in the year 183 there could be no longer any prospect of a grand alliance against Rome. In only eleven years the term *Diadoch*, or Successor, i.e, to Alexander the Great, had ceased to have any meaning. "Macedon had been driven out of Greece, and Syria out of Asia Minor, while Egypt had lost all her foreign possessions except Cyprus and Cyrene."

Rome was now protectress of myriads of human beings. How could she sustain that role? Was she even willing to sustain it? Would not greed for wealth and for power undermine her; would not her ancient virtues be corroded with new vices? Would not the state yield to the faction, the faction to the egotist? Yes, alas, all these things would happen to Rome. But before we trace the decline to its end in the abyss—for such is the theme of this study—it would be pleasant, and instructive, too, if we could have some picture of Rome in the hey-day of her righteous glory. As it happens, just such a picture has been painted for us, and by a master hand. We have already come in contact with Polybius; it is now time to take him more closely into our confidence.

CHAPTER V

HEY-DAY

PHILIP of Macedon remained loyal to his treaty with Rome until his death, in the year 179, when he was succeeded by a crafty and ambitious son, Perseus. Already related, by his sister's marriage, to the king of Bithynia, he himself wed the daughter of Seleucus IV, who had succeeded Antiochus. With foredoomed folly, Perseus now fomented anti-Roman feeling throughout Greece, which, among the bird-witted Hellenes, was not difficult. Relations with Rome grew steadily worse until Perseus denounced the treaty with the Romans, who were compelled once again to intervene by force of arms. The Aetolians and Achaeans were predominantly loyal, and Roman diplomacy succeeded in dissolving the very coalition on which the foolish Macedonian had counted for support. The end soon came: the victory of Pydna, beneath Mount Olympus, for ever extinguished the power of Macedon. Perseus was banished to Italy, his kingdom partitioned into four fragmentary states, half the former revenues appropriated to Rome. Harsh reprisals were taken on those states who had been so improvidently rash as to side with Perseus. From the Achaean *poleis* more than a thousand persons were simply rooted up and taken off to Rome, without any pretence of a trial, as hostages. Among them was a youth from Arcadia called Polybius. He was a native of Megalopolis, the "great city" founded by the Theban Epameinondas to be a counterpoise to Sparta and the capital of the Arcadian federation. Polybius, whose father was a distinguished soldier and diplomatist, was brought up as a countryman, devoted to country sports and ways, and remote from the intrigues and temptations of the cities. He never, so far as we know, visited Athens. As Glover points out, his criticism of Demosthenes is significant— "measuring everything by the interests of his own city, thinking

that all the Greeks should keep their eyes on Athens, and if
they did not, calling them traitors, he seems to me ignorant
and very wide of the truth, especially since what actually be-
fell the Greeks then bears witness that he was not good at foreseeing the future." Polybius was: he was an exceptionally far-
sighted man, unbiased and uncommitted to any petty loyalty.
He was a man of practical bent. He had studied geometry as
well as literature. He was interested in medicine and surgery and
in astronomy and geography. He even devised a method of fire-
signalling which employed an alphabetical code, instead of the
set and limited vocabulary hitherto in use. Not only by his
father but from his own experience Polybius was early introduced to affairs. He took a professional interest in war, and
wrote a work on tactics. He discusses the strength and weakness
of the Macedonian phalanx, notes modern improvements in siege-
engines. One of the most famous and longest sections of his book
is devoted to the Roman army. His life was remarkably varied:
he accompanied his father on military and diplomatic occasions,
and at the time of the battle of Pydna was himself Master of the
Horse of the Achaean League. Most of the thousand deportees
appear to have had a hard time in Italy, because when after sixteen years' detention without trial they were at last allowed to
go home, less than three hundred had survived. Polybius was
one of them. During the final campaign against Perseus he had
become acquainted with the Roman commander, an impoverished but upright nobleman called Aemilius Paullus, who was a
friend of the Scipios and of their brilliant and liberal circle. Now,
Polybius was allowed to remain in Rome to act as tutor to Paullus' two sons, whom he had also met in Greece. He had lent
them books which he discussed with them. The elder boy, not
unnaturally, claimed the larger share of Polybius' attention; but
one day the younger lad—he was only eighteen—"in a quiet and
gentle voice and blushing slightly" asked Polybius why he always
seemed to address all his remarks to his brother: did he think
that people were right in saying he himself was a listless, idle
boy? Not a bit, said Polybius; he would love to help him in any
way he could. The boy caught him by the hand, and begged

him to join lives with him. This, naturally, pleased Polybius, but he says he was embarrassed when he "reflected on the high position of the family and the wealth of its members," for the boy had been adopted by the Scipios and was now one of that exalted breed, being known as Publius Scipio Aemilianus. "However, after this mutual explanation the young man never left his side, and preferred his company to anything else," and they became as father and son.

Nothing could have been more fruitful than this friendship, both for the two men themselves, and for us too; because it gave Polybius the ideal background and bent for interpreting Greece and Rome to each other, and that is precisely what he set out to do in his history. It has been well said that it was the first recorded attempt to write *universal* history, that is the story not of one great national struggle, like Herodotus', or of one disastrous conflict, like Thucydides', but of the interplay of forces which were to reshape the Mediterranean and the Levant. For Polybius had no doubts on that score. He was one of that rare breed of men who recognize a new world when they see one. He saw that the future lay with Rome. To anticipate a little, when Polybius was at last free to go back to Greece, he found it hard to settle down after so long an absence. He was, as we shall see, at Scipio's side when Carthage fell, and witnessed the sack of Corinth in the same year, 146. He was with Scipio again in Spain, twelve years later. He visited Alexandria, where he noted the violence of the mob and the propensity of the school-children for taking part in riots. He traced Hannibal's passage of the Alps, he explored the Atlantic. He is said to have died at the age of eighty-two of a fall from his horse.

Being an educated Greek, Polybius naturally began by a brief résumé of Greek political theory and the three sorts of government known to Greece—monarchy, aristocracy and democracy. There are really six, though, says the practical Polybius, because monarchy degenerates into tyranny, aristocracy into oligarchy and democracy into mob-rule. But he is not concerned with theory. "It is not fair to introduce Plato's *Republic* which also is much belauded by some philosophers. For just as we do

not admit to athletic contests, artists or athletes who are not
duly entered and have not been in training, so we have no right
to admit this constitution to the competition for the prize of
merit unless it first gives an exhibition of its actual working."
No, let us stick to actual constitutions. Sparta and Carthage
are both reviewed, and their virtues and defects described.

To modern minds, it seems strange to direct attention to Sparta,
and even Carthage, and not to mention Athens. The very name
Athens has come to epitomize for us "the glory that was Greece,"
in Poe's famous phrase. But in antiquity this was by no means a
universal opinion. It was Sparta that was praised for its stability,
and praised even by Athenians, and eminent ones at that, men
of the stamp of Xenophon for instance. Polybius says in so
many words that he does not propose to linger long over the
Athenians, or the Thebans either, because they never knew a
really great expansion, and their prosperity lasted but a short
time. The Athenians he compares to "a ship without a master."
Chaos replaces discipline, and shipwreck follows, as constantly
happened at Athens. The Spartans, on the other hand, had
built into their constitution the three elements of royalty,
aristocracy and democracy. At the head of the state were the two
kings, then came the *Boule* or Senate, and then the assembly of
citizens. Carthage, with its *Suffetes,* or kings, its Senate and its
popular congress, had very much the same polity, not unlike that
of Rome. But when the balance is struck between the three—
and we must remember that Polybius, unlike modern theorists,
had had personal experience of Carthage, Sparta and Rome in
war and peace, in the field and at the conference-table—Polybius
has no doubt that Rome is superior to the only two contemporary
states worthy even to be compared with her. In the first place,
the Romans are practical people: theory means little to them,
results everything. Secondly, their constitution is an ideal balance
between the three elements of monarchy, aristocracy and democracy. The consuls are, for their year of office, kings; the
Senate is the organ of oligarchy, the Comitia of democracy. "As
each element in the state can either help or obstruct the other,
they act in perfect unity in any sort of emergency, from which

one may deduce that it would be impossible to establish a better form of republic." Then, too, religion is a powerful bond among the Romans. Polybius' observations on the subject are of particular interest to a modern reader. He himself, as a free-thinking Hellene, affects to despise any talk of gods or hell, which are not "necessary" for men of sense; but a democracy is not composed of men of sense, and therefore religion and its sanctions become a necessity. "What in other peoples may be regarded as a fault, is what holds the Roman republic together, I mean superstition." It pays off, too. "If you lend a Greek the sum of one talent only, even if you had ten securities and as many promises and twice the number of witnesses, it is out of the question that he should keep his word, nor can you make him do it. Whereas among the Romans, however large are the sums to be disposed of, whether in the magistracies or the provinces, they keep faith to the letter, on account of the oath they have taken. In other peoples it is rare indeed to find a man who refrains from laying his hands on the public funds; among the Romans on the contrary it is very seldom that anyone is accused of peculation."

This picture of a republic sounds as though it were drawn in Polybius' native land, Arcadia, rather than from real life; but the most significant factor has been left until last: the army. Polybius devotes the greater part of one whole book to the Roman army, writing what is, in fact, a textbook on the subject which is still a classic. He describes first the chain of command from the consuls down through the tribunes to the centurions and legionaries. Then we are told how the men are recruited, how enlisted and sworn in; what is the order of battle of the legions and their auxiliaries, the disposition of the infantry and cavalry, the Romans and the allies. Their armament is recorded in detail, their methods of attack and defence. The famous Roman camps, of which the relics may still be found all over Europe and beyond, are described with meticulous precision. They were, as Polybius says, miniature towns, with every quarter laid out four-square according to a standard plan, on a grid-pattern of streets, the whole surrounded by a palisade and ditch. How different, notes Polybius, from the bivouacs of the Greeks, who simply

halted when they felt like it, and disposed themselves as the lie
of the land dictated. At the very beginning of his history, Polybius
says he is writing it because he sees in the rise of Rome a
wholly new phenomenon. "The very element of unexpectedness
in the events I have chosen as my theme will be sufficient to
challenge and incite young and old alike to peruse these pages.
Can there be anyone," he asks, "so gross and dull as not to
want to know by what means, and by what sort of conduct,
the Roman people subdued almost all the nations of the world
in fifty-three years?" (That is, by his reckoning, from the beginning of the Second Punic War down to the battle of Pydna.)
"By what sort of conduct" we have already seen: "by what
means" we have seen, too. It was the army, and even to-day to
read Polybius' account of the army of the Roman republic is to
be convinced that it inevitably must vanquish and overcome all
its enemies. That it was to do for some time, indeed until the
end of the Roman dominion nearly six centuries later, with only
a few major set-backs. But the conduct was to decay far more
rapidly, and it was that decay which, using the army as its
weapon, was to cause Rome to commit suicide.

It is desirable at this juncture to make a point which will be
cardinal to the understanding of the stages by which the republic
sank to its end. Historians of the eighteenth century wrote in an
age of stability. Wars there were, but they were conducted by
professionals, and did not affect the ordered ways of society. In
that age, therefore, any decline or dissolution, be it political or
social, was regarded as unthinkable and, if it had actually occurred in the past, utterly reprehensible: only wicked men could
have brought it about. Then came the revolutions: first the
American, then the French, and new ideas were abroad. But
not new states, with the sole exception of the American Union.
Elsewhere, reaction won all along the line. Napoleon had betrayed the revolution for which Byron, the admirer of Washington and Bolivar, bitterly reproached him. The Habsburgs, the
Romanovs, the Bourbons, the Ottomans, all went on as before.
Greece was grudgingly given limited freedom. Italy was not.
The fetish of stability, therefore, still bemused men's minds, and

so it was that history (which always records present ideas as much as past events) continued to proclaim that states, unlike people, have only to be just to be immortal. Our own age knows that this is not true. So did Polybius.

"Such is the cycle of political revolution," he writes, "the course appointed by nature, in which constitutions change, disappear and finally return to the point from which they started. Anyone who clearly perceives this may indeed in speaking of the future of any state be wrong in his estimate of the *time* the process will take, but if his judgement is not tainted by animosity or jealousy, he will very seldom be mistaken as to the stage of growth or decline it has reached, and as to the form into which it will change. And especially in the case of the Roman state will this method enable us to arrive at a knowledge of its formation, growth and greatest perfection, and likewise of *the change for the worse which is sure to follow some day*. For as I said, this state more than any other has been formed and has grown naturally, and will undergo a natural decline and change to the contrary."

The change which Polybius foresaw was already at work during his lifetime. Roman pride was to degenerate into arrogant violence, Roman rectitude into casuistical egotism. Public life no less than private morals was to be tainted and corrupted by greed and indulgence. As regards public policy, three events were to prove how imperious Rome had become.

Antiochus III "the great" of Syria was succeeded by a son, Antiochus IV, "Epiphanes" or "manifest," because he regarded himself, and expected to be regarded by others, as a deity. Like his father he had designs on Egypt, and in 169 and again in 168 invaded that country. Rome was now ready to expel him. But not by force of arms. She simply dispatched thither an ex-consul called Popilius Laenas. Popilius and Antiochus had known each other in Rome, where the king had at one time been a hostage. As Popilius approached, Antiochus went out to meet him, and hailed him from afar. When the Roman reached him, the king held out his right hand, glad, after so many years, to see his old acquaintance once more. In reply, Popilius coldly gave to Antiochus the tablets he held in his hand, and bade him read them. Antiochus opened the tablets and was appalled by what he read within: a resolution from the Senate bidding him clear out of Egypt. "I must consult my friends," he said; whereupon Popilius, with his walking-stick, simply drew a circle in the sand around Antiochus, and said: "I want your answer before you step out of that circle." For some moments Antiochus was struck dumb. Then he said: "I will do what the Roman people want." Only then did Popilius hold out his own right hand, and salute Antiochus as a friend. Such was the new method of conducting Roman foreign policy. But worse, far worse, was to come.

Carthage, after her defeat at Zama, loyally observed the terms of her treaty with Rome. She scrupulously abstained from any provocation. Hannibal himself had put her finances in order. The instalments of the indemnity were duly paid. But Roman greed and jealousy would not let well alone. Hannibal was forced to flee his country and Rome then intrigued with a neighbouring ruler, Masinissa of Numidia, to humble Carthage. He was encouraged to encroach on what was left of Punic territory until finally, after many vain appeals to Rome, Carthage was exasperated into an attempt at self-defence. Roman hatred, rapacity and sheer thirst for revenge, stimulated by the iron-hearted Cato, who ended every speech with the sentence "Carthage must be wiped out," finally brought about the wanton destruction of the detested city. After a terrible siege the city fell in 146 B.C. The inhabitants were sold into slavery, the town was burnt. Polybius was present at the final scene, with his pupil and friend Scipio, who was in charge of the disgusting havoc. As he watched the flames engulf Carthage, and they burned for seventeen days, Scipio is reported to have predicted, quoting Homer, that his own city would one day suffer a like fate. He left behind him a wilderness, the site ploughed over and sown with salt.

In this very same year, 146, yet another famous city was to be destroyed by vengeful Romans, namely Corinth. The removal of the Achaean leaders referred to above had left the Peloponnese

in a state of bewilderment, which gave a fair field for the
innate Hellenic love of intrigue.

Rome finally intervened and in the summer of 147 informed an
assembly at Corinth that the Senate had decided to dismember
the Achaean League. The Achaeans were goaded into resistance.
Despite the warnings of the governor of Macedonia (for since
148 the four petty Macedonian states had been amalgamated as
a Roman province) the Achaean general replied that the
Achaeans wanted the Romans as friends, not masters. The
Romans wanted to be both. War followed, the Greeks were overcome, and Corinth opened its gates. Polybius was here, too, to
witness the savagery of those whose temperance he had lauded
when he had lived among them. The inhabitants fled, the city
was burned by express order of the Senate, and its art treasures
were looted, the first of many to go west to Rome.

Thus was the last flicker of Greek freedom extinguished. Not
until the early days of the nineteenth century A.D. would that
flame be rekindled. And this had happened only twenty years
after Flamininus had proclaimed the freedom of Greece!

When it comes to private morals, and their degeneracy, one
example may suffice, and it is drawn from the life of Flamininus'
own brother, Lucius. In the year 192 Lucius was consul, and
was encamped at Piacenza in northern Italy, bent on humbling
the rebellious Boii, who lived between Piacenza and Rimini. He
had with him a young male favourite. This effeminate creature
was complaining to his patron one day at a banquet about the
hardships of campaigning, specially when "on the staff" of the
commander-in-chief: he never saw anyone killed nowadays—so
different from Rome where at the "games" he could watch
gladiators slaughter each other to his heart's content. Flamininus
was piqued: he assured the youth that he had no cause for
self-pity, and thereupon ordered that a certain Boiian chieftain
should be brought into the banqueting-hall. This man had taken
refuge with the Roman general, and so was entitled to the immunity of a suppliant. Nevertheless, there and then, with his own
hand, the Roman killed him, to satisfy the whim of a catamite.
What is more, he got away with it. He was never brought to trial;

Cato, who belonged to the opposite faction in the Senate, acting as censor, struck his name from the roll of senators and so deprived him of his privileged seat in the theatre. But his supporters soon had him back in the front row.

"Lilies that fester smell far worse than weeds." The Roman garden had already begun to wilt and decay.

CHAPTER VI

THE FATAL FLAW

T HE foregoing chapters have been devoted to demonstrating how a little Italian town became mistress of most of the known world, and the methods by which it did so. Its virtues were recorded, and finally the beginnings of decay, both of character and fabric, were mentioned. It was suggested that a decline was not far away; indeed, had already set in.

We must now examine in more detail the nature of this decline and the consequences, dire in themselves, but fraught with utter ruin, which sprang from it.

The government of Rome was not in reality quite the ideal harmony of the three elements of monarchy, aristocracy and democracy that Polybius described. In action, it became ever more oligarchic, more monolithic. The fall of the patriciate and the admission of the plebeians to the highest office did not alter the essentially aristocratic colour of the whole fabric. Nowadays the word "plebeian" connotes a member of a class that is poor and underprivileged. But in the Rome of the second century B.C. it denoted no such person. Once the plebeians were admitted to the consulship they must attain the same distinction and the same hereditary privileges as the patricians, so that, in the words of the great historian Mommsen, "the Romans had again arrived at the point whence they had started; there was once more not merely a governing aristocracy and a hereditary nobility—both of which had in fact never disappeared—but there was a governing hereditary nobility." The Senate had become to all intents and purposes independent of the people.

The nobility similarly contrived to establish their hold on the second rank of society, namely the *equites*, or knights, who voted in the Comitia Centuriata. Wealth here had the preponderance of votes because (as later in the days of European chivalry) only rich men could afford to maintain horses. Originally the state did actually deliver 1800 horses to citizens of substance who, being selected by the censor, were simply the nominees of the nobility. But because they were rich and because to them fell an ever larger share of public contracts, they became a party in the state, a plutocracy in fact, whose power as a political factor was destined to grow until the equites would challenge the Senate itself.

The alliance of privilege and wealth—and Rome's conquests had enormously increased Roman riches—always bodes ill for a state. Its influence on eighteenth-century England, as on nineteenth-century America, was uniformly bad. But here we come to the basic difference between Rome and modern democracies. In both England and the United States, corruption was eradicated and honest government restored by the action of ordinary citizens proceeding by ordinary methods, that is by the use of the ballot-box. The ordinary citizens of Rome had no such recourse. To start with, as has already been noted, the only body in which debate was possible was the Senate. Only the Senate had any continuity of purpose. The Comitia were simply mass meetings in the open air which showed by their "ayes" and "noes" whether or not they approved the motions put to them. It was all done by hands and lungs; heads hardly entered into it.

Secondly, and here we touch on the most important flaw in the whole of Roman polity, representative government as we know and practise it was completely unknown not only in Rome, but in antiquity in general. In a Greek city-state, this was no drawback. The Aristotelian ideal for a city-state was one small enough for every citizen to be able to take his part in governing it. And in Athens and Thebes, Sparta or Corinth, it was possible. Every inhabitant of Attica was an Athenian citizen; but so small is the region, less than fifty miles wide in any direction, that it really was possible for the remotest farmer to find time for civic duties. Similarly at Rome, in the days of her infancy. But when the citizens were distributed among the colonies, and with the growth of Rome itself, the citizen body, the sum of civic-minded burgesses, was diluted and dissipated. Had the burgesses been

divided into wards, each entitled to return a member to a central
parliament or congress, the whole history of Rome would have
been different. But representative government in the modern
parliamentary sense is the invention of king Edward I of England
in the year 1295. For those who have been brought up to regard
"politics" as synonymous with "representative government" it is
hard to divorce the two. But in discussing Rome, it is essential to
do so. The mere idea of representation is irrelevant to the whole
question.

It is hardly to be wondered at, therefore, that deprived of any
effective say in the conduct of affairs, the common people of
Rome became demoralized and more than ever disposed to sell
their hands and voices to the highest bidder, the nobleman who
would pander to them most brazenly. The relationship of patron
and client had always existed in Rome, as it does to this day in a
tribal society; but what had started as a natural and paternal
nexus was now prostituted into becoming a commercial trans-
action.

This debauchery of the people, bad enough in itself, was aggravated by two other factors, which in retrospect are generally
regarded as one, *panem et circenses*, bread and circuses, in
Juvenal's bitter gibe. Ever since the conquest of Sicily, foreign
corn had found its way to Rome, to supplement and to undercut
the harvests of the Italian yeomen. As the empire grew, so did
the influx of corn, either sent by the provincial governors or
delivered free in Rome by the provincials themselves, in order
to curry favour with particular magistrates, a bribe in kind. The
aediles, who were responsible for the corn-supply, were thus
able to gratify the populace with grain at ever cheaper prices.
This had a doubly evil consequence. It debauched the rabble so
that, as Cato said, "it is no wonder the burgesses no longer listen
to good advice: the belly has no ears." Secondly, it ruined the
farmers, who were, as in every land, the backbone of society.

Popular amusements increased alarmingly. For half a millennium the community had been content with one festival a year,
and with one circus in which to celebrate it. Rome's first professional demagogue, Gaius Flaminius, added a second festival

called significantly "plebeian" and a second circus in 220 B.C. (He is remembered to-day for his still-existing Via Flaminia, which starts from the Porta del Popolo in Rome and ends at Rimini.) A third festival in honour of Ceres soon followed, a fourth in celebration of Apollo in 212. Eight years later came the fifth, dedicated to the Great Mother, who had recently been imported from Phrygia in Asia. Flora followed in 173. These games were paid for by the magistrates whose duty it was to furnish the festivals. The curule aediles took care of the old national festival and those of the Great Mother and Flora, the plebeian aediles provided the plebeian festival and that of Ceres, the urban praetor that of Apollo. Thus, to provide "games" and so to conciliate the people by amusing them soon became practically a qualification for holding the highest office of state. It did no harm to a man's prospects if he threw in an extra performance, a gladiatorial show at his own expense. The lavishness of the games became the standard by which the electors judged the fitness of a man for the consulship. This was a costly form of bribery—a good gladiatorial show even then cost the equivalent of $100,000—but it was worth it, if only because it excluded anyone who was not rich from political power.

From the Forum corruption spread to the army. The old citizen militia thought itself happy if it returned with some compensation for the toils of war and, when victorious, a trifling honorarium. But now the new breed of generals led by Scipio Africanus lavished the wealth of Rome, not to mention the spoils as well, on their troops. They came home rich men. It must be remembered in this connection that in those days a general had perforce to carry around with him large quantities of bullion or specie in order to pay his army, and to maintain it in the field. To capture a general's headquarters was almost as lucrative as robbing a temple; temples being the safe-deposits of antiquity. The Romans often did both, and enriched themselves accordingly. So quickly did this cancer spread that when a general like Aemilius Paulius, the victor of Pydna, insisted that movable spoil was state property, his own soldiers, specially the volunteers who had joined the campaign solely for what they could get out of it, very nearly refused him his triumph by popular decree, having already thrown away the honour on anyone who had sacked a few villages in Liguria. The venality and cupidity of the army was to be one of the vices which would dig the grave not only of the republic but, in its turn, of the empire which followed it.

Thus was the government of Rome ruined by Romans. "Never," says Mommsen, "even in the most limited monarchy was a part so completely null assigned to the monarch as was allotted to the sovereign Roman people . . . The government of the Senate might be bad; the primary assemblies could not govern at all."

When we turn to the department of economics, the prospect is no less bleak. Roman economy was exclusively agricultural. Rome never produced manufactures, even on the limited scale of a pre-industrial era such as Greece did, pottery (which in antiquity furnished many household goods which to-day would be made of other materials) or metal-ware, textiles or glass. The farm had been the self-sufficing unit. It furnished corn, wine and oil for food, with an occasional joint of meat, oxen for ploughing, sheep for woollen clothing, supplemented by a hide or two for a shield or a pair of sandals. This yeoman economy was now being undermined by two things. One was the increasing importation of corn, which has already been mentioned. The other was slavery. The richer a man was, the more slaves he could afford, and so the larger became his holding at the expense of the "little man." The slave-holder was ruined morally, as slave-holders always are. "The whole system was pervaded by the utter regardlessness characteristic of the power of capital. Slaves and cattle stood on the same level; a good watchdog, it is said by a Roman writer on agriculture, must not be on too friendly terms with his 'fellow-slaves.'" The austere and upright Cato expressly says that slaves should be sold when they are too old for work. No wonder there was a Roman proverb: "So many slaves, so many enemies."

Thus the Roman economy was ruined in the interests of the rich and of the rabble. "Any representative system, however meagre, would have led at least to serious complaints and to a perception of the seat of the evil; but in those primary assemblies of the burgesses anything was listened to more willingly than the warning voice of a foreboding patriot."

In this world of callous capitalists and a brutalized rabble, it is hardly to be supposed that the spiritual climate would be very elevated. Nor was it. Primitive Roman religion has been described as "a well-developed Animism." Most primitive peoples believe in spirits of some sort, and not infrequently give them "a local habitation"—a grove, a tree, a stone, "and a name." The Romans in their primitive beliefs as in their later outlook were practical, and so the spirits must have functions, rather than mere dwelling places. With typical Roman orderliness, (with almost military precision), we find spirits detailed for every process of the agricultural life, or of human life in general. With the development of the city, a cult of Rome developed which gradually displaced the rural cults, for in a predominantly urban society the old rural *numina* of seed time and harvest, of flocks and vines, had little place. In this atmosphere it is hard to detect any trace of personal religion, and in fact there was almost none. Rome was to import her religion, or rather religions, from without. First came Etruscan strains. In place of the vague *numina*, the Etruscans introduced definite gods in human form, and gave them statues as representatives, and temples for them to live in. This was no improvement; on the contrary, it was a retrograde step: the *numina* were at least spirits, whereas the Etruscan gods were little more than "Big Brother and Sister." Another bad Etruscan influence, which was to cramp the official Roman mind throughout the whole history of pagan Rome, was the practice of divination. The art, if so it may be called, was in itself of Roman origin, as is proved by the Latin words *auspicium* and *augur*, both of which have survived in our own language. But the elaboration of the whole business, the mumbo jumbo of entrail-quizzing and the working out of a sort of code whereby the import of a bird's flight depended on which "temple" or "region" of the sky it appeared in, and in which direction it flew, all this was due to Etruscan soothsayers. So was the practice of divination by lightning. Thus the Etruscan influence, far from purifying primitive Roman religion, debased it: it increased superstition

and made religion a ready-to-hand instrument for political manipulation. This, combined with the anthropomorphism of the
temple-cults, had, as we shall see, a lasting influence for evil.

From what quarter, then, was any elevating, spiritual influence
to come? To this question there are two answers. The first is
Greece. It was the Greek colony of Cumae, on the northern horn
of the bay of Naples, that first, being the Greek city nearest to
Rome, gave the religious ideas of Greece to its future mistress.
Not only was Cumae a famous centre of Apollo-worship, but it
was also the home of one of the Sibyls, whose dank and echoing
grottoes inspire an eerie sort of awe in a modern visitor. The
Sibylline influence on Rome can be traced back to the beginning
of the fifth century B.C., and that of Apollo to the same remote
epoch. Other Greek deities soon followed, not seldom through the
direction of the Sibylline oracle itself. These gods might be
roughly Latinized, as when Asklepios, god of healing, became
Aesculapius. Often they were identified with some Latin *numen*,
as Hermes was with Mercurius, or Poseidon with Neptune. The
stresses of the Hannibalic War produced two opposite religious
phenomena. On the one hand, the Romans actually buried alive
a Greek man and woman and a Gallic couple, a revolting revival
of a long-discarded barbarism. On the other, the internationaliza-
tion of the Roman pantheon was carried much farther. An assembly of twelve gods, Greek and Roman side by side, was exhibited
and worshipped according to Greek rites. Henceforward, the religion of Rome ceases to be Roman and becomes Graeco-Roman.

Hitherto the newcomers had all been Greek. But now the vastly
important step was taken, again at the instance of the Sibyl, of
bringing the Great Mother from Asia. The black stone which
was held to embody her was greeted by Scipio and a band of
noblewomen and housed in the temple of Victory on the Palatine
itself. All too soon, the true nature of the worship of this alien
deity became apparent, and the Senate formally forbade any
citizen to take part in her orgiastic rites. Twenty years later,
the Senate was constrained to lay a similar ban on the Bacchana-
lia, the worship of Dionysos; and on this occasion they even ex-
ceeded their constitutional prerogative, and forced the Italian

allies to observe a similar restriction. The repression availed
nothing. The gates were now open to the Orient, and it was from
the East that new cults were to enter Rome for centuries to come.
Among them were to be two of the utmost import not only to
Rome, but to mankind at large: Judaism and in due course Christianity itself. The first comers were hardly what we should call
"spiritual." It was only natural, therefore, that more elevated
minds should turn to Greek philosophy, which in the second century meant predominantly, as it would mean in the days of St.
Paul, two hundred years later (*Acts* XVII), Epicureanism and
Stoicism, of which more will be said in Chapter X.

Not even philosophers received a universal welcome in Rome.
The earliest of them, who had arrived as diplomatists rather than
as teachers, were promptly expelled as soon as they began to
discuss ideas. But gradually Greek philosophy, like Greek and
Oriental cults, became acclimatized in Rome. The "old school,"
typified for all time by the uncorruptible, cold and cruel Cato,
deplored anything and everything un-Roman, simply because
it was un-Roman. On the other hand, the Scipios and their circle,
whom Cato detested for personal no less than political reasons,
welcomed the "new learning." They spoke Greek, wrote in Greek,
welcomed Greek philosophers and artists. Given the rigidity of
Roman institutions and ways of thought, it was inevitable that the
impact of so much seductive novelty would provoke a clash. But
it was to be no mere academic dispute. For centuries the Romans
had been governed, and had governed others, by the *mos
maiorum*, the custom of their fathers. Now, in the sudden "mir-
acle" that Polybius set out to analyze, they had been well-nigh
engulfed in a flood of riches and power. Wealth, and the insolence that goes with it, had assumed control, the public property had been diverted to the profit of the few. Slaves had supplanted free men, a greedy and venal rabble had jostled the sons
of Romulus from the assemblies and the voting-booths. Could a
"state so constituted" endure? This question was to be the
subject of the debate which would only end a century later
with the death of the republic itself.

CHAPTER VII

THE GRACCHI

FOR a whole generation after the battle of Pydna the Roman state enjoyed a profound calm, scarcely varied by a ripple here and there on the surface. Its dominion extended over the three continents; the lustre of the Roman power and the glory of the Roman name were constantly on the increase; all eyes rested on Italy, all talents and all riches flowed thither; it seemed as if a golden age of peaceful prosperity and intellectual enjoyment of life could not but there begin." Thus does Mommsen describe the high noon of the second century B.C.; but he adds: "So it seemed at a distance; matters wore a different aspect on a closer view. The government of the aristocracy was in full train to destroy its own work."

Yes, Rome was now a city of gold, and of golden opportunities for amassing more. So rich had the spoils of Pydna been that since the triumph of Aemilius Paullus, no Roman citizen had been required to pay any direct tax. To the mere description of that triumph, as given by Plutarch, the debased word "fabulous" may for once be truly applied: it reads like a fairy-tale. Paullus, we remember, was almost deprived of his triumphs by his own troops, because he had preserved the booty intact for the Roman people, and had not allowed the soldiers to filch it; this no doubt accounted in some degree for its profusion. Since triumph will figure largely in the ensuing narrative, it may be well to give an account of this one, taken from the vivid narrative of Plutarch. It lasted for three days. Aemilius had already attracted attention by cruising up the Tiber in the galley of the defeated king Perseus, which was richly adorned with captured arms and costly textiles. Now, for the great festival, the people put up scaffolds in the Forum and in the circuses and along the streets through which the procession would pass. Everyone wore white.

The temples were open, festooned with garlands, and fragrant with incense. On the first day, "which was hardly long enough for the sight," two hundred and fifty chariots went by laden with statues, pictures and colossal images, all taken from the enemy. On the second morning, a train of wagons carrying the magnificent arms and armour of the Macedonians, both steel and bronze, swords, spears, shields and targets, all artfully disposed so as to rattle and clash with the movement of the vehicles, was followed by three thousand men carrying gold and silver coins in great vessels, while others bore exquisitely wrought silver goblets and cups.

The third day was ushered in by military trumpeters sounding the charge. The procession was headed by young men in embroidered smocks, leading a hundred and twenty fatted calves for sacrifice, their horns gilded, their heads decked with garlands and ribbons, with boys carrying gold and silver libation-bowls walking beside them. Next came seventy-seven vessels filled with gold coin, and the great sacrificial bowl, encrusted with precious stones, which Aemilius was to dedicate. The next exhibit was the table-service of the defeated king Perseus, all of gold, followed by his chariot, bearing his armour, surmounted by his diadem. His poor little children came next, not really understanding how miserable they were, a sight which moved the sentimental Romans (because, like so many cruel people, they were sentimental) to tears. Then Perseus himself, clad in black, looking utterly stunned, followed by his staff and suite. Finally, preceded by four hundred gold crowns, the offerings of obsequious cities, Aemilius himself appeared, seated in a magnificent chariot, clothed in a robe of purple interwoven with gold, and holding in his right hand the laurel-branch of victory. His entire army followed, bearing likewise boughs of laurel, and singing songs of raillery or triumph. The death of Perseus sealed the solemnities.

Such was a Roman triumph, such the display of pomp and power, of authority and riches which now adorned, or disfigured, the Roman capital. One single campaign had garnered this profusion. But it was not only from Greece and Africa that riches had flowed into Rome during the lifetime of the generation after

Pydna. During the final struggle with Carthage, and as its concomitant, Rome had waged war with the peoples of Spain. The Celtiberian War, as it is known, lasted, according to Polybius' reckoning, for twenty years. Roman losses were enormous, and helped create the climate for the reforms of Tiberius Gracchus, who sought to increase Rome's man-power resources by increasing the numbers of her yeomen. This conflict also, like all great wars, led to the making of exceptional laws. The ten-year interval between consulships was dispensed with, the prohibition of re-election to the consulship was waived. It even led to the beginning of the official year on the first of January instead of on the first of March, so that our modern New Year's Day is a by-product of the Celtiberian War. Moreover, so barefaced and gross had been the extortions of certain Roman commanders in Spain that a permanent court was now established at Rome to deal with such offences.

After many vicissitudes, Scipio Africanus the younger, the man who had seen the end of Carthage, again accompanied by his tutor Polybius, captured the last Spanish stronghold, Numantia, thereby laying the foundations of what was later to be Rome's richest single province. That was in the year 133. In this very same year the great revolution started which was to last for a century, and to see the extinction of the republic. That result in itself would be enough to make the period of abiding interest; but another factor, subsidiary it may be, but intensely human, enlarges that interest into fascination. It so happens that the epoch we are about to consider is the most richly documented of any era in recorded history before the invention of printing. Many of the chief actors, indeed, have left us their own memoirs of the events which they helped to mold, among them two of history's most famous names, Cicero and Julius Caesar. Of others, we have contemporary or near-contemporary records so vivid that they have served to immortalize those whom they describe, not least in the *Julius Caesar* and *Antony and Cleopatra* of Shakespeare himself. Hitherto, if we except Cato, whose book on estate management has already been cited, Polybius, a Greek, has been our only surviving eyewitness of Roman history. Under the influence of Hellenism, an indigenous Latin literature came to life. The first Roman historian, Fabius Pictor, still wrote in Greek; but soon, both in poetry and prose, Roman chroniclers were writing in their own vernacular. We therefore have Latin histories of much of the great struggle, based on Latin records. Above all, we have the great anthology of Plutarch's *Lives*. Reference has already been made to Plutarch: he was a philosopher and priest of Apollo, who lived in Greece during the second half of the first century A.D. and the first quarter of the second. He was a native of Chaeronia in Boeotia, just north of Athens, of which city Plutarch became an honourary citizen and was a priest at Delphi. He visited Rome and lectured there. He wrote, in Greek, on many subjects, moral and philosophical; but it is for his *Parallel Lives* that he is best known, and always will be; because as long as men and women read history, they will study the *Lives*. For the earlier ones, Plutarch relied perforce solely on other writers; but for the later years of the republic not only were such sources far more copious, but he was able also to tap oral tradition. He specifically mentions his great-grandfather and grandfather as authorities for certain events. As a result, his later Roman lives, such as those of Cicero, Julius Caesar and Antony, are not only longer than those of earlier subjects, but far more actual, more "three-dimensional" as it were. Finally, to stimulate our imagination, we have the "visual aids" of actual representations of the chief actors, in busts, statues and above all, coins. Of those who have so far sustained the action of the drama, we have no authentic image. There are, it is true, a few busts, mostly funerary, in bronze and stone, of men and women of the earlier republican epoch. They show hard, rigid, almost simian features. For the later republic, on the other hand, we have a number of authentic likenesses; so that we feel we really know Cicero, Pompey, Caesar, Antony and Cleopatra, Octavian and his family. Even for the earlier period, before portraiture was developed, the characterization of Plutarch is clear enough to enable us to feel that we are taking part in the events he describes. Let him, therefore, introduce the Revolution.

"Of the land which the Romans gained by conquest from

their neighbours, part they sold publicly, and turned the remainder into common; this common land they assigned to such of the citizens as were poor and indigent, for which they were to pay only a small acknowledgement into the public treasury. But when the wealthy men began to offer larger rents, and drive the poorer people out, it was enacted by law that no person whatever should enjoy more than 300 acres of ground. This act [known as the Licinian Rogations of 367 B.C.] for some time checked the avarice of the richer and was of great assistance to the poorer people, who retained under it their respective portions of ground, as they had been formerly rented by them. Afterwards the rich men of the neighbourhood contrived to get these lands again into their possession, under other people's names, and at last would not stick at claiming most of them publicly in their own. The poor who were thus deprived of their farms were no longer either ready, as they had formerly been, to serve in war or careful in the education of their children; so that in a short time there were comparatively few freemen remaining in Italy, which swarmed with barracks full of foreign-born slaves. These the rich men employed in cultivating the ground of which they had dispossessed the citizens."

> "Ill fares the land, to hastening ills a prey,
> Where wealth accumulates and men decay."

In eighteenth-century England, where this same blight of "enclosure" and heartless capitalism spread across its once fair fields, there were remedies to hand. Although Goldsmith's "Fair Auburn" might become "The Deserted Village," a firmly-established economy already welcomed the dispossessed into the new world of America and the Indies. At home, industry and manufacture, however grim and destructive they might be, would at least provide some sort of livelihood for the rural unemployed. Rome had no such resources. Peasants simply became vagabonds. The census figures tell their own tale. From the end of the Hannibalic War until 159, the number of the citizens increased steadily, the chief cause being the continuous distribution of domain-land. In 159 there were 328,000 citizens capable of bearing arms. After that year there is a marked falling-off. In 147, the total is 324,000, in 131 only 319,000, and this in a time of profound peace at home and abroad. If things went on like that, the sovereign people of Rome would be corrupted into a mob of planters and slaves. Who was to stop the rot? Old Cato was dead. He died in 149, three years before his vindictive dream came true. His hereditary rival was now the most respected man in Rome, Publius Cornelius Scipio Aemilianus Africanus, to give him his full title. He was the favourite son of Aemilius Paullus, the adopted son of the great Scipio, whose glorious addition of Africanus he too now bore by personal right. He was, besides, the hero of Numantia. Initiated by Polybius into the graces of Hellenism, he had grown up to be a man of complete probity, in a world which was becoming ever more venal and dissolute. It was on him, therefore, that the eyes of the citizens were turned: he was in truth "first in war, first in peace and first in the hearts of his countrymen." He had already helped in the reform of abuses. It was chiefly due to him that Lucius Cassius had been able in 137, against bitter opposition, to carry his law introducing the secret ballot for the popular tribunals which still dealt with much of the criminal jurisdiction, thereby greatly lessening the efficacy of the open bribery which had by now become part of the Roman concept of politics. On his campaigns in Africa and Spain, Scipio had excluded women from the camp and had restored and maintained the ancient discipline of the army. As censor in 142 he had discouraged the "Greek" innovation of shaving and had earnestly exhorted the citizens to adhere to the "custom of their fathers." The manifestations of deterioration which Scipio had reprobated were but symptoms: the disease remained. Scipio refused to treat it. It was as though Washington had said "no," or Churchill had been afraid. Rome's greatest citizen was unwilling to save Rome. He temporized, and so in the end he met the fate that awaits all moderates in the day of extremes. In the year 140, Scipio's friend and political mentor Gaius Laelius, then consul, had proposed a scheme whereby domain-land which without being alienated had been temporarily occupied should be reimpropriated and distributed to distressed Italian farmers. Seeing the storm this would raise, he drew back, thereby earning the name of Sapiens, "prudent." Scipio agreed with him. This attitude naturally displeased the popular party; but Scipio had already outraged the aristocrats by his support of Cassius. Down to Scipio's time, it had been customary for the censors, on relinquishing office, to implore the gods to increase the power and glory of the state. Scipio only asked them to preserve the state. In that phrase lies all Scipio's philosophy and his tragedy.

Where the greatest Roman of the day, one of the greatest Romans of all time, despaired, a young member of his family circle, unknown and untried, dared to hope—and to act. His name was Tiberius Sempronius Gracchus (163–33). His father, who bore the same name, was a model aristocrat. The latter had twice been consul, in 177 and 163, censor in 169. The lavishness of the games which, as aedile, he had exhibited in 182, achieved only at the cost of oppressing dependent communities, had drawn upon him the deserved disapproval of the Senate. On the other hand he had shown himself generous, when as tribune in 184 he had saved the elder Africanus and his brother, both of whom he disliked, from public disgrace. As censor, he had prevented freedmen from voting. Most important of all, by his bravery and moderation in Spain he had won the hearts of the Spaniards, at a time when his countrymen were universally and justly detested. The great Africanus major (as we may call him), touched at Tiberius' support, gave him in marriage his daughter Cornelia, a woman of superior education and great force of character. Tiberius and Cornelia had twelve children, of whom three survived—a sad commentary on the expectation of life of the ancients, and indeed of most generations until almost our own day. When Tiberius died the reigning Ptolemy wanted to make Cornelia queen of Egypt; but she preferred to remain a widow, and devote herself to the task of being the mother of the Gracchi. Of her three children, the daughter married Africanus minor, already their cousin, who thus became by marriage the brother-

in-law of the very men who were to attempt to succeed where
he had been unwilling to try.

Of the two boys, the elder was called Tiberius after his father,
the younger, nine years his junior, Gaius. Tiberius was of a
gentle, reasonable disposition. He received the best education
that the Rome of his day could furnish, that is at the hands of
the leading resident Greek practitioners, one being a Stoic
philosopher and the other a rhetorician. Tiberius opened his
public career when he was co-opted into the college of augurs
and—no less important—married Claudia, whose father, Appius
Claudius Pulcher, was not only the senior representative of one
of Rome's most famous families, but was chief of the Senate,
princeps senatus, as well. Africanus minor, although he was not
on good terms with his father in-law Appius, nevertheless took
his young relative Tiberius, then aged seventeen, to Africa as a
member of his staff, a "tent-mate" or *contubernalis,* as it was
officially styled. Tiberius served at the siege of Carthage and
again, in 137, this time as quaestor, during the Numantia
campaign. This episode was to have a twofold bearing on his
future career. First, it was on his journey towards Spain, Plutarch tells us, that Tiberius saw with his own eyes the depopulation of Tuscany: "Finding hardly any free husbandmen or
shepherds, but for the most part only foreign, imported slaves,
he then first conceived the course of policy which in the sequel
proved so fatal to his family." Then when he reached Spain his
father's reputation there for justice and clemency enabled
Tiberius to extricate a Roman army from a desperate situation
into which it had been led by an utterly incompetent general.
The composition which Tiberius was able to make with the
Numantines was repudiated by the Senate, but his action naturally won him wide-spread gratitude among the troops and
their dependents.

Meanwhile, another series of hostilities, wholly unconnected
with the Spanish campaign, had a powerful influence in setting
Tiberius irrevocably on the path of reform. The corrosion of
society by slavery has already been mentioned; but depopulation
and unemployment were not the only evils it produced. The

concentration in the rural districts of gangs of desperate and revengeful men, treated like cattle, imperilled the general peace, because if these men could combine against their masters, they could threaten the state with internecine war. And that is what they did. The Hannibalic War had enormously increased the number of slaves available to Roman cruelty and greed, and from time to time there had been slave revolts. Two generations later the disorders were renewed—and repressed. In the year 133, 150 slaves were executed at Rome, in Minturnae 450, and in Sinuessa no less than 4000. In the island of Delos, now one of the largest slave-markets of the world, and in the silver-mines of Attica, force was needed to quell the slave insurrections. Worst of all was the outbreak in Sicily. Brigandage has always been endemic in Sicily, specially in the gaunt plateaux of the interior, which seem designed by some lunar landscapist to favor guerrilla warfare. A rich planter of Enna was murdered by his exasperated slaves. A massacre followed, whereupon a Syrian and a Greek formed a slave "kingdom" with its own army. It took Rome no less than three years to subdue the insurgents, and the campaign is rightly dignified by the name of the First Servile War. If slavery could produce such terror, was not this yet another, and very practical, argument in favour of the revival of free agriculture?

It was in this atmosphere, both personal and political, that in December 134 Tiberius sought the tribunate for the following year. One of the consuls was in Sicily, fighting without success against the slaves, the other, Africanus himself, was detained for months in Spain, in order to subdue a small country town. Clearly, the state was in danger; to Tiberius fell the task of seeking to save it.

> "The time is out of joint: O cursed spite,
> That ever I was born to set it right."

It was indeed the predicament of Hamlet that now confronted Tiberius.

The popular young nobleman, the "soldier's friend," was elected by acclamation. His father-in-law promised to help him, and he could look for benevolent aid to the jurist Scaevola, who was to be one of the consuls for the fateful year 133, and to Crassus, the *pontifex maximus*. With this prospective support Tiberius, immediately on entering office, proposed the enactment of an agrarian law. It was in substance largely a renewal of the Licinian law: state lands occupied by possessors without re-muneration—those that were let on lease, such as the territory of Capua, were not affected—were to be resumed by the state; but as an easement each occupier might reserve three hundred acres for himself and one hundred and fifty for each of two sons, not more than six hundred in all. The resumed lands were to be let in eighteen-acre lots, as inalienable, heritable leaseholds, to citizens and Italian allies. The lots must be used for agriculture, and a small rent was to be payable. A permanent land-board was to superintend the whole scheme. "Never," says Plutarch, "did any law appear more moderate and gentle especially being en-acted against such great oppression and avarice. For they who ought to have been severely punished for transgressing the former laws, and should have at least lost all their titles to such lands as they unjustly usurped, were notwithstanding to receive a price for quitting their unlawful claims, and giving up their lands to those fit owners who stood in need of help." Neverthe-less, the rich could not stomach even so mild a measure. They did all they could by slanderous misrepresentation to wreck it: Tiberius, they said, was out to procure a wholesale redivision of land, to subvert the government and to produce general chaos. They had no success. Tiberius had not studied oratory for nothing. "The wild beasts," he told the people, "have their own lairs, they have places of rest and refuge; but the men who bear arms, the men who risk their lives for the safety of their country, all they can enjoy is air and light; they have no houses or dwell-ings of their own, and are compelled to wander from place to place with their wives and children." What a mockery it was, when their commanders told them to fight "for their sepulchres and altars." They had no sepulchres nor altars, not even a house or hearth to defend. They fought and died, but only to maintain the luxury of others. "Masters of the world" they were called, these warriors, and yet they had not a single foot of land to call their own!

No one could withstand this sort of harangue, specially when it was addressed to an audience who were already in passionate sympathy with the speaker.

But if Tiberius was to be beaten, it must be on his own ground, that is by another tribune, for there were ten of these officers elected annually. The landholding interest therefore approached one of Tiberius' colleagues called Octavius, who seems to have been honestly of the opinion that the proposed law was contrary to the public interest. The debate between the two tribunes, who had been friends, was conducted with decorum and politeness, but it produced no agreement. Tiberius thereupon withdrew his bill, and introduced a more stringent one, as if to show the rich that he was stronger, and the poor that he was more their friend, than had been supposed. Still Octavius would not yield, so that in the end Tiberius imposed his veto on all public business. The courts were deserted, the treasury was sealed. Tiberius was now under the threat of personal violence, and when he walked abroad went armed with a sword-stick. When Tiberius again put forward his bill, there was a scuffle during which his opponents made off with the voting-urns. The Senate attempted a composition. Tiberius welcomed this move, being convinced that all reasonable men must be on his side. But in the house the rich prevailed: his bill was thrown out.

In times of less tension, as in a modern democratic legislature, the bill might have been withdrawn, reintroduced a year later, and if not accepted then, revived at intervals until public opinion swung in its favour: such a process is constantly observable in the legislatures of Britain and America. But Tiberius felt that he had reached the point of no return: either he must accept total eclipse, or else he must start a revolution. He chose the latter course. He told the citizens that either he or Octavius must be deposed from office, and proposed that the question be put to the vote. Octavius naturally resisted the suggestion, whereupon Tiberius moved that Octavius be deposed. Plutarch and Appian give us dramatic descriptions of the scene which was to prove the first in the great drama of the Roman Revolution. There were thirty-five tribes in the assembly, each of which had one vote. When the first tribe voted for Octavius' deposition, Tiberius turned to Octavius and begged him to give in. In vain; and so the voting went on, tribe after tribe voting against Octavius. Seventeen tribes had thus voted; if but one more cast its vote into the same urn, Octavius would be ousted in disgrace. In one of those emotional scenes that the Romans, for all their "gravity," deeply relished, Tiberius stopped the proceedings, crossed over to Octavius, embraced and kissed him before the whole assembly, and implored him not to suffer such dishonour, nor to put upon Tiberius the odium of having inflicted it. Octavius was moved, and his eyes filled with tears, but the sight of a group of land-owners who were watching the struggle stiffened his resolution, and he bade Tiberius do his worst. The eighteenth tribe voted, and Octavius was reduced to the rank of an ordinary citizen. He no longer enjoyed immunity, and so was dragged from the rostra by one of Tiberius' own servants. A riot at once broke out, from which Octavius was only saved with difficulty by his rich friends. Tiberius succeeded in quelling it and then, amid general rejoicing, his law was enacted and the land-commissioners appointed. As though to exacerbate the landowners, the board was to consist of Tiberius himself, his brother Gaius, then aged twenty, and his father-in-law, Appius Claudius. It was to be a family affair.

The aristocrats now made no secret of their intention to get even with Tiberius. That they would impeach him when his term of office expired was the least of their threats; so that Tiberius was now attended by a bodyguard of three or four thousand men whenever he appeared in the Forum. He himself wore mourning, and paraded his children before the people, asking them to provide for them and their mother, because he now despaired of his own security. Tiberius was, truly, at the end of his tether. Gratitude is a frail flower, whereas hatred is a very tough weed. The agrarian law was enacted, the board set up; but it was clear that unless Tiberius could find some new interest to exploit, some new hope to nourish, he was a doomed man. It was at this juncture that a wonderful windfall came his way. Attalus III, king of Pergamum, cannily anticipating the inevitable, "bequeathed" his kingdom to Rome. Tiberius proposed that Attalus' wealth, which was very great, should be devoted to providing the poor citizens who were to be beneficiaries under the agrarian law with implements and stock for their new farms; and claimed that the citizens should determine how the new province of "Asia," as the Pergamene kingdom would become, was to be administered. This infuriated the Senate still further, if that were possible, so that Tiberius saw that his only hope of survival lay in being elected tribune for a second year. He came forward with a "popular" program: shorter military service, the right of appeal to the Comitia, the inclusion of equites among the panel of judges. When the tribes met to elect the tribunes for the ensuing year, the first to vote favoured Tiberius, but his opponents imposed their veto, and the assembly broke up, the election being postponed until the next day.

On the following morning, the tribes assembled in front of the temple of Jupiter on the Capitoline hill, just above the Senate-house and Forum. At first all went well for Tiberius, who was given a rousing reception when he entered the hustings; but almost at once disorder broke out. Tiberius' partisans smashed the halberds of the police and the lictors' fasces, and put themselves in readiness to combat the skirmishers of the opposite party, who were trying to force their way into the assembly. At this juncture, Tiberius raised his hand to his head to signify, above the noise of the riot, that his life was in danger. One of his enemies at once ran down to the Senate-house and announced that Tiberius was asking the people to crown him. The senators, who must already have been perturbed and excited by the sound of the struggle on the Capitol, were themselves a prey to confusion. Nasica, the son-in-law of Africanus major, and now *pontifex maximus*, a harsh and vehement reactionary, jumped up and urged the consul presiding to punish the "tyrant." When, very properly, the consul replied that he could do nothing contrary to law and would equally resist any unlawful decision provoked by

Tiberius, Nasica called on all those who wished to defend the laws to follow him, and "wrapping the skirt of his toga over his head, hastened to the Capitol." The sight of the chief priest, followed by a number of senators marching up the slope of the Capitol with murder in their eyes, affrighted the followers of Tiberius. At his first election and during his agrarian campaign these had been predominantly farmers, countrymen who had found it worth while to come into the city to advance their own interests; but on this occasion, we are told, there had been no time to get them in, and so the crowd consisted of the urban rabble. They soon gave way. Tiberius was isolated. He tried to escape by flight. A pursuer caught hold of his toga: Tiberius let it go, but the man snatched at his shirt; Tiberius stumbled and fell, and before he could get up again was hit on the head with the leg of a stool. He was soon dispatched. Three hundred more were killed, "not one by an iron weapon," and their bodies, including that of Tiberius, thrown into the Tiber. So ended the first civil bloodshed since the kings had been expelled nearly four centuries before, and so began the revolution which was to end one century later.

The aristocrats were jubilant. Even the moderate Africanus, when he heard of the death of his brother-in-law, is reported to have exclaimed (characteristically quoting Homer): "Even so perish all who do likewise." But the oligarchs did not dare to attempt to abolish the land-board, which had, after all, been constituted by a law legally enacted. A court was set up to punish everyone who had been guilty of helping Tiberius. Nasica, the ringleader of the noble mob who had murdered Tiberius, was a member of the court, and they showed little mercy. Now that the Senate had regained control, however, Nasica was an embarrassing ally. A rising in Asia led by a certain Aristonicus, a pretender to the throne of the deceased Attalus of Pergamum, furnished a convenient pretext for dropping him. He was packed off to Asia on a commission of enquiry and died there shortly afterwards.

The land-board nevertheless soon ran into difficulties. Most of the public domain of Rome lay in or near territories occupied not by Roman citizens but by Latin or Italian allies. Naturally, portions of these lands unallocated to citizens had been appropriated for use by members of allied communities who hated to see them lying idle; any enterprising farmer would have done the same. Now, the discontent of the allies, their feeling that they were being exploited for the benefit of Rome, has already been mentioned. The arrival of the land-board and the steps they took to reallocate the domain, giving portions of it to "citizens" who had never even served in the legions—this really was the last straw. Scipio now, in the year 123, contrived to have the commissioners warned off allied lands, and to confine their work to lands indisputably belonging to citizens. This pleased the allies, but laid Scipio open to vituperation both from the Gracchan party, who felt that he was curtailing their activities, and from the landowners, who feared that they would now be the sole target of the reformers. After one of these angry exchanges in the Senate, Scipio went home, and before lying down, put by his bedside the tablet on which he intended to write during the night his speech for the morrow. This speech was never delivered. Scipio was found dead in his bed the next morning. No one has ever known how he died. His widow (Tiberius' sister), Tiberius' brother, all three members of the land-board were accused, even Cornelia herself. The official version was that he had died of natural causes, and this view is supported by the fact that Scipio's friends never succeeded in bringing a charge of murder home to any individual. But Scipio was only fifty-six, and he himself had mentioned, shortly before his death, that he knew his life was threatened. He was buried hugger-mugger: no one was allowed to see the dead man's face, nor his body, which according to Plutarch showed signs of violence, and the funeral pyre did the rest.

The great commoner was dead, the prototype of the moderate doomed to martyrdom; but the agitation went on. The work of the land-board was at a standstill. The Gracchan party suggested that the Italian allies should be granted citizenship, so as to be brought once more within the purview of the agrarian law. The Senate countered this by contriving that one of the tribunes for the year 126 should propose that all those who were not citizens should be dismissed from the capital. Among those who championed the allies was Gaius Gracchus, Tiberius' brother, but the proposal was carried. This odious discrimination brought the discontent of the allies to a head. One of the most prominent of the Latin colonies, one moreover that had an unbroken record of loyalty to Rome—it had been steadfast even in the darkest days of the Hannibalic War—Fregellae, some sixty miles south-east of Rome, broke out in open revolt. For the first time in a century and a half Rome was involved in an insurrection against her hegemony not brought about by a foreign power. Fregellae, at that time probably the second city in Italy, was simply wiped out. Its inhabitants were spared, but the very name was erased from the map. Endless impeachments for high treason followed. Gaius Gracchus was among those who were arraigned and thus it was that he entered the domestic drama by standing for the tribuneship for the year 123.

Gaius was only thirty, but he had already made a name for himself. He had, like his brother, served with distinction before Numantia. He had been a member of the land-board. Later, as quaestor to a tactless consul in Sardinia, he had by kindness induced the Sardinians to yield the much-needed winter clothing which they had refused to hand over on the consul's brusque requisition. A little later, ambassadors from Micipsa, son and heir of the collaborating king Masinissa, told the Senate that their master, "out of respect for Gaius Gracchus," had sent a large quantity of corn to the troops in Sardinia. The senators were furious. They dismissed the ambassadors, and prolonged the command of the unfortunate consul, thinking thereby to keep Gaius at a distance in Sardinia. He boldly returned to the capital and was able to show that he had already served twelve years in the army, instead of the statutory ten, and had been a quaestor for three, two years more than he was required to. What was more, he had returned no richer than he set out.

He was elected tribune, and his fiery oratory soon marked him out as a popular champion. He was far more of a demagogue than Tiberius. He invoked the memory of his brother, he in-

voked the name and fame of Cornelia "the mother of the Gracchi." He was out for vengeance, and for power. Tiberius had
been content to propose a single reform; Gaius planned an entirely new constitution. Already, at some time after the death
of Scipio (who was opposed to the measure) a law had been
enacted allowing a tribune to be re-elected, thus removing one
of the obstacles which had thwarted Tiberius. First of all, he
had to establish a hold over the city voters; and the method by
which he did so has laid him open to much unfair criticism.
The corn-supply had hitherto been in the hands of amateurs,
young aediles just entering on a political career, with no experience and no knowledge of economics. Shortages, due to failure
of deliveries or foul weather, were a chronic occurrence. Gaius
therefore arranged to have large granaries built, to hold a reserve,
and then organized a monthly distribution to every resident
citizen who applied for it in person. It was to be had at half
the current market price; but it amounted to no more than the
equivalent of one two-pound loaf a day, not much for a family
whose staple food it was. The measure did, it is true, set a
precedent which other demagogues, not excluding Julius Caesar
himself, would find it convenient to follow; but it was not in
itself subversive, any more than the first-aid measures adopted
by Britain during the aftermath of war, or by America during
the Depression were subversive. It did, of course, strengthen
Gaius politically, if only because it undermined the hold of the
rich on their "clients," who could now turn to Gaius instead.

The small farmers may not have been best pleased by this
measure, although it must be borne in mind that they had
long ceased to be the only or even the chief providers of corn
for the metropolis. But Gaius had a plan for conciliating them,
too. He set about improving the road-system, so as to enable the
countrymen to get their produce to the city speedily and conveniently. His roads became the model for later engineers. He
designed them not only as utilities but as amenities, too. They
traversed the countryside in a straight line, were partly paved,
and partly surfaced with pounded gravel. Valleys were crossed
on embankments or viaducts, so that steep gradients were elim-

inated. Milestones were erected to show the distance between places, and little mounting-blocks were provided at intervals. This may seem a superfluity, but it must be remembered that stirrups were unknown in antiquity. If you were rich you had a groom who would help you to mount; but Gaius was, as usual, thinking of the poor, who had no grooms. They must have blessed him as they jogged along his lovely level roads.

He brought the land-board back to life; but realizing that townsmen make poor farmers, he hit on the idea of founding new colonies, not only on the site of Capua, still derelict from the Hannibalic War, or at Tarentum, but actually across the sea at Carthage. Next it was the turn of the commercial classes. The taxes of "Asia" were no longer to be farmed out, because under that system, so long as a certain sum found its way to the treasury, no one could possibly tell how much had originally been extorted from the unfortunate provincials, specially in the years when the harvest failed. Perhaps the tithe system would be better? It was accordingly introduced, and the contract for its collection was to be allocated in Rome, not in Asia. This meant a handsome annual profit for some of Gaius' rich friends.

Gaius would beyond doubt have liked to cripple the Senate. He had a plan for so doing, by increasing its numbers from three to nine hundred, and thus swamping his opponents. But he had to abandon so audacious a scheme. Instead, he managed to have the jury-courts transferred from the Senate to the knights, a class which was now to include any citizen worth about ten thousand dollars or more.

The equites, or knights, were henceforth to be reckoned as a definite order in the state, second only to the senators. When we take into consideration that it was before the jury-courts that retiring provincial governors had to account for their administration, we can see what a whip-hand the equites were now to wield over their "superiors." What Gaius could hardly have foreseen was that both as tax-gatherers and as judges the equites were to be every whit as grasping and corrupt as the Senate.

Gaius had no difficulty in getting himself elected for a second year. He had, to all intents and purposes, and in a bewilderingly short time, imposed a new constitution on Rome, "insomuch," says Plutarch, "that all persons, even those who hated or feared him, stood amazed to see what a capacity he had for effecting and completing all he undertook. As for the people themselves, they were transported at the very sight, when they saw him surrounded with a crowd of contractors, artificers, public deputies, military officers, soldiers and scholars. All these he treated with an easy familiarity, yet without abandoning his gentleness." He was, in fact, the uncrowned king of Rome.

Gaius would have gone far to mitigate, if he could not remove, the grievances of the allies. First he would have given the limited franchise to all the allies, so that they would have enjoyed the citizens' privileges in regard to commercial transactions, testamentary dispositions and the like. Those who already possessed this status were to be allowed to opt either for full citizenship (which would allow them to vote, but would compel them to serve as soldiers or pay the exemption-fee) or for the right to appeal to the Assembly against the sentence of flogging often awarded by army officers. These moderate proposals might have been accepted, but for the cunning tactics of the Senate. They dared not oppose Gaius openly, so they descended to the artifice of setting a tribune to catch a tribune.

They put up a limp and odious creature called Livius Drusus, simply to outbid Gaius in every possible way, with promises which his masters had not the slightest intention of honouring. At this juncture for some reason Gaius went off to Africa to supervise the founding of the new colony of Carthage. Stories got about that the omens were unfavourable, that hyenas had dug up the boundary-marks, that the site was for ever accursed. When it came to the next elections, Gaius' rural supporters were out of town. The mob, as fickle as it was greedy, deserted him, and he was not re-elected for a third term.

The end soon came. Opposition to the Carthage scheme erupted into violence. Gaius was declared an outlaw; he retreated first to the Aventine, and then across the wooden bridge which Horatius had defended "in the brave days of old" up onto the Janiculum, watched by all, aided by none. He was killed, at his own command, by a devoted slave.

Thus ended the reign of king Gaius, and the Gracchan dream of a reformed state. Thus started the hundred years of violence which was to end in the elevation of Octavian to very much the status which Gaius had sought to occupy.

Until recently it has been the habit of historians to decry the Gracchi as self-seeking revolutionaries out only for their own aggrandizement. They have generally been regarded as being the authors of the century of strife that followed Gaius' death. But until recently history was written by men of upper- or middle-class sympathies. Nowadays, in an age which has seen a New Deal and a Welfare State, under both of which the lot of millions has been marvellously ameliorated, it is possible and fitting to take a more liberal view of the Gracchi. That they were clever politicians, that they exploited their hereditary charm and abilities for their own ends, is not to be denied. Is it to be denied of the majority of politicians so gifted? But their reforms were salutary, their aims enlightened. It was not their fault that corruption had already eroded Roman society like the death watch beetle, so that only the façade remained intact. The tribulations of the next century, which was to end in the death of the republic, were due far less to the Gracchi than to those who selfishly, irresponsibly and successfully opposed them.

CHAPTER VIII

INTER ARMA SILENT LEGES

W HEN fighting begins, the law keeps silence." This dictum
was to be the motto of the age which followed that of
the Gracchi, and the man who first uttered it would be that
age's artificer. His name was Marius.

Hitherto the action described in this narrative, in so far as
it concerns the rise and decline of the Roman republic, has been
political action. Riots there have been, battle, murder, sudden
death, privy conspiracy and rebellion; but the outcome has
always been some new political development, some new electoral
or constitutional balance, ratified, in the end, by the Senate and
people of Rome. Now, and until the end of the republic itself,
the sword was to be the only arbiter of success, the only key to
power. That was to be the harsh fact of Roman life for the next
seventy years. Moreover, whereas the principal agents in the
formation of the ideas of the Gracchi had been Greek, and it
was from the Greek world that the chief influences on Roman
thought and motives had long been transmitted, Africa was
now to supplant Hellas, and intrigue, not philosophy, would
nourish the springs of action.

When Gaius Gracchus fell, in the year 121, the Senate was
technically the victor. But they had rid themselves of this dangerous radical by violence, only nominally disguised under a pro-
cedural innovation, the passing for the first time of the *senatus
consultum ultimum,* the "final decision" of the Senate. They had
only just got away with it; and so they must proceed carefully
on their myopic way. Their first step was taken in the very year
of Gracchus' death: the allotment-holders were permitted to sell
their holdings, which soon passed once again into the hands of
the large landowners. In 118, the land-board was abolished, which
meant that no more allotments could be made. In 111 all the

squatters on the public domain were deemed to be legal owners in freehold; so that the rich usurpers could feel as secure as the privileged "receivers" of Church property would in the England of Henry VIII. So much for the land. What about the law-courts? Could the Senate regain control of them? They could not: in 106 the issue came to a head. A law was introduced by the consul Quintus Caepio which would have restored the courts to the Senate, but it was not carried, or if carried, very soon repealed. The equites would have none of it: squandering public land was one thing, trying to curtail their privileges was another. The equites had proved the power of their order, for such, largely owing to the measures of Gaius Gracchus, it had now become. It was at this period that the equites, that is the plutocrats, acquired the right to sport a golden finger-ring, like the senatorial aristocrats; but not until 67 were they allotted their own seats, just behind the senators, at the games. It would be misleading to say "at the theatre," because Rome did not possess a permanent theatre until 65. "About this time"—actually in 111—Appian tells us, "the consul Scipio Nasica demolished the theatre begun by Lucius Cassius, and nearly finished, because he considered this also was a likely source of new seditions, or because he thought it far from desirable that the Romans should become accustomed to Grecian pleasures."

In the struggle now beginning between the oligarchs and the people, the equites, being in the middle, would play an ever-increasing role, with the popular party relying more and more upon their interested support: "the enemy of my enemy is my friend."

It was, as noted at the beginning of this chapter, from Africa that the spark was wafted that was to set Italy alight. Micipsa had bequeathed his kingdom not to any one heir but to three. He may have thought thereby to avert strife; he should have known that he was making it inevitable. His two sons, Adherbal and Hiempsal, were to share the legacy with a nephew, Jugurtha. Jugurtha was older and bolder than his cousins. Micipsa had sent him off in 134 at the head of a Numidian contingent to help Scipio at the siege of Numantia, probably hoping that he would not come back. But Jugurtha did come back—as Scipio's admired friend, and with an intimate knowledge of Roman character, its strength and its weakness. Jugurtha, now the adopted son of Micipsa, calmly and deliberately set about "liquidating" his rivals. Hiempsal was the first to go, in 117. Numidia became a prey to civil war, the majority remaining loyal to Adherbal. Jugurtha beat him in the field, whereupon Adherbal went to Rome to engage the support of his suzerain, closely followed by an embassy from Jugurtha bent on the same mission, but with far greater skill in knowing how to bring it to fruition. Gold, and plenty of it, was what Jugurtha relied on. As a result of his manoeuvres, instead of Jugurtha's being denounced as an aggressor, a commission was appointed in 116 to visit Numidia and to define the boundaries between his realm and that of Adherbal. Jugurtha, ready as ever with solid cash, was awarded the east, Adherbal the west. He was not to keep it for long. Less than four years later, in 112, Jugurtha invaded his territory and after contemptuously rebuffing a second Roman mission sent at Adherbal's request, besieged and captured Adherbal's capital, where he killed not only Adherbal but also a large number of Italian merchants who, at first constrained to fight for Adherbal, had in the end opened the gates of his citadel to Jugurtha. This was not only a crime but a blunder as well: not merely honour, but money was now at stake. One of the tribunes forced the Senate into action. An embassy from Jugurtha was sent home unheard, an expeditionary force was recruited, commanded by a notoriously bribe-prone consul, Bestia. No sooner had he entered Numidia than Jugurtha induced him to leave it by the surrender of thirty elephants, a quantity of cattle and horses (which he was at once allowed to buy back) and some money. Public indignation seethed in Rome. A praetor was sent to bring Jugurtha to the city so that he might reveal the names of those whom he had bought. Jugurtha willingly came—under a safe-conduct, because it gave him an opportunity for showing his contempt of Rome, and his power. When the tribune who had led the indignant patriots demanded of the African that he name his agents, another tribune ordered him to be silent. Jugurtha had won without saying a word. But he now overreached himself. A rival to his throne, a cousin, was being supported by one of the consuls for 110. Jugurtha ordered one of his suite, called Bomilcar, to have the man murdered, there in Rome, where he had come to press his claim. The murder was bungled, the assassin caught, and Jugurtha's complicity established beyond doubt. Even now, the government did nothing. Jugurtha went bail for Bomilcar, and then both of them simply made off to Numidia. It was on this occasion that Jugurtha uttered the famous taunt: "A city for sale, and soon to go down, if it could find a buyer." It must have stung the Romans, because this gibe by an African prince showed up the rottenness of Rome. It also, as men saw afterwards only too well, fired the fatal train of doom for the republic.

The war was resumed, so was the story of disaster: a Roman army was trapped in the desert. Its commander, though absent at the time, was exiled. Rome at last determined to avenge the humiliation and defeats she had suffered, not least because the plutocrats were burning to get their hands on the riches of Numidia. An old-fashioned and uncorruptible aristocrat, Quintus Metellus, was given the command, and arrived in Africa in 109, bent on reorganizing the demoralized army, whose principal occupation had now become the looting of any available property, including that of the settlers in Roman Africa. Among Metellus' subordinates was a man of forty-eight called Gaius Marius. He had no third name, or cognomen, because he was the son of obscure peasants who worked as day-labourers near Arpinum, a district to the south-east of Rome which was later to give Cicero to the world. Metellus and Marius had known each other for many years, because Marius' family were "clients" of the great Metellan family. It was through the influence of a Metellus, a consul in 119, that Marius entered the political field by becoming one of the tribunes for that year. He had already made a name for himself as a soldier. Like Jugurtha, whom he could hardly have failed to meet, he had fought with Scipio at the siege of Numantia. He not only displayed great personal bravery in the campaign, but was a willing supporter of Scipio in his efforts to improve the lax discipline of the Roman army. He had several times been decorated. One day, at a reception, a flatterer asked Scipio where the Romans would find another general like him. "Here, perhaps," replied Scipio, putting his hand on the shoulder of the young man next him. It was Marius, and it was this commendation of Scipio's, we are told, that first, "as by a divine admonition," spurred Marius to aspire to greatness.

The friend of Scipio, the protégé of the Metelli, the rough, tough peasant's son, the man who in Plutarch's phrase "never sacrificed to the Graces," remained true to his class and his heredity. As tribune he proposed some measure which would have further curtailed senatorial judicial privileges—we do not know how—whereupon he was summoned to appear before the Senate. Marius did so, and calmly told Metellus' brother-consul Cotta, that if he pressed his opposition he would have him arrested. When Metellus, Marius' patron, said he supported Cotta, Marius ordered that he be taken into custody. The Senate was aghast, but not one of the other tribunes dared gainsay Marius; the opposition simply collapsed and Marius' measure became law. Marius was now a popular hero; but he had no intention of being a slave of the people: he would be their master, as he was shortly to prove. A law was introduced which would have increased the distribution of subsidized corn; Marius, being himself of yeoman stock, vetoed it. He was now "honoured by both parties, in gratifying neither contrary to the public interest." Even so, his brusque manners did not help him in his career. He failed to be elected an aedile, and only just scraped home as a praetor. After an undistinguished year of office he went off to govern "further Spain," where he successfully repressed banditry. When he came home he opened up new horizons by marrying Julia, a member of an old family called Caesar. Julius Caesar, born some two decades later, was her nephew. We must now return to Africa and to Q. Caecilius Metellus. Marius had humiliated his brother, but the general nevertheless took Marius with him as his *legatus,* or second-in-command. They very soon fell out. Marius, who by nature and heredity had far more in common with the soldiers than with his aristocratic patron, deliberately courted their favour. He lived hard, ate the soldiers' rations, and stood up for them against their superiors. The final breach occurred when Marius, wrongly as it turned out, insisted that Metellus execute for cowardice an old family friend. When the error was discovered Marius merely boasted that he had involved Metellus in the guilt of putting his friend to death. Disloyalty could hardly go further. And yet, in Marius' hands it did. The troops had been writing home that the man to be consul was their friend Marius. And so Marius, in the summer of 108, demanded leave to go to Rome and stand for the supreme office. Metellus openly jeered at him. Would it not be more seemly, said the nobleman, if the peasant waited until he could stand together with Metellus' son? Metellus detained Marius as long as he dared; but with only twelve days to go before polling-day, Marius succeeded in leaving Africa. He just made it, arriving in Rome in time publicly to decry Metellus, and to assure the sovereign people that he, Marius, would either kill Jugurtha or bring him home alive.

Marius was elected, the first man of his stamp and class ever to become consul. At once he set about making himself supreme, and very cunningly he did it. He was, with his fellow consul, commander-in-chief, and as such responsible for recruiting. Hitherto recruits had been enlisted from among citizens and allies "whose property was a sort of security for their good behaviour." Marius now threw open the military career to anyone, paupers and slaves included, who chose to follow it. This meant that Marius' soldiers would be attached to Marius, not to Rome, that their interests lay in war, not peace. This step was to lead to measureless evils; Marius was Rome's first war-lord, the first Roman for whom Rome was to be as a harlot, not a mother.

Marius again flouted the Senate. It was their prerogative to assign commands outside Italy: Marius insisted that he be sent to Africa, and by a special decree of the people, to Africa he was sent. Metellus, now superseded, could only retire, leaving Marius to reap another's hard-won laurels. In this Marius was only partly successful; because although his long-range desert group did ultimately prove itself Jugurtha's master, the final capture of the African was secured by the treachery of a rival chief, and it was to a well-born subordinate called Sulla, now aged thirty, that Jugurtha was delivered. Sulla had a seal engraved showing the surrender of Jugurtha. Marius was awarded his triumph, and Jugurtha was starved to death or strangled in the prison below the Capitol; but between Marius and Sulla the ultimate clash was inevitable.

It was averted by an external threat far more dangerous than that of Jugurtha. It came from the north, as it had done in the dread year of 391 B.C., and would again at the beginning of the fifth century A.D. The nomad tribes, great blond giants who fought in serried lines linked to one another by chains, terrified the southerners, as they had done before and were so often to do afterwards. They were once again on the move. Hitherto Marius had not in fact shown any great military aptitude; but he had established himself as a man with a star, a child of good fortune and, above all, as the friend of the people. In 113, again in 109, and yet a third time in 105, Roman armies, led by incompetent amateurs, had suffered crushing defeats. The road to Rome lay open: it was only the whimsical wanderlust of the northerners that prevented their taking it. They tended either to swerve to the west, lured by the riches of Spain, or to return to Gaul. But their awful menace remained. It was at this point that Marius came back from Africa. Strict legality had been waived, and he had already been elected consul a second time for the year 104. His prestige boosted by his triumph and by the end of Jugurtha, not to mention the enormous quantities of coin and bullion he had brought back with him, Marius proceeded to train a new army on his own lines. As before, they were recruited from the lowest strata of society, men who had nothing to lose and everything to gain from war and pillage. The strictest discipline was supplemented by rigorous training. Each man had to carry his own baggage and rations, so that the troops came to be known as "Marius' mules." The order of battle was overhauled. The legions had formerly been drawn up in three lines, graded according to age with the youngest men in front. The unit of manoeuvre was a maniple, or section, each maniple being at some distance from the next to allow freedom of action. This formation had shown itself no match for the packed barbarian onslaught. Marius decided that the unit of manoeuvre must be made larger and more solid. He therefore divided each legion into ten cohorts of six hundred men each. The age distinction between the ranks was done away with. This made for greater cohesion; and the nascent regimental spirit was fostered by the introduction of what we should call "colours," that is the famous standards or "eagles." The arms were improved. The throwing-spear had formerly had the head attached to the shaft by two metal rivets. Marius substituted a wooden pin for the second bolt. The pin broke on impact, thus making the spear useless for throwing back. Finally, and most important, Marius (or if not he, one of his followers) amended the system whereby regimental officers were chosen from among decorative young aristocrats who possessed the necessary influence but seldom the slightest military qualifications. Instead, each legion was now to be commanded by a competent officer chosen by the commander-in-chief, the ornamental young gentlemen being relegated to administrative duties.

These changes, viewed from the professional point of view, were the most important "reforms" ever undertaken in the organization of the Roman army; it would be whole centuries (when it was already too late) before any radical alteration in strategy, tactics or equipment would be adopted to counter the resurgent power of Persia; but seen against the background of political and social life, the new model brought nothing but bane. Rome was now ready to be the prey of any general who could cajole or seduce enough troops to fight for him, and through him, for loot and power. Since the chilling experience of Cromwell and his major-generals, England has always refused to be dominated by soldiers, or to countenance a standing army (the army is technically only kept in being by the annual re-enactment of the Mutiny Act). America has inherited and maintained the same wholesome aversion to military dominance. In each case their instinct has been right, and the basis of their state's stability. If more nations had heeded the terrible example of post-Marian Rome, the world would to-day be a more tranquil place.

Marius' second consulate was spent in reorganization and training; he still had not met the enemy—would the people grant him a third term? Such a thing was unheard of. But just at the right moment an incident occurred of the kind that Marius knew so well how to turn to account. It happened that a nephew of Marius called Lusius who was serving under him was, despite his acknowledged merits, a pederast. He had made repeated advances to one of his own soldiers, Trebonius by name, who had refused to respond to them. Finally Lusius ordered Trebonius to come to his tent, a command the soldier could not refuse. Once there he was subjected to violence, whereat to save his honour the lad drew his sword and ran Lusius through. Marius was away at the time. On his return he fixed a day for Trebonius' trial. It is typical of the morals of the day that no one would risk giving evidence against the commander-in-chief's nephew: on the contrary many came forward to testify against Trebonius. Trebonius with great courage told the whole story, bringing witnesses to support his assertions of innocence. When he had finished, Marius ordered that a garland be brought into court, and himself placed this signal mark of valour on the head of Trebonius "as having performed an excellent action at a time that very much wanted such good examples."

This vindication of morals—for the Romans were no less hypocritical than more recent sinners—combined with the news that the barbarians were once again coming southwards, helped Marius to his third consulship. He moved north, but still the enemy, with their by now established disregard of time and place, held off. Another year had gone by. Marius must be, and was, elected a fourth time, largely by the help of a theatrical tribune called Saturninus. While waiting for the northerners to return, Marius had fixed his headquarters near the town of Arelate, or Arles as it now is. This had the advantage that it was far removed from the strife and tension of Rome, besides being in an area which allowed Marius plenty of room for manoeuvre. But it had one disadvantage: the mouth of the river

Rhône on which it stands had become silted up—an occurrence
which repeatedly strangled towns in antiquity, when mechanical
dredging was unknown. Marius solved the problem, and kept his
troops actively employed, by digging a canal from Arles to the
sea, thereby laying the foundation of Arles' commercial prosperity, its administration being in the experienced hands of the
citizens of Massilia or Marseilles, an ancient Greek colony which
had always been on good terms with Rome.

At last in the year 102 (the probable date of Julius Caesar's
birth) the northern horde approached. They were a formidable host indeed, if only by mere weight of numbers. But they
played into Marius' hands: they split into three bodies. The most
westerly came down towards Marius. He cleverly allowed them
to by-pass Arles and then, by outmarching them, confronted
them in a carefully chosen position near Aquae Sextiae, or
Aix. The result was an overwhelming victory for Marius and his
professionals. Rome had triumphed once again. The remaining
enemy hordes were annihilated in the following year near Milan.
Italy was saved, and Marius was her saviour. He was now the
greatest man in Rome, hailed, after Romulus and Camillus (who
had rescued Rome in 390), as the third founder of the city. But
his star was already setting. He had no political flair whatever.
Everything, he thought, could be won by steel or gold. It was
he who first contemptuously coined the phrase with which this
chapter opens. By flagrant bribery he did succeed in becoming
consul for the sixth time; but he was now compelled to rely on
the support of Saturninus and a creature equally odious called
Glaucia, the former as tribune, the latter as praetor whose aid
was ineffective in the troubled scene which Rome and her
empire now presented. There was resentment against the Senate
and its incompetent generals, there was unrest in Sardinia. Piracy was rampant in the Aegean, and the slave-markets from
which Roman capitalists obtained their servile labour-force were
replenished by corsairs who defied Rome's authority. In Sicily
a more terrible sequel to this vile traffic now showed itself. It
happened that a client-prince of Bithynia, in what is now north-
western Turkey, had complained to Rome that he was unable to

send a contingent of troops to help fight the northern invaders because half his fighting-men were already serving on Roman territory—as kidnapped slaves. The Senate ordered an investigation, and hopes of liberty ran high among the Sicilian captives. The slave-owners protested, and the governor of the island called off the enquiry, which had already resulted in the liberation of some eight hundred men. The slaves, far more numerous and lusty than their masters, again broke out in rebellion. The revolt took three years to quell, at enormous cost in human lives. Even then, nothing was done to remedy the evils which had caused it. Only the capitalists had gained.

Marius was no match for the combination of greedy knights and scheming demagogues of the stamp of Saturninus and Glaucia. This ignoble couple simply used Marius, now consul for the sixth time, as a front for their reckless prostitution of power. Colonies for the veterans were to be founded in Cisalpine Gaul, in Greece and in Sicily. The supreme authority of the Comitia was to be established by the impeachment of anyone who "diminished the majesty of the Roman people," and every magistrate and senator was to take an oath to support the proposals. Marius jibbed, but swore. His rival Metellus preferred exile and retired to Rhodes. Rioting broke out, and by the most flagrant piece of "tacking," backed by hooliganism, the measures were enacted. In the summer of 100 Glaucia stood for the consulship. His rival, Memmius, was simply murdered by hired thugs. This was too much, even for Rome: the Senate passed the "ultimate decree," which meant that Marius, as consul, must now proceed against his disreputable friends, who as though preparing for civil war had occupied the Capitol. Marius cut off the water-supply, and thus forced them to surrender. He tried to save their lives by locking them up in the Senate-house; but the mob climbed onto the roof, tore off the tiles, and pelted them to death.

The republic was dying, but it would take a long time to die —that was, in brief, the lesson of the shoddy, shabby events recorded above. Metellus was recalled; Marius, accepting this bitter signal of defeat, left Rome for Asia in 99 B.C. He had for ever turned his back on glory, but not on Rome.

CHAPTER IX

SULLA

MARIUS was no statesman; his political abilities were contemptible; and yet it was Marius who had molded the pattern of Roman politics for almost a century to come. The reason for this paradoxical achievement is as simple as it is sad. The replacement of the citizen militiaman by the professional soldier inevitably meant that the future now lay with the warlords, with individuals not legislatures, with adventurers not maintainers of tradition—in short with tyrants, not servants. This ruinous syndrome has, over the last century, bedevilled and wrecked much of Europe. For us it started after the French Revolution when the "popular general" whose inevitable appearance Burke had at once foretold arose in the person of Napoleon, and was to be even more active for ill in our own generation. That is why the story of Rome in the last days of the republic has for us such a poignant and personal interest, quite apart from the intrinsic drama of the events themselves.

For nearly a decade after Marius' departure the capital made the most of an uneasy peace. The Senate and the knights scored off each other so far as they dared. The Senate carried a law forbidding "tacking" such as had been flagrantly employed against their interests. The knights, as to show that when it came to corruption they were just as efficient as their rivals, made use of their control of the courts to harry senatorials, even going so far as to exile a just man, Rutilius Rufus, who had tried to protect the people of Asia from the extortions of the tax-collectors. It was this blatant piece of malpractice that provoked the clash. One of the tribunes for the year 91 was Marcus Livius Drusus, a rich and upright man who conducted his life, as Mommsen says, on the principle that *noblesse oblige*. His father had been one of the chief opponents of Gaius Gracchus, but the younger

Drusus was to be dubbed by a contemporary critic "a pale reflection of the Gracchi." Drusus was out for a compromise, a *modus vivendi* which would restore the "Harmony of the Orders." But first he must win the hearts, that is the stomachs and pockets, of the people. He proposed the founding of more colonies, distribution of more public land. He lavishly increased the corn-dole, and to meet the run on the treasury which it caused had to debase the currency. This done, he proposed to restore the control of the courts to the Senate, and at the same time to double the size of the Senate by promoting three hundred knights to membership of it. This "package deal" pleased neither side, but Drusus contrived to force it through the Assembly. The Senate, quite justly, declared that Drusus' enactment was a breach of the "anti-tacking" law mentioned above and therefore without effect.

Faced with dead-lock on this issue, Drusus now proceeded to tackle another, equally urgent and far more potentially dangerous—the enfranchisement of the allies. As with all civil wars the chief emotions aroused in retrospect by what is known as the Social War are, even after two thousand years, surprise and pity—surprise that so late in the evolution of a republic such an issue should have been left unfaced and unsettled, pity that so many innocent lives on both sides were sacrificed to intransigence. Of the actual conduct of the war we know little, because our sources are so meagre; but we do know—and this is important—why it began, and what remarkable changes in the fabric of the Roman state it was to produce. It is a classical illustration, this war, of Aristotle's dictum that "wars arise out of small things, but not about small things." The "small thing" which touched it off was the knife of an anonymous assassin. Drusus, it was known, was the champion of "allied rights." For centuries now Italians had waged Roman wars—but always subordinated to Roman commanders; Roman officials could fleece, seize or bully them, and they had no right of appeal or redress. Even the courts were closed to them, save through the humiliating device of conciliating or buying the good offices of some Roman patron. All this injustice, this frustration and animosity could be swept

away by one single concession—the franchise. But that is just
what the proud and obstinate men of Rome would not yield.
Only a few years before, in 95, a number of Italians who had
migrated to the capital and had thus managed to have their
names inscribed on the voting list were struck off it and sent back
to their towns of origin. This callous rebuff to national feeling
brought matters to a head. Secret organizations came into being
in many towns, plans were formed for taking by force what
could not be obtained by peaceful means; and it was to Drusus
that the nationalists looked. Then one fatal night, as Drusus was
going home after a rally in the Forum, he was murdered. All
hope of a compromise now vanished. Freedom armies were reported to be forming. The Senate sent a praetor with proconsular powers to reconnoitre the position in Picenum, on the
east coast south of Ancona. Hearing that Asculum, the chief town
of the district, had exchanged hostages with another town, an
obvious preliminary to joint military action, he behaved with
such insolence to the citizens of Asculum that they murdered
not only him but every Roman in the town. They immediately
dispatched an embassy to Rome, to press their demands and
complaints, but the Senate, not unnaturally, refused to meet
them unless they were prepared to make amends for the massacre. War was now inevitable.

At this point it may be observed that the sequence of events,
of ignorance, lack of sympathy, obstinacy, the preference of
privilege to principle, leading to disaster, and the final victory
of the nationalist cause, the determination of the colonial government "not to yield to violence," its ultimate yielding to nothing
less than violence—this whole process was to be repeated over
and over again in the history of later European empires. That
Rome's Social War is the first recorded example of the sad
syndrome is not the least of the reasons which make it of such
interest to us to-day. For, of course, in the end the allies won;
they were bound to, if Rome itself was to survive.

Not all the allies joined the nationalists. The Latins and the
Greeks of the south, the Etruscans and Umbrians of the north,
and at first the Apulians of the south-east—these all remained

loyal to Rome. The insurgents consisted of eight Apennine tribes and the Picentines with their southern neighbours. A confederate capital with a government modelled on that of Rome was established at Corfinium, in the central Apennines, and a new state proclaimed under the name Italia. Of all these proceedings this choice of name for the state is the most historically proleptic; because, if we except the "kingdom of Italy" of Theodoric at the end of the fifth and beginning of the sixth centuries A.D., it was not until 1870 that Italia would cease to be "a geographical expression" and become what she now is— a state.

Mommsen calls the Social War "the most fearful civil war that has ever desolated the fair land of Italy," and in our own day we know how disastrous such wars can be.

Although Rome had the advantage of interior lines of communication, with better-trained troops and more experienced generals, she was compelled to fight on two fronts, the northern and the southern, and suffered initial reverses. During one of these a Roman general was routed and lost his command. This was transferred to Marius, who in the hour of crisis had returned to the army as one of the five subordinates of the consul Rutilius. Marius advised Rutilius to train his levies before rushing into battle. Rutilius ignored the old man's counsel, and pushed on up a river valley into enemy country. Marius, in position lower down the valley, saw numbers of bodies floating downstream, and by this macabre signal-system realized that the consul was in action. Marius, now more than sixty-five years old, had been accused of lethargy in this campaign; but he now showed his old mettle. He crossed the river, seized the enemy camp, forced the enemy to retreat and killed eight thousand of them. Nevertheless, the exhibition in Rome of the bodies of the fallen consul and his officers so depressed the citizens that it was ordained that in future those who were killed in battle should be buried where they fell. Marius was soon made sole commander in the north, and laid siege to Asculum, the Picentine capital. Many of the sling-stones used by the besiegers have come to light. No doubt the rude messages scratched upon them, just like the inscriptions on shells in more recent wars, added to their efficacy. Meanwhile, the other consul, Lucius Julius Caesar, had realized that political ills can be cured only by political remedies. Not only was the war going badly both in the north and in the south, but disconcerting news now arrived from the east: Mithridates, king of Pontus, was threatening Roman Asia. Moreover in Gaul beyond the Alps there was tribal unrest. Julius therefore put forward a proposal that all allied *communities* who either had not revolted, or were prepared to lay down their arms at once, should be granted citizenship. The measure was passed, and Etruria immediately took advantage of it. Other tribes began to waver. Early in the next year, 89, at the instance of two tribunes, yet another law was passed, granting citizenship to all *individuals* who were registered citizens of allied communities and were domiciled in Italy, provided they applied for it within sixty days. One of the consuls had even gone so far as to enfranchise thirty men of a squadron of Spanish cavalry for exemplary conduct during the siege of Asculum, an act which the Cambridge Ancient History terms a landmark in the history of Western civilization, because here for the first time Roman citizenship was conferred on dwellers outside Italy. Thousands of Italians flocked to Rome to take advantage of the measure and by the end of the year only the Samnites and Lucanians were still at odds with Rome.

For the rest, Italy was at last united. Every freeborn dweller south of the Po, Gauls included, was now a full Roman citizen, and the towns enjoyed municipal government on the Roman model. The law-courts, the markets, the rostra, the hustings, the legions—all were now equally open to every Italian.

Everything now seemed set fair for tranquil progress. But alas for Rome! Her statesmen had not yet learned the hard lesson that it is more blessed to give than to concede. The old reactionaries, with Sulla at their head, were by no means content to see the legislature thronged with all these "new" citizens; they tried therefore to have them registered in eight only of the thirty-five tribes which made up the Comitia, so that their voting-power would be restricted and largely annulled. The moderates wanted the newcomers to be distributed evenly throughout all the tribes, which was clearly the just and proper thing to do. The leader of the progressive party was a youthful tribune called Sulpicius Rufus, the most polished and persuasive orator of his day—Cicero, now rising eighteen, took him as his model. Sulpicius, like the Gracchi and Drusus before him, was a young aristocrat in a hurry: he was eager to promote not only the interests of the "allies," but those of the commonalty as well, but in his haste he made a fatal error, fatal alike for himself and for Rome. Sulla, who had been conspicuously successful in the southern command, and whose troops were devoted to him (even when they murdered one of their senior officers, Sulla had merely told them to make up for it by bravery in the field!), had been elected one of the consuls for the year 88, the other being a nobody called Pompeius Rufus. Sulla had already been awarded the Eastern command, that is in the forthcoming campaign against Mithridates, while his colleague was to remain in Italy. Sulpicius, in order to curry favour with the populace and so secure the necessary votes to pass his citizenship law, now proposed, quite illegally, that Sulla should be denied his command and Marius appointed in his place. The consuls declared a religious *hartal*, and so suspended business. Riots broke out, and Sulla himself only escaped by taking refuge in Marius' house, the old man kindly letting him out by the back door. He was forced to yield. He countermanded the solemnities and returned to his army, which was still besieging Nola. Sulpicius was now able to force through his measures. But that was far from being the end of the matter. Mommsen sums up the situation as follows: "Sulla himself was a hardened, cool and clear-headed man, in whose eyes the sovereign Roman burgesses were a rabble, the hero of Aquae Sextiae (Marius) a bankrupt swindler, formal legality a phrase, Rome itself a city without a garrison and with its walls half in ruins, which could be far more easily captured than Nola." He set out to capture it.

Something has already been said of Sulla; it is now time to present him more in the round, because he is the first of the great "stars" as we should now call them in the final drama. Sulla

—Lucius Cornelius Sulla—was born of a noble patrician family which had for long been obscure and indigent. He himself was called "Sulla" from his complexion, which was blotchy, what an Athenian jester called "a mulberry covered with meal." He had fair hair and blue eyes, very keen and piercing, and made all the more so by contrast with his hectic cheeks. As a youth he liked low company, a taste he never abandoned. He had amours with both sexes, an actor called Metrobius being his first love, and was fortunate in being bequeathed two fortunes, one by a Greek lady, a rich vulgarian called Nicopolis, and then another by a doting stepmother. He was beyond doubt fortunate —"Felix" was what they called him, and the name he himself assumed. He was a mass of contradictions. He was rapacious yet open-handed, generous one minute, vindictive the next, now cringing, now domineering, "so that it was hard to tell whether his nature had more in it of pride or of servility." But he was destined never to lose a battle, never to retrace a step, and to become the sole master of Rome. He was now fifty years old, a consul, who had already proved himself as a soldier in Numidia and Italy and in the East, where as governor of Cilicia he had pacified Cappadocia and had even impressed the Parthians with the might of Rome. To crown his contradictions, Sulla, the man who by heredity and upbringing was the upholder of the old republican tradition, was to be the very man who set it quite shamelessly at naught, and the first Roman to capture Rome by the sword.

This was no difficult task. As usual, Sulla acted on the spur of the moment. He recorded in his memoirs, now lost to us but used by Plutarch, that all his most successful enterprises were thus undertaken. When the tribunes arrived from Rome to take over Sulla's army and conduct it to Marius, they were stoned, and Sulla set out for Rome. Meanwhile Marius and Sulpicius, who had enlisted a gang of braves which Marius called his "anti-Senate," started massacring Sulla's friends and looting their property. The Senate, now powerless, sent two praetors to prohibit Sulla's approach. The soldiers wanted to lynch them, but contented themselves with tearing off their badges of office and breaking their ceremonial rods, and so sending them back. When a second deputation arrived saying that the Senate had promised to do everything he wished, if he would only halt his march, Sulla pretended to be about to mark out a camp, and then the moment the deputation was out of sight, sent an advance guard ahead to secure the gate and the wall on the Esquiline, that wall of which part is still to be seen outside the Termini railway station. Sulla followed soon after, and finding that his men were hard pressed, took the lead himself and ordered his archers to fire incendiary arrows "letting fly at the tops of the houses . . . and made his entry by fire, which knows no distinction betwixt friend and foe." Thus was Rome for the first time taken by a Roman, and a consul at that.

Marius withdrew to the temple of Tellus, or Mother Earth, and thence issued a proclamation offering freedom to the slaves if they would rally to him; but he was overpowered and fled the city. His later adventures will be related in their place. Sulla summoned the Senate and dragooned it into passing a decree of doubtful legality outlawing Marius, Marius' son, Sulpicius and a few other ringleaders. Their lives might be taken with impunity, and their property was forfeit. Sulpicius was betrayed by a slave, in return for a promise of enfranchisement. Sulla accordingly first freed him, and then had him hurled headlong from the Tarpeian Rock on Capitol hill, the traditional punishment for traitors. Sulpicius' head was nailed up on the rostra.

Sulla was now anxious to get away to the war in the East. He had only induced his soldiers to follow him to Rome by holding out to them the prospect of loot in the gorgeous East from which, he said, Marius would certainly debar them, by leaving them behind in Italy and taking men of his own choosing. Clearly Sulla must not delay his departure if he was to retain his troops' loyalty, could such a word be applied to such an army. At the same time, something must be done to ensure the stability of the state, now shaken to its foundations. Sulla compromised. A complete overhaul of the machinery of government must await his return; but he could and did enforce some interim measures. Sulpicius' laws were repealed, thus not only postponing the problems raised by the granting of burgess-rights to the allies, but also stiffening the resistance of the Samnites and Ligurians, who were still fighting. Next it was ordained that in future no measure could be brought before the people unless it had been previously approved by the Senate. Thirdly, the Comitia Centuriata, in which wealth had the greatest influence, was to be the only active assembly; the Comitia Tributa was to do nothing, and the only function of the Concilium Plebis would be the election of its tribunes. Sulla wanted also to double the size of the Senate; but choosing new senators would take time, and so he postponed that major task with others, until after the war. These were but rough and ready measures—"first-aid to the constitution," they have been called. They looked well on paper, but would they be proof against a second Sulla, an "anti-Sulla"? We shall see.

At the elections for the magistracies for the next year, 87, Sulla suffered an ominous rebuff. Two of his protégés, one being his own nephew, were rejected in favour of two men known to be his opponents, and of the consuls, although one, Gnaeus Octavius, was a "sound" conservative, the other was a snake of a man called Cinna, to whose election Sulla had been forced to agree to appease his adversaries. He bound him with a great traditional oath to do as he (Sulla) wished. Holding a stone in his hand, Cinna stood in the Capitol, and prayed that if he were false to Sulla, he might be cast from the city as that stone from his hand—throwing it to the ground before the assembled throng. Cinna had no intention of keeping this or any oath. Hardly was Sulla's back turned, when he started a process for his impeachment.

For Sulla was now on his way to Greece. His departure, already dangerously postponed, was precipitated by the murder of his colleague, the consul Pompeius Rufus. He had been appointed to succeed Pompeius Strabo as commander on the northern front. Strabo's soldiers were having none of that, so they simply murdered the new general in order to keep the old. Sulla took the hint and moved against Mithridates. The eclipse of the Macedonians and the enfeeblement of the Seleucids had left a power-vacuum in the Levant and Near East. Rome had accepted the Pergamene bequest in 133 and twenty years later had occupied the Cilician shore; but for the rest Asia Minor had been left to its own devices, which meant that it would fall into the hands of the first strong man armed who chose to take it. That man was to be Mithradates VI, king of Pontus. Descended, as the name implies, from the old Persian nobility— Mithras was the Persian sun-god—the dynasty first became prominent in the third century B.C. Gradually their authority spread, until it included a number of the ancient Greek colonies on the Black Sea coast. The Pontic kings now boasted of their Greek culture and were proud of their family connections with the Seleucids. Towards the end of the second century Mithradates V had occupied the seaport of Sinope, on the Black Sea, itself a Greek city, and had made it his capital. The Greek cities of the Crimea were soon subject to Pontus, and so was Trapezus, or Trebizond. Mithradates V was assassinated in 121, and was succeeded by his son Mithradates Eupator, a boy of seven, watched over by the queen mother. She was soon got rid of, and spent the rest of her life in prison. Mithradates then liquidated his younger brother, and was left to rule alone. He was a remarkable man, full of energy and guile. He saw himself, although he was a Persian, as the last champion of Hellenism against Roman aggression, of the East against the West. Pontus, like the other principalities of the region, was technically a "friend and ally" of Rome, in reality her vassal. Rome had whittled down much of the dominions won by Mithradates' father, and the proud youth felt that he had a score to settle with her. The Greek cities of the Crimea asked for his help against the Scythians. Mithradates was glad enough to give it, and thus to secure not only the hegemony of the Black Sea but also access to timber with which to build a fleet. Next, turning his eyes from the sea to the land, he occupied Lesser Armenia in what is now eastern Turkey, and then part of Paphlagonia to the west. Moving south, he laid hands on Cappadocia, but here he had been foiled by the aforementioned mission of Sulla in 92. Bithynia was his next goal, the region on the Asian shore of the Bosporus. Here again a Roman envoy confronted him, and not content with urging Mithradates to withdraw, incited the Bithynians to invade Pontic territory. This goaded the restless and ambitious monarch to action. Rome was now preoccupied with the Italian War: now was the time to turn Rome out of Asia. In the year 88 Mithradates swooped. With his command of the Bosporus he was able to bring his fleet into the Aegean, thus supporting his land-forces. He easily overran Asia and made Pergamum his capital. The provincials, after fifty years of exploitation by Roman officials, tax-gatherers and crooks, welcomed him as their liberator. He took a frightful revenge. He massacred every Italian in sight. Eighty thousand are said to have perished. In Delos, the island formerly sacred to Apollo and now a thriving slave-market, the Italian dealers were similarly slaughtered. The Athenians, with that flair for backing losers which had never deserted them since the days of Demosthenes, thought the hour ripe for rebellion, under the leadership of a self-seeking and self-satisfied philosopher of servile origin called Aristion. Aristion murdered the pro-Roman party. Mithradates sent over his general, Archelaus, and his fleet now had a secure base in Piraeus, the port of Athens, from which Delos and the Cyclades were occupied without difficulty. The Thracians were encouraged to invade Macedon, Euboea was conquered and it seemed as if the whole of Greece would be subject to Mithradates before Sulla could leave Italy. Such was the situation when, in the spring of the year 87, Sulla landed in Greece.

Sulla's Greek campaign is chiefly remembered for the siege and sack of Athens, so that Sulla has always had "a bad press." His military prowess, moreover, tends to be overshadowed by that of Julius Caesar. But in fact, considered purely and simply as an example of the military art, Sulla's Greek campaign is among the most remarkable on record. There was this solitary Roman with his five faithful legions, with no fleet, no reserves and no support from home—on the contrary, he had been declared an outlaw. More, an army was actually dispatched from Rome to supplant him. And yet Sulla prevailed, and was to return in triumph.

The sight of a Roman army brought the majority of the Greeks to their senses: they fell over each other in their eagerness to "show willing" to Sulla, who at once sent off his quaestor to assemble a fleet from Rhodes, Cyprus and Phoenicia. This officer's name was Lucullus, who is chiefly remembered as a gourmet and as the man who introduced the cherry into Europe, but who was in his prime a very capable commander. Sulla meanwhile was besieging Athens in a characteristically Sullan fashion. This lover of things Greek was utterly ruthless when it came to subduing the city which was the glory of Greece, "the violet-crowned city" as Pindar had called it. Having no funds of his own, Sulla robbed the sanctuaries of Epidaurus, Olympia and Delphi. Being short of timber, he felled the groves of the Academy and the Lyceum—the abodes of Plato and Aristotle respectively. How different were the Romans of to-day, commented the Greeks, from the upright republicans of the preceding century, Flamininus and Aemilius Paullus! Aristion, it is true, did all he could to infuriate Sulla, shouting scurrilous insults at him and his wife Metella (his fourth) from the walls. The city was now starving, and its inhabitants were eating old shoes, when finally a deputation approached Sulla to ask him to spare them. The scene is described by Plutarch, himself an honorary citizen of Athens. The suppliants started on a long harangue, in the typical Greek manner, citing all the great names of Athenian history from Theseus onwards. Sulla cut them short. "Shut up and get out," he said, "I wasn't sent here to learn history, but to crush rebels." The end soon came. Some old men, down by the Ceramicus, the potters' quarter which gives us our word "ceramics," where the roads for Piraeus and Eleusis still start, were overheard to say that a certain part of the defences was unguarded. Sulla himself made a reconnaissance in the dark, located the fatal postern, and ordered a general attack by night. The adjacent curtain was soon levelled and the Romans poured into the city. The slaughter was appalling. The market-place ran with blood. The massacre was only stayed when Sulla, sated and cynical, told two Athenians "I forgive the few for the sake of the many, the living for the dead." It was 1st March, 86. Aristion held out on the

Acropolis for a few weeks and then was forced to surrender for lack of water to one of Sulla's lieutenants. Sulla himself, after taking and burning Piraeus, marched north to meet Archelaus' army in Boeotia where, on the historic field of Chaeronea, he soundly defeated it. Next year he similarly routed another Pontic army at a point a little farther north. The army which had been sent to supersede him disintegrated. Its commander was murdered, its second-in-command committed suicide, and the men came over to Sulla: his "fortune" was certainly holding. He now summoned Mithradates to a conference not far from the site of Troy, and there dictated his terms. These were surprisingly moderate—too moderate for the liking of his troops—but Sulla was anxious to get Asia off his hands so that he could return to Rome. Mithradates was to surrender his fleet, to withdraw to his original Pontic frontiers and to pay an indemnity. The provincials fared worse. Asia was fined twenty thousand talents, the equivalent of some thirty million dollars. The provincials could not raise this huge sum, and so in no time the Italian money-lenders were back again.

Sulla's troops, now swelled to seven legions, were billeted on the inhabitants, who had not only to feed and clothe them, but to give them pocket-money as well.

Ominous news had arrived from Rome, brought by refugees from Cinna's reign of terror. Sulla's wife Metella barely escaped with the children. All his houses, she reported, both in town and country, had been burned. It certainly was time he hurried home. Leaving the two legions that had come over to him to maintain order in Asia, he set sail from Ephesus, stayed a few months in Greece, and then marching north prepared to cross to Brundisium (Brindisi). With him went much loot, the most interesting item being the library of a certain Apellicon "in which were most of the works of Theophrastus and Aristotle, not then in general circulation." After lying in obscurity for so long, they were now to be published to the world.

Sulla had been away from Rome for four years, a period during which, in Cicero's words, "the state enjoyed neither justice nor dignity." To add to the general distress Cinna had announced that he intended to revive the program of Sulpicius in regard to the newly-enfranchised citizens. This at once provoked rioting, aggravated by the crowds of new citizens now in Rome, who rallied to the side of their patron. There was a fight in the Forum which Octavius, the other consul, won, and soon Cinna, after trying once again to raise the slaves in revolt, was forced to leave the city. He was declared to be an enemy of the state, and in his place a certain Merula was made consul, a high priest of Jupiter or Flamen Dialis who was forbidden by traditional taboo to look upon a corpse, or even to enter the presence of an army. Clearly he was intended to be a cipher, and to leave the direction of affairs to Octavius, who was but little equipped to manage them. While Octavius was theorizing about the constitution, Cinna was raising an army. He simply appropriated that of the praetor Appius Claudius in Campania, and marched on Rome at its head.

At this point Marius re-enters the story. His adventures after his flight from Rome had been picturesque. He had embarked in a friend's ship at Ostia, but was blown back by a storm and forced to land near Minturnae, on the coast north of Naples. When he and his famished companions were about three miles from the city, they saw a troop of horse coming in pursuit of them. Back they darted to the beach and regained the ship which was anchored close to the shore. The horsemen demanded Marius' surrender, which the crew refused. Nevertheless, as soon as the troop was gone the crew, playing for safety, landed Marius at the mouth of the river Liris, hard by Minturnae. Here, after hiding in a swamp, and being befriended by an old man who recognized him, he was at last found by a search-party, dragged naked from the pool in which he had sought refuge, and taken before the magistrates of Minturnae. They confined him in the town jail while they debated what to do with him. In the end they decided that he should die, and sent the executioner to dispatch him. The man was a Gaul, one of those whom Marius had defeated. But in the shadows of the dungeon, he caught sight of Marius' eyes "which seemed to dart out flames at him," as he roared: "Fellow, do you dare kill Gaius Marius?" The tribesman

dropped his sword and ran out crying "I cannot kill Gaius Marius."
The magistrates now changed their minds, and escorted Marius to
a waiting ship—to go whither he would. After a narrow escape in
Sicily, where he had been compelled to put in for water, Marius
at length reached Africa, and landed on the desolate site of
Carthage. The Roman governor of the province, who was neither
a friend nor an enemy of Marius, but a loyal servant of Rome,
sent at once to tell Marius that he might not set foot in Africa,
and that if he did the senatorial decree would be put into
execution and Marius treated as an enemy of the Roman people.
Marius was dumbfounded, and was silent for some time. When
the messenger asked what answer he should give the governor,
Marius replied: "Go and tell him that you have seen Gaius Marius
sitting in exile among the ruins of Carthage." Marius' son meanwhile had found a refuge with Hiempsal, king of Numidia,
but that shifty prince would have detained him as a hostage,
had not one of his concubines fallen in love with the handsome
lad and enabled him and his friends to escape and join his
father. They got away just in time: as they were putting to sea,
a troop of the king's horse came galloping up to arrest them.

Thus Marius returned to Italy, a vindictive dotard, with hatred
in his glaring eyes, his unkempt hair and beard adding to his
terrifying aspect. He soon assembled a ragged regiment of slaves
and shepherds and made common cause with Cinna. Repulsive,
physically and spiritually, as he had now become, Marius was
still Marius. In no time he cut off the corn-supply with an improvised navy, confiscated the merchants' stocks of grain, took
Ostia, Rome's port of entry for provisions, by treachery, and
closed the harbour. He then moved on Rome and encamped on
the Janiculum, from which he could survey the whole of the city
from across the Tiber. Rome was at his mercy, but of mercy he
had none. Cinna, as consul, received a deputation from the
Senate with courtesy, and would have treated them with leni-
ency; "Marius stood by him and said nothing, but gave sufficient
testimony by the gloominess of his countenance and the stern-
ness of his looks that he would in a short time fill the city with
blood." His band of slaves became his executioners; at a word,

or even a nod from their master, they killed. It was enough that Marius did not return a man's salute that the man should instantly be butchered. Treachery and denunciation were rife; no one felt safe and very few were. The streets were choked with maimed and headless corpses; and Marius' assassins were now murdering innocent people in their own houses, defiling their children and ravishing their wives. Finally, when the blood had flowed for five days, Cinna sent to the butchers' camp a gang of Gauls who killed the lot as they slept.

For the consulship of the year 86, no election was held. Cinna and Marius simply nominated themselves, for Marius had always said he would be seven times consul. He only lasted thirteen days, and then died. Among the victims was poor Merula, who was replaced as Flamen Dialis by a nephew of Marius' wife, young Julius Caesar, aged fourteen! Marius had saved Rome from the northern barbarians; but he had destroyed her with those of his own breeding. It is a sad, but very Roman, epitaph.

Cinna somehow held the state together for two more years. Economic chaos had followed on the loss of Asia to Mithradates, aggravated by the civil strife in Italy. Some attempt was made to restore the debased coinage; and a drastic scaling down of debts was enforced whereby creditors were compelled to accept a *sestertius* in the *denarius*, a quarter in the dollar, in full payment. But the régime was chiefly notorious for the dispatch of the army destined, unsuccessfully, to stab Sulla in the back, as already mentioned. Meanwhile, the newly-enfranchised citizens were being enrolled; eventually, it seems, being spread over all the tribes so that their votes would be effective. Some Italians were still in arms in remote parts, but "the principle of the settlement," in the words of the Cambridge Ancient History, "was irrevocably fixed. All the free inhabitants of Italy were to be equal members of a single state. The unification was achieved."

In the spring of 84, Cinna was murdered; but the troops he had raised to oppose Sulla were still under arms. When a year later Sulla landed at Brundisium he could, for the first time in his career, afford to wait. The aura of triumph which now surrounded him—his "felicity," in fact—was bound to undermine the

loyalty of his opponents even more effectively than it had done
in Greece. Of the Italians, only the Lucanians and the Samnites
remained in the field against him. Of the consuls, both of whom
were adherents of Marius, Norbanus was soon shut up inside
Capua, and Cornelius Scipio's troops, seduced by bribery and
promises, simply deserted, which caused Cinna's late colleague,
Carbo, to remark that in Sulla's breast there was a lion and a fox,
and that the fox was the more troublesome. Carbo's own troops,
in the north, were scattered by Licinius Crassus and a young
man not yet twenty-four called Gnaeus Pompeius, the brilliant
son of an incompetent father, known to history as Pompey the
Great. The younger Marius was driven back to Praeneste (Palestrina). Sulla entered Rome unopposed. As Sulla moved south-
east to press the siege of Praeneste, a Samnite and a Lucanian with a considerable levy slipped in behind him and
encamped before the Colline gate, on the site of the Termini
railway station. Sulla hastened back and, allowing his troops no
respite, against the advice of his lieutenants, attacked at four in
the afternoon. The engagement turned out to be the fiercest of the
whole civil war. The citizens were terrified, and the issue was
for long in doubt. Many civilians were killed or trampled to
death; but in the end, after a brilliant action by Crassus on the
right wing, and the defection of a division of the enemy, Sulla
was victorious. Praeneste soon fell, young Marius committed
suicide, and the war was at an end.

Three days after Sulla's victory, the senate met in the temple
of Bellona. While Sulla was addressing them, a ghastly confusion
of cries assaulted the ears of the assembly. Sulla continued speaking unperturbed, bidding them listen to him, because the noise
outside was merely the punishment of some offenders. In fact, the
uproar was caused by the dying shrieks of six thousand prisoners,
who were being slaughtered in the Circus Maximus by Sulla's
express orders. "This," says Plutarch, "gave the most stupid of
the Romans to understand that they had merely exchanged, not
escaped, tyranny." That indeed was the truth. Sulla was to outdo
in barbarity any of his predecessors. It was just over half a
century since violence had been the arbiter at Rome. Three times

in seven years Rome had witnessed political murder, twice it
had been seized by Roman arms. Marius had massacred his
enemies, but Sulla would be more thoroughgoing, colder, cru-
eller and more calculating. All those who had opposed him
were to die; and his friends were given *carte blanche* in deciding
whom they should murder, which resulted in the deaths of
many out of sheer personal spite. A brave young senator rose
one day and asked where the massacre would stop. "We do not
ask you to pardon those whom you have destined for destruction: we only want you to relieve the anxiety of those whom
you have decided to spare." Sulla was not sure whom he would
spare, but agreed to draw up lists of those who were to die.
The first list contained eighty names, the next two hundred
and twenty, and the third the same number. He announced that
he had put down as many as he could remember, but would add
those who had escaped his memory in due course. Death was the
punishment for harbouring a proscribed person, three thousand
dollars the reward for killing one, even if it was a slave who had
killed his master or a son his father. The proscription raged all
over Italy, and many were slaughtered simply for their property.
"Alas! my Alban farm has betrayed me," cried one innocent
man: he was dispatched without delay. Nearly five thousand
citizens lost their lives. The confiscated property brought in an
enormous sum. Many of the estates were acquired by Sulla's
minions for next to nothing.

Sulla had indeed "shut the gates of mercy on mankind"; he
had dared "to wade through slaughter to a throne." He was now
the sole ruler, the monarch, of Rome. He had himself proclaimed
dictator, an office which had not been revived since the days of
the war against Hannibal. But Sulla was to be absolute ruler not
for six months, as of old, but for as long as he saw fit, and with
untrammelled powers to reshape the constitution.

This, after celebrating his triumph over Mithradates in January
81, Sulla proceeded to do. His breadth of vision, the scope of his
aims, his care for the sound administration not only of Italy but
of the provinces as well are as remarkable as any element in his
genius; yet here again we come up against that contradiction

which was engrained in his character, because his methods, his judgement of political realities were reactionary to the point of archaism. Sulla regarded his legislation as a return to tradition, the reinstatement of the Senate as the repository of authority, as a restoration, in fact. But, as Mommsen pointed out, all restorations are revolutions. Sulla's certainly was. Before his Eastern campaign he had enacted certain "first-aid" laws, as we have seen. These had been disregarded during the ascendancy of Cinna and Marius, so that the dictator had to start all over again. In what order he tackled each particular problem, we cannot be sure, but of the final result we have a clear picture.

First, in regard to the Italians, he accepted the *fait accompli*. The Social War was at an end, and with it the very use of the word *socius*, "ally," as applied to any inhabitant of Italy. All were now to be citizens, though—and here again we see the limitations imposed by the absence of representative government—only for those living near Rome can their new status have involved any direct participation in politics.

Next, the powers of the Assembly were curtailed by reducing those of the tribunes. Their veto might no longer be used to frustrate legislation or blackmail opponents. It was restricted solely to intervention on behalf of individuals—its original function. The corn-dole, which had been one of their chief political props, was abolished. To discourage ambitious young men from seeking the office, Sulla ruled that the holding of it disqualified for any higher office.

Thirdly, it was ordained that no bill might be introduced into the Assembly unless it had the prior approval of the Senate. This ensured that the Senate should be supreme not only in framing and conducting policy both domestic and foreign, and in the carrying out of it, but in legislation as well. The Senate itself was now enlarged by the addition of three hundred new members, chosen for their known conservative sympathies. The censors' powers of scrutiny and selection were superseded by a new method of recruitment. Twenty quaestors were to be elected every year, and at the end of their term of office would automatically become senators. This meant that men in their thirties would enter the legislature. At the same time, the downward age-limits for office were rigorously reimposed: thirty for a quaestor, thirty-nine for a praetor, and forty-two for a consul. To attain a higher office a man must have served in the lower. It thus became impossible, on paper, for an ambitious newcomer to rocket to power.

Rome now ruled ten provinces. Like later imperial powers she had acquired them haphazard. Sulla knew from his Eastern experience that Rome must now adopt a uniform and practical system of administration. His provincial reforms were to prove not only his most beneficial legacy, but also his most enduring. At the end of his year of office a consul or praetor would automatically take up a provincial command; and the number of praetors was raised from six to eight to furnish the necessary annual output. No troops were to remain in Italy—Italy had suffered too grievously from them of late. To American or English readers, for whom the absence of a standing army on domestic soil is part of their constitutions, this may appear to be the most obviously admirable of all Sulla's reforms. In fact it was to prove the most disastrous. Since all the legions were to be abroad, the consuls, having no one to command, would no longer be commanders-in-chief. Whereas the proconsuls and pro-praetors in the provinces would have individual armies at their disposal. True, it was laid down that no provincial governor might move outside his province, which meant he might not wage "private wars," and that at the end of his term he would be answerable for his actions to a senatorial court—one of six new ones to deal with cases of high treason, public disorder, corruption, murder, fraud and embezzlement. But it meant that an ambitious and unscrupulous governor, specially of Cisalpine Gaul, where the defences of the northern frontier lay, and now elevated to provincial status, could easily defy the defenceless Fathers. All too soon this very thing was to happen.

As a comprehensive system of legislation, administration and constitution-building, Sulla's enactments, the Leges Corneliae as they are known, deserve our admiration; but the spirit behind them was corrupt, the power that enforced them sinister. They

were intended as a salute to the future; they were but a sad
farewell to the past. Yet Sulla remained a contradiction to the
end. He had done his work in no more than two years. In 79 B.C.
he laid down his authority, and retired to private life, devoting
himself to finishing his memoirs. And he had married again. At
a gladiatorial show one day he found himself sitting next to a
beautiful divorcée called Valeria, the sexes not being yet separated in the theatre, as they later were. As she passed behind
him, she leaned on his shoulder, and plucking a bit of wool
from his toga, sat down. Sulla looked up, wondering what it
meant. "What harm does it do you, you great man, if I want a
tiny share in your 'felicity'?" she asked. They flirted for the
rest of the performance. Sulla sent to find out who she was, and
all about her, and they were soon married. He was sixty, and
she was his fifth wife. But despite this match, he still devoted
himself to his old pleasures and his old companions, chiefly
actors—Metrobius his first love "for whom though past his prime
he still professed a passionate fondness," Roscius the comedian
and Sorex the brilliant mime. In his feasting, as in his late
wife's funeral, he cynically transgressed all his own sumptuary
laws, which like all such enactments were never capable of en-
forcement. Sulla may have known that his end was near. In
Athens he had had to resort to medicinal springs to combat the
first "shadow of gout." He was now assailed by a loathsome
putrefaction, probably the result of arteriosclerosis. He finished
the twenty-second book of his memoirs, in which he records
having seen his son lately dead, beseeching him to come and join
him and his mother Metella. The next day, hearing that a certain
magistrate had put off paying a public debt, in expectation of
Sulla's death, he had the man hailed before him, and in a
paroxysm of anger ordered him to be strangled then and there.
This last fit of brutality exhausted him, and he died the next
day. His funeral was magnificent. His epitaph, of his own composition, was to the effect that no one had ever outdone him in
returning good for good, nor evil for evil. A statue of him was
erected in the Campus Martius; but his most permanent memorial
was the new *tabularium* or record-office on the Capitol. It was

erected the year after his death, but to his own design. Large parts of it still stand, and it is interesting as being the first surviving building in Rome to incorporate the Greek column flanking the Roman arch—a feature which was to be developed into the standard triumphal gateway. It would have been well if that had been Sulla's chief bequest to posterity. But it was his baser lessons that his Roman pupils had learned, and not triumphs, but disasters were to be his legacy.

CHAPTER X

POMPEY—THE FIRST PHASE

SULLA'S death left not what he had intended to bequeath, a Rome restored, but the very opposite, a Rome distracted. Just why he abandoned power after having made himself Rome's monarch we cannot know. Was he weary? That he was very ill is beyond doubt. Did he realize, in the end, that his system would not work, that its very rigidity would lead to its destruction? Or was he just cynically indifferent to what might overtake his country? It is impossible to say. Sulla dead remained the enigma that the living Sulla had been. What is certain is that the scramble for power which had been started by Marius had now become so headlong that it would not end for another forty-five years.

In trying to form some estimate of the motives of the oncoming war-lords, it is well to remember that we simply cannot judge them by modern standards. Neither the Greeks nor the Romans ever produced the "gentleman," as he was to be known, honoured and imitated in the society of modern Europe and America. As Burke pointed out in his famous lament for Queen Marie Antoinette, our standards of decent and laudable conduct, the rules of our game as it were, have come down to us from the age of chivalry, which was itself a fine distillation of the spirit of Christianity. We have, it is true, adapted many Greek ideas, and some Roman ones, but as Matthew Arnold puts it, "conduct is three quarters of life," and our conduct is or should be regulated by the standards of a Judaeo-Christian ethic which was wholly lacking in the ancient world.

There were, nevertheless, as in every age, men of upright and enlightened character who did sincerely strive to live a life of integrity and rectitude. For them, philosophy supplied what religion could not supply. Roman religion was a hidebound affair.

The countryman would worship his ancestral gods, calling on Priapus to bless his flocks, Autumnus to increase his harvests, and his wife would intercede with Artemis in childbed. For the city-dweller, these simple deities had no meaning. The only religion he knew was a matter of formulae, legalistic and dry as dust. There was nothing there to inspire him. From the East, more personal and exciting cults were beginning to arrive, and many of them would find eager adherents in Rome. Of those Eastern importations only two flourish to-day, Judaism and Christianity: the rest have long since perished. In the last days of the Roman republic, Judaism had, as we shall see, arrived in Rome, but its teaching was, to begin with, confined to members of the Jewish community. Other Oriental religions made more converts. Isis from Egypt followed upon Cybele from Asia. Mithras the sun-god of Persia became ever more popular. Other cults came after them. None claimed universal authority—it was a matter of choice for the individual; but what all of them did promise was *salus*, health, or, as applied to the soul, salvation.

Many of these cults were orgiastic and from time to time gave rise to scandals, and foreign gods were "banished" from Rome. But they contrived to find their way back, being most popular among women and the illiterate.

The upper-class educated Roman, bred on Greek scepticism, and yet mindful of the old-fashioned virtues of the Roman, his gravity and his dignified fortitude, spurned both the old religion, though he would generally observe its forms, and the new alien imports. For him the guide would be philosophy, which meant by and large one or other of the two most favoured systems, that of Epicurus or that of Zeno the Stoic. Both were basically materialist, being founded on earlier Greek systems worked out in Ionia. Epicurus in the year 306 had founded what amounted to a sect in his garden at Athens. His philosophy is essentially contemplative, what we should call "escapist" to-day. Epicurus sought a rational basis for the pursuit of happiness and found it in scientific materialism. He was an atomist—one to whom there were only two realities, atoms and the void. This theory, be it noted, was founded not on observation, as modern atomic notions are, but on speculation pure and simple. It thus led to many conclusions connected less with scientific fact than with philosophic postulates. If it is atoms that make the world go round, then there is no place in it for gods. They may exist, but if they do it is in some calm abode in space. With human affairs they are not concerned. So we need not fear them, nor anything else, particularly death. Thus is opened the way to happiness. The true Epicurean will not seek it in gross pleasures, but rather by exercise of the mind and the finer feelings. It is best not to meddle in public affairs, to avoid matrimony even.

It is not hard to see how such a negative scheme could lead to abuse. It was alien to the main fibre of the Roman texture of soul. But it did inspire one of the greatest of Roman poets, Lucretius, who wrote what is still the only atomic epic and one of the world's great poems, which was deeply to influence Virgil himself, and to wake admiring echoes in the English poets Gray and Tennyson. It was, too, the creed held, if lightly, by Rome's most human and charming poet, Horace.

Stoicism was a far more positive creed, and harmonized far better with the Roman attitude to life. Zeno, the founder of Stoicism, became a philosopher by accident. He was a well-to-do merchant from Cyprus, a Phoenician, that is a Semite, not a Greek at all. This is significant, for it is with Zeno, long before the introduction of the Judaeo-Christian ethic, that the idea of aspiration, of the sublime, a typically Semitic concept, and quite un-Hellenic, enters Greek philosophy. Zeno was shipwrecked near Piraeus, and walked up to Athens, a penniless castaway. Entering a bookseller's, he started browsing and picked up a copy of Xenophon's memoirs of Socrates. He was so fired by them that he asked the bookseller how he could learn philosophy. It chanced that the leading Athenian philosopher, Crates, was passing the door at that very moment. "Follow him," said the bookseller. Zeno did so, and after a period of novitiate under Crates, started his own lectures. Being too poor to hire a hall, he talked in a painted porch, or *stoa*, whence the name Stoic.

That was in 300 B.C. Like Epicurus, Zeno was concerned to

find the *summum bonum* for the *individual,* the best way for him
to live, in the new Hellenistic age which had followed Alexander's
conquests and the break-down of the old city-state with its
communal loyalties. For Zeno, world-soul and world-body are
united, in Armstrong's words "like the obverse and reverse of a
coin." The Stoics are pantheists. "The conception is well expressed in Pope's *Essay on Man:*

> All are but parts of one stupendous whole
> Whose body nature is, and God the Soul."

Nature is the key: since nature is governed by rational law,
it is enough to follow nature to secure happiness. Stoicism is
rigid, and active. Above all, Stoicism had a developed ethical
system. We are responsible for our actions and therefore we are
free. Virtue is the sole end of man: everything else is either bad
or "indifferent." This elevated, if cold, creed was to become in
effect the state religion of Rome. It would inspire a slave, Epicte-
tus, and an emperor, Marcus Aurelius, both of whose writings
have come down to us. Much of its preaching passed into Christian thoughts and practice and has in essence lasted to this day
in what is least repellent in English and American puritanism.

Thus we see that in republican Rome, while the old religion
was being abandoned, men's minds were finding new refuges
either in the Oriental cults or in philosophy. But they were nearly
all united in being pathologically superstitious. Unbelief and
superstition go hand in hand; but the extent to which Romans
were dominated by superstition would be hard to credit were
there not such abundant evidence for it from the very beginning
to the very end of the Roman world. Marius carried round with
him a female Syrian soothsayer in a litter, Sulla was guided
by dreams and visions. Everybody believed in omens, official and
unofficial alike. The colour of a hen's liver, the flight of a crow,
even the braying of an ass was taken to indicate what action
should be taken or what avoided. A Roman was haunted by day
and night, from the cradle to the grave, by these "supernatural
solicitings." Unless he were a philosopher, or an adherent of a

"salvation" cult, how could he be expected to have the time or the will to lead his own, independent, responsible, good life?

In such an atmosphere of spiritual instability it was hardly possible that political stability could be attained, even had Sulla's death not of itself thrown all into confusion. Trouble began at once. In the very year of Sulla's death, the first attempt was made at undoing his work. One of the consuls was M. Aemilius Lepidus, who as governor of Sicily had pillaged the province so scandalously that he was threatened with impeachment. In order to forestall the prosecution Lepidus deserted the Sullan party and set himself up as champion of the mob. So successful was he that he not only succeeded in deterring his accusers from prosecuting their attack, but actually became one of the consuls for the year 78. He then proposed the restoration of the corn-dole, the recall of the victims of Sulla's proscriptions (from which Lepidus himself had not scrupled to profit) and the restoration of the tribunes to their former position. Catulus, the other consul, was a staunch Sullan; but he could not prevail against the apathy and bewilderment of the now headless party. Lepidus retired to Etruria, where he raised a nondescript army and marched on Rome. Catulus defeated him on the Campus Martius, and Lepidus was forced to flee to Sardinia where he died shortly afterwards of consumption. This episode, shabby and squalid as it was, is of less importance in itself than in its sequel, a mere by-product as it were, which was to shape the fate of Rome. For the rounding-up of the malignants was entrusted to a young lieutenant of Sulla's. His name was Gnaeus Pompeius, or as he is generally known, Pompey.

Of all the train of war-lords, beginning with Marius and ending with Caesar, none is more humanly attractive than Pompey. Plutarch liked him, Mommsen hated him, but so dear has he always been to English-speakers that, like Marcus Antonius after him, he has been granted English nationality and has for centuries been known by his English name. Pompey also has a further claim on our affection: we know what he looked like. He is the first man to play a "lead" on the Roman political stage of whom we possess an authentic portrait bust. It is in Copenhagen, and is one of the finest of a school that was to give us representations of men and women which would not be equalled until the days of the Renaissance. The Copenhagen head shows a man with a broad brow, a genial aspect, and a most attractive distinction. Firm, temperate and very "Roman" it is. And that is how he appeared to his contemporaries. His father, the general, had been so unpopular owing to his grasping covetousness that when he died in 87, his corpse was dragged from the bier on its way to his funeral. Pompey, on the other hand, remained the people's darling throughout his career. He had charm, he had beauty. "No man ever asked a favour with less offence, or conferred one with a better grace. When he gave it was without assumption; when he received, it was with dignity and honour." "His beauty even in his bloom of youth had something in it at once of gentleness and dignity; and when his prime of manhood came, the majesty and kingliness of his character at once became visible in it." People said that from "the languishing motion of his eyes" he resembled Alexander the Great. Pompey liked that. In after times a famous old harlot called Flora used to say, when she was recalling her golden youth, that she never could part with Pompey without giving him a little bite.

Pompey first saw service with his father in the campaign against Cinna. He evaded a plot against his own life, and single-handed quelled an attempted mutiny against, and murder of, his unpopular father. After the general's death his enemies tried to be avenged on the son by suing him for misappropriation. Pompey cleverly admitted that he had received from his father some hunting tackle and a few books after the siege of Asculum, but had lost them when his house had been broken into and looted by Cinna's thugs. The judge was so much impressed by the young man's ability—he was only twenty-two—that he offered him his daughter Antistia in marriage, whereupon, when he was acquitted, the bystanders greeted him with the old Roman wedding-paean. "Talasio," they shouted. After Cinna's death Pompey retired to his estates in Picenum, where he was popular among the countryfolk; so much so that when Sulla landed next year, young Pompey took it on himself to hold an assize in the market-place of Auximum, in the north of the district, expelled two citizens, brothers, who were active in Carbo's interests, and then proceeded to raise, organize and commission three complete legions—officers, men, commissariat, transport, munitions —in fact, a complete expeditionary force. In his march southward to join Sulla, young Pompey met and defeated no less than five hostile forces, the last being led by Carbo himself. Sulla thought it impossible that so errant a knight (for such was Pompey's status) could survive, pitted against such experienced adversaries; but when he beheld this splendid and victorious host approaching, he dismounted (then, as still in the Orient, a sign of respect), and having been saluted as Imperator, as was his due, "returned the salutation upon Pompey, in the same term and style of Imperator, which might well cause surprise, as none could ever have anticipated that he would have imparted, to one so young in years and not yet a senator, a title which was the object of contention between him and the Scipios and Marius, father and son." Sulla was naturally delighted to find that one young Roman captain at least had been moved to take up arms for him, not against him, and paid him the same sort of honours as Scipio had paid to Marius. He went further: after Pompey had returned from a successful campaign in Gaul, Sulla and his fourth wife, Metella, decided that Pompey should be bound to them more intimately by wedding Metella's daughter Aemilia by her former husband. Aemilia was already married and with child. Antistia, whose father had only a short time before been murdered in the very Senate-house because he was a supporter of Pompey and Sulla, was divorced, and the wedding took place. No good came of it. Aemilia died in childbed almost as soon as she had entered Pompey's house, and Antistia's mother committed suicide out of shame and misery. Plutarch calls these disgusting proceedings "the very tyrannies of marriage." They were to be repeated over and over again in the insensitive power-market of the republican dynasts, and into the days of the first emperor himself.

Sulla's opponents were still active, in Sicily and in Africa. Pompey was dispatched to deal with them. He was uniformly successful, but it was in these campaigns, trifling as they were compared with his later triumphs, that Pompey disclosed the flaw in his character which was to be his undoing. He was hesitant. Ruthless, like all Romans, he could be; but he was never able to think more than one move ahead. He had to stop to work things out; and if ever there was a world in which he who hesitates is lost, it was the world into which Pompey was born. Even ruthlessness must be immediate to be acceptable. For instance, when the egregious Mamertines of Messina tried to argue that they were the heirs of special privilege, Pompey quelled them by saying: "What? Will you never stop prating about the law to people like us, who wear swords?" But when he captured Carbo, instead of killing him straight away, which would have meant that he was merely obeying superior orders, and would have been regarded as the fortune of war, he hesitated. He had Carbo, who had been three times consul, brought before him in chains, into a court-room, examined him with all due legal formality, and then sent him off to be executed. People did not like that; it put them against Pompey. On the other hand, his hesitancy sometimes worked in his favour. He had decided to punish the people of the Greek colony of Himera, famous for the Greek victory over the Carthaginians in 480 B.C., because they had sided with the anti-Sullan party. Their leader, begged leave to speak. Pompey granted it, and the man then told him that if he did what he intended he would punish the innocent, and absolve the guilty. "And who is the guilty man?" asked Pompey. "I am," replied the leader, whereupon Pompey pardoned not only him but the whole town.

Leaving his brother-in-law to govern Sicily, Pompey then crossed into Africa, cleared the province of the rebels, went on into Numidia, and having "revived the terror of the Roman power," in Plutarch's significant phrase, went off to hunt lions and elephants. All this in forty days, by a young man not yet twenty-five.

It was too much for Sulla. He sent Pompey orders to disband his army, except for one legion, and to await the arrival of a successor. The soldiers simply refused to accept the orders. They forced Pompey to continue as their general, whereupon Sulla, making the best of a *fait accompli*, put himself at the head of the welcome deputation, and greeted Pompey when he reached Rome by the title of Magnus, Great, by which he was thereafter known, though Pompey himself was reluctant to use the title and only adopted it officially some time later. Modest as he might be, he did nevertheless demand a triumph. This was contrary to custom, which allowed a triumph only to a consul or a praetor. Scipio the elder, who had defeated the Carthaginians, had never, Sulla pointed out, demanded such an honour. It would do Pompey no good, he said, a man who had scarcely grown his beard and was too young to be a senator, to enter the city in such a grand manner. It would only arouse envy. To which Pompey calmly replied that more people worshipped the rising sun than the setting sun. Sulla did not catch what Pompey had said, but saw the look of amazement on the faces of his suite, and asked them to tell him. When he understood, he seemed flabbergasted at Pompey's effrontery, and cried out, twice over: "Let him triumph, let him triumph." And triumph he did, despite the clamour of his soldiers, who thought they had not had a large enough cut of the spoils. The only enforced modification of his original plan was that his chariot had to be drawn by horses instead of the elephants he had brought from Africa for the occasion, because the city gate was too narrow to admit them. "He could have been a senator too, if he had wished, but he did not sue for that, being ambitious, it seems, only for unusual honours. For what wonder had it been for Pompey to sit in the Senate before his time? But to triumph before he was in the Senate was really an excess of glory."

Pompey was now in a position to dominate Rome, a triumphant general, and a popular idol. But, as usual, he had no plan. He was merely a simple knight again after his triumph, and instead of seeking his own immediate advancement, he committed a crass political blunder. He secured the election of Lepidus as consul for the year 78. Sulla, who had but a few more months to live, was stung to reproach: "Well, young man, I see you rejoice in your victory, and well you may! You've contrived that the consulship should go to the vilest of men, Lepidus, instead of to the worthiest and best, Catulus. But you'd better look out: you've made your enemy stronger than yourself."

Sulla made no mention of Pompey in his will, which was the last, unkindest blow one Roman could deal another, because there was no way of answering back.

Sulla may have been jealous, but he was right. And so we find Pompey taking the field against the very man whose election he had promoted, with the successful result already noted. It was not, however, the end of the war. Rome was not yet at peace. Just as a seismic shock may cause destructive waves to lash far-distant shores long after its epicentre is calm, so now unrest and rebellion still distressed Spain and the East; nor would Italy itself be spared. Spain was, and would for long remain, Rome's most important province. For one thing, it was the vital link between Italy and Africa, for Rome's empire was from first to last predominantly a land empire, like that of Turkey or Austria, not a sea empire as the Portuguese or Dutch, among others, were to be. It was on roads, not ships, that the legions primarily depended. Ships were for commerce, and the protection of commerce. Secondly, Spain was extremely productive, particularly of precious metals. It was Rome's El Dorado. In the year 83, the democrat régime had sent to Spain a capable general called Sertorius. He was a Sabine, which, coupled with the fact that he had served with distinction under Marius, was enough to make him doubly obnoxious to Sulla. He was to become "the last and greatest name in the story of Spain under the Roman Republic"; but Sulla proscribed him at once, and in 81 sent a lieutenant with two legions to recover the opulent province. Sertorius was forced to flee to Africa. He fell in with some pirates, who he had hoped would take him to the Islands of the Blest (the Azores) where he could pass his days in tranquil ease; but the pirates "desired not peace nor quiet, but riches and spoils," and forsook him. Nothing daunted, Sertorius made himself master of Mauretania, captured Tingis (Tangier) and brought orderly government to the whole region. The people of western Spain, to whom he had endeared himself by his straightforwardness and fair dealing, now begged him to come back and be their leader against Rome. He crossed the narrow strait, landed near Trafalgar, and soon had the country under his control. Sertorius was an organizer and commander of genius. He captivated the inhabitants by moving freely among them and getting to know every part of the terrain. He was also shrewd. He appealed to the superstition of the natives by having always at his side a tame white fawn, which he said possessed a spirit of divination. When news arrived, he would keep it dark, merely saying that the fawn had something momentous to divulge, and then after solemn consultation with the gifted creature would announce the tidings, which would later be confirmed from official sources. He also opened a free school at Osca (Huesca) for the sons of chieftains, where they were instructed in Greek and Latin. Their fathers were delighted to see them parading in smart purple-edged gowns, and learning to be good administrators when they grew up. So was Sertorius: they were the best possible hostages, even if he did disguise the fact by acting as their examiner, giving away the prizes and hanging golden amulets round the necks of the brightest pupils.

For eight whole years (79–72) Sertorius remained undefeated, and had meanwhile founded a Romano-Iberian power, which was to have incalculable benefits in store for Rome. Not only some of her most brilliant men of letters, Seneca, Martial and Quintilian among them, but two of her greatest emperors, Trajan and Hadrian, were to spring from Roman Spain.

The word guerrilla comes from Spain, and it was Sertorius' foe who "suffered all the inconveniences of defeat, although he earnestly desired to fight, and Sertorius, though he refused the field, reaped all the advantages of a conqueror." To Sertorius also must go the credit for the invention of the precursor of tear-gas. A certain tribe of freebooters lived up in the mountains, beyond the Tagus, in caves which faced north, impregnable and unapproachable. Sertorius noticed that at the foot of the cliff the soil consisted of friable earth and dust. He also noticed that the wind blew consistently from the north, thus fanning the rapacious cavemen. One morning they awoke to find that far from cooling them, the wind was killing them: Sertorius had simply ordered his army, foot and horse alike, to stir up as much dust as they could. The breeze, growing stronger as the day advanced, carried the dust into the caves where "it quickly blinded their eyes and filled their lungs, and all but choked them." After two days of this they surrendered.

There was a real danger, the Senate thought, that Sertorius—he was not a native Roman anyway, but a Sabine—might set himself up as a second Hannibal. They therefore reluctantly appointed Pompey to the Spanish command. So incompetent were the consuls of the year 77 that when someone asked whether Pompey was being sent out *pro consule* ("for a consul"=proconsul) the answer was "No, *pro consulibus*," i.e. for both of them. By the time Pompey arrived in Spain in 76, Sertorius had been reinforced by the remains of Lepidus' army, under Perperna. He had, too, some capable pirates on his side, and had even negotiated a lease-lend agreement with Mithradates, whereby in return for some Roman officers the Pontic king lent him a fleet. But Pompey soon established his ascendancy.

Perperna was doing his best to undermine Sertorius, who for his part, under the pressure of adversity, became overbearing and cruel. He actually put to death some of his boy-hostages, and sold others. The end came when Perperna arranged for him to be assassinated at a banquet. Perperna was soon captured, and tried to save his skin by handing to Pompey Sertorius' papers, which included a number of most incriminating letters from men in high places in Rome, inviting Sertorius to come and start yet another revolution. Pompey did what few other Romans would have done: he threw the lot, unread by either him or anyone else, into the fire. He then executed Perperna.

Sertorius was a great Roman, or perhaps it would be truer to say, a great servant of Rome. His provincial policy alone shows him to have been well in advance of his age. It was part of the Roman tragedy that so many of its greatest sons should fall fighting not Rome's enemies but each other. Both England and America have known civil war; but in each case, harrowing as the conflict was, the result enriched national life. In England, parliamentary government, in America the preservation of the Union and emancipation—these were the abiding benefits of such bitter strife. In Rome, no such results were to be achieved. Civil strife begat nothing except more civil strife, until in the end one man was left the victor. Thus it came about that when Pompey returned to Italy he did not return to peace.

The immediate reason for continued anxiety was almost fortuitous. Once again the slaves had risen in revolt. It happened that in the year 73 a Thracian gladiator called Spartacus, together with seventy-three companions, broke out of a training-jail in Capua, and established themselves on the summit of Mount Vesuvius. As we have seen, unrest among the slaves, who were treated with the utmost barbarity, was endemic in Rome; but whereas the former revolts in Sicily had been the work of desperate Orientals, this outbreak was manned by tough Europeans, Thracians and Gauls with a few captives from the Teutonic invasions. Fighting was their business, and Spartacus had actually served with the Roman forces. They were a very formidable menace, and the attempt to surround the insurgents atop of the volcano met with no success. They were soon masters of the whole of southern Italy, and new recruits poured in.

Spartacus was wise enough to realize that although he might defeat an incompetent praetor, Italy would not fall permanently under the control of a gang of slaves; whereas if they could once get beyond the Alps, they might disperse to individual freedom. In pursuit of this bold plan he set out for the north and managed to reach Picenum. There Spartacus trounced each of the consuls for the year 72 in turn, and opened the way to the mountains by routing the forces of the governor of Cisalpine Gaul. Then, with freedom within his grasp, Spartacus fatally reversed his plan and moved south again, perhaps even with the idea of marching on Rome. In the event, he went back to his old haunts. Here he was finally cornered and killed. The standards and colours, the consular insignia, which had been lost in former battles were recovered. The heroic gladiator, who with his improvised army had defied Rome for two years and had nine times defeated her army, was no more.

Five thousand stragglers were wiped out by Pompey; but the *coup de grâce* had been given by another commander, Marcus Licinius Crassus, a sinister and revolting figure even by Roman standards. He celebrated his début as general by crucifying six thousand prisoners along the Appian Way between Capua and Rome. Pompey in his official dispatch to the Senate pointed out, truthfully if tactlessly, that although Crassus had overthrown the slaves in battle, he, Pompey, had torn up the whole war by the roots; meaning that had he not reduced Sertorius, Rome would never have been able to concentrate her attention and her arms on the rebel gladiator. Unfortunately, Crassus failed to grasp this. He thought that he himself was a great general, and that Pompey was his enemy.

Both these misconceptions were to lead him to disaster. But first of all, it will be well to examine the character and rise of Marcus Crassus, millionaire.

CHAPTER XI

POMPEY AND CRASSUS—ENTER CICERO AND CAESAR

MARCUS LICINIUS CRASSUS possesses a double interest for the twentieth-century student of minds and morals. First, because he was responsible, through his own pride and folly, for the most appalling disaster to Roman arms since the battle of the Allia, and secondly because he is a frighteningly contemporary type: a thoroughgoing, ruthless, millionaire tycoon.

He was born about 115 B.C., the second son of a worthy father, Publius Crassus, who was consul in 97 and then governor of Farther Spain for three years. When he came home he celebrated a triumph over the Lusitanians. During the Social War, Publius held a command in Lucania, where he was defeated by the Italians. It is quite possible that young Marcus served with him both in Spain and in Italy. What is certain is that when in 87 the followers of Cinna and Marius seized Rome, Publius committed suicide rather than see his enemies triumph. His eldest son apparently died at the same time, thus leaving Marcus, at the age of twenty-eight, heir to the family fortune and to his brother's wife Terentia, to whom he remained faithful to the end of his days. The fortune was not a large one, only three hundred talents, about forty-five thousand dollars. Thirty years later, he was worth the equivalent of ten million dollars. How was it done? Like other millionaires, Crassus started off quietly. He lay low, hidden in a cave, until Cinna's death. Back in Rome he lived unostentatiously, and had no use for grandiose buildings: he had no need of them, for as will be seen he would live in those of others. He studied history and cultivated rhetoric, made a point of returning every man's salute, and was soon known as the poor man's friend in the courts. This affability was the cover for Crassus' ruling passion, avarice, which showed itself even in small things. For instance, Crassus decided to become an adept in the philosophy of Aristotle, which was now becoming fashionable. So he hired a poor philosopher called Alexander, who went about with him on his travels, and so bestowed the cachet of learning on his patron. Alexander was so poor that Crassus had to lend him a travelling-cloak. But when they got home he would take it back again; and that was all Alexander got for his labours.

Crassus, with his father and brother to avenge, willingly joined Sulla on his return from the East, and played a not inconspicuous part in the battle of the Colline gate. This did not make him a general, and he was not to be seen in the field again for nine years; but unfortunately he thought of himself as a military figure, and from this epoch dates his emulation of Pompey, nearly ten years his junior, and the *folie de grandeur* which was to goad him to his doom.

He was now able to set out on his career as a financier. He lent money, and was very strict at calling it in when it was due. The only concession he made to his "friends" was that he charged them no interest. We are told that he rejoiced in the misfortunes of others; he not only rejoiced in them, he knew how to profit from them. When Sulla started his proscriptions, Crassus was a privileged bidder at the auctions of the property of the pro-scribed, as one by one they were hunted down and butchered. Within a few months he had acquired not only considerable estates, but also the slaves that went with them. It was now that he showed what a sharp operator he was—no wonder people called him unreliable and shifty. He even contrived, without Sulla's knowledge, to slip into the proscription list a rich land-owner whose estate he coveted, after which Sulla never trusted him again. Having thus acquired a working capital, Crassus proceeded to exploit it. Plutarch says that he acquired most of his fortune by "fire and rapine, and by taking advantage of public calamities."

Rome was chronically subject to disastrous fires. The streets were narrow, and most of the populace lived in tall apartment houses. Only the rich had water laid on in their homes, and there was as yet no fire-brigade. This was Crassus' opportunity. His army of slaves was organized in regular departments, readers (essential in the pre-printing age), secretaries, silversmiths (Crassus owned a number of silver-mines), stewards and waiters. He also trained his own fire-brigade. Whenever a fire broke out, his men would go to the scene, ostensibly to help in quenching the flames, but in reality to buy the burning building, and those threatened by the fire, at give-away prices. Then his architects would get busy, with his builders and masons, and up would go a new block, which Crassus would let at a handsome figure. It is no wonder that "the greatest part of Rome came at one time or another into his hands." Sulla had promoted three hundred knights to membership of the Senate and these newcomers needed stylish homes to live in and possibly estates as well. "Supply and demand," in Sir Frank Adcock's words, "did their perfect work, as he moved from one market to another." He became richer and richer.

No one had more to fear from a slave-revolt than this man whose wealth was generated and increased by slaves, no one more reason to do all in his power to repress it, nor to rejoice at its collapse. The six thousand crucified men on the Appian Way were Crassus' "collateral" as it would now be called.

Pompey and Crassus: it was impossible that they should agree, essential that they should co-operate. Just how unfriendly they really were to each other it is difficult to judge: their enemies, and each of them had many, naturally did all they could to create a breach, through which they could penetrate to wealth and influence. Crassus was a scheming townee, Pompey a carefree countryman. Crassus was jealous of Pompey, to whose support he owed his consulship, and Pompey was not as deferential as he might have been to his older colleague. Pompey had triumphed magnificently a second time; Crassus, having defeated not a regular army but a slave commando, had to be content with an ovation, that is a civic welcome in which the successful general walked into the city on foot, wearing a crown not of laurel but of myrtle. Nevertheless it was clear that they and they only could be consuls for the year 70. Pompey in one of his speeches to the people tactfully said that the honour of having Crassus as his colleague was as great as that of being

consul; but once they were in office they were continually at log-
gerheads. The year 70 B.C. thus became one of the great missed
opportunities of history. Pompey and Crassus had, as yet, no
serious rival, and they had humbled all their enemies, domestic
and foreign. They might have restored the republic and prevented its death. Instead they were destined to mould the
destinies of Rome not in Rome itself, but, each of them, in the
Orient; Crassus disastrously both for himself and Rome, Pompey
beneficially for Rome and posterity. Both were to die defeated
in battle. So devious, so unpredictable and contrary, can history
be.

Politically the consulate of Pompey and Crassus was barren.
Pompey had no political flair, Crassus was out for money. What
remained of the Sullan constitution was scrapped. Already in
75 the regulation which debarred tribunes from further office had
been repealed. Their full powers were now restored to them. The
only other important piece of legislation was a law which removed the jury-courts from the exclusive control of the Senate
and manned them instead by senators, knights and *tribuni
aerarii*, who were of much the same standing. The new arrangement was a compromise: senatorial justice had become dis-
credited, and more jurors were needed in any case, because of
the increase of business brought about by Sulla's expansion of
the criminal code. The corn-dole had been reinstituted in 73.
Crassus, to show the people that Pompey was not the only one
worthy of their gratitude, provided a three months' supply from
his own pocket, and gave a grand banquet at which the citizens
were feasted at ten thousand tables. Pompey replied with an
equally theatrical but less expensive gesture. According to ancient custom, when a knight had completed his term of military
service he led his horse into the Forum before the censors and,
after giving an account of the campaigns in which, and the
commanders under whom, he had served, asked for his discharge.
When the two censors of the year, Gellius and Lentulus, were
holding their inspection and the knights were passing before
them, Pompey was seen coming down into the Forum, with the
full insignia of a consul, and leading his horse. When he came

to the bench, he bade his lictors—there were twelve of them each carrying a bundle of *fasces*—make way, and led his horse up to the tribunal. The populace fell silent with amazement. The senior censor duly examined him. "Pompeius Magnus, I demand whether you have served in the wars the full time prescribed by law?" "Yes, I have," answered Pompey in a ringing voice. "I have served all, and all under myself as general." The people were entranced by this display, and shouting for joy, insisted on the censors' rising from their seats and escorting Pompey home; the people followed after, cheering and clapping their hands.

In such play-acting the year passed. The final scene took place by the rostra, when a certain knight who was a stranger to politics, a countryman, declared he had had a dream in which Jupiter had commanded him to tell the citizens that they must not allow the consuls to lay down their office without being reconciled. Pompey, who was now becoming rather vain, made no move; but Crassus offered him his hand and said: "I cannot think, fellow-citizens, that I do anything humiliating or unworthy of myself, if I make the first offer of accommodation and friend-ship with Pompey, whom you yourselves styled the Great when he scarce had a hair on his face, and granted the honour of two triumphs before he had a seat in the Senate."

So closed this unremarkable year. At its end neither consul proceeded to a province. Crassus was busy in Rome, making money and keeping an eye on Pompey, who had, as so often, no plans for the immediate future. He had best bide his time, he reckoned, for some big military command was bound to come his way soon.

Spain was now tranquil. Lucullus was in control in Asia, Bithynia and Cilicia; his brother had coped with the Balkans. Though by no means wholly subdued, Crete had been declared a consular province in 70, and so one of the consuls for 69, Q. Metellus, went out to attempt to govern it. It was now becoming apparent that a unified Mediterranean command could not be postponed much longer, and no doubt Pompey saw himself as the man born to hold it. He was right. At this point we must introduce two more characters who were to play their parts in the grand drama, as opposed to the private farce just recorded. They are two of the greatest names in history, Cicero and Caesar.

For two thousand years these two figures have occupied the minds of men wherever politics have been debated. There would be epochs, there would be regions in which the names of Scipio, of Marius, of Sulla and of Pompey would be but dim memories, "shadows of great names," dim rays of stars long since cold. But never would men cease to laud the language of Cicero, even when they were unable to imitate it, nor to recall with admiration or revulsion the deeds of Julius Caesar, the man whose very name was to become a synonym for monarchy, not only within the wide confines of the Roman world, but as "Tsar" and "Kaiser" in lands which had never known the Roman dominion. The reputations of the two men have undergone astonishing vicissitudes, depending on the moral and political climate of different ages and countries. Until the end of the eighteenth century, Cicero was the admired orator, philosopher even, the creator of the Latin prose which still had a general vogue as a language of expression and communication among scholars and in diplomacy. (In the preceding century John Milton had been Cromwell's Latin secretary, charged with drafting his foreign dispatches.) During the nineteenth century, when history came to be written more and more by German scholars, Cicero's pusillanimity as a statesman began to overshadow his brilliance as an orator, specially as the use of Latin declined. Even to the English and Americans, he was no longer "Tully" as he had affectionately been dubbed in the age of elegance. This decline in Cicero's fortunes reached a nadir with Mommsen. That great man, who has had many critics, many imitators, but no rival, relegated Cicero to the lowest rank as a sort of untrustworthy journalist. To-day he would be rated far higher by many; but he has never regained the pedestal of grandeur he formerly occupied, and it is unlikely that he ever will.

Caesar has known similar ups and downs. For centuries he was venerated as the founder of the only polity under which men thought it possible to live. To the Renaissance he was the embodiment of the armed might which they admired and sought to foster. Shakespeare made him immortal: "O Julius Caesar, thou art mighty yet"—the line was to be prophetic. With the birth of romantic humanism, the tone changes. "The strongest poison ever known, Came from Caesar's laurel crown," Blake declared. During the nineteenth century, republics became more and more fashionable, empires less and less laudable in the eyes of enlightened folk—unless they happened to have an empire of their own: that was "different" and uniquely benign. The absolute corruption of absolute power—Lord Acton's mous thesis—found a multitude of adherents. Then at the end of the century Mommsen was to proclaim Caesar as the greatest Roman of them all, the inevitable, the necessary, complete man of destiny. The Cambridge Ancient History took much the same line. In our own day, which has seen a tyranny or two, dictators are not so popular, and Caesar, like Napoleon, has had as many critics as admirers.

But this continual assessment and reassessment of these two personalities only serves to make characters which would in any case be interesting more fascinating than ever. After two thousand years they still hold us, not least by the clash and conflict of their outlook and abilities.

Cicero came, like Marius, from Arpinum, in the hill country south-east of Rome. His full name was Marcus Tullius Cicero. Marcus was proud of his cognomen for as Plutarch tells us: "he who first of that house was surnamed Cicero seems to have been a person worthy to be remembered; since those who succeeded him not only did not reject, but were fond of the name, though vulgarly made a matter of reproach. For the Latins call a vetch *cicer*, and a nick or dent at the tip of his nose, which resembled the opening in a vetch, gave him the surname *Cicero*." Such is the modest origin of one of history's most famous names. Cicero's origin was modest, too. His father was a simple country gentleman, married to a well-born lady called Helvia. As soon as little Marcus was old enough to start lessons he was hailed as a prodigy. Parents used to visit the school in order to hear him, his fellow-pupils eagerly sought his company. All of which was very bad for the boy, because with all his talents he had his besetting sin, vanity. As he grew older he was to display other flaws of character which were to be the foil of his brilliance and ultimately to bring him to disaster. But in the bright springtime of youth his genius blossomed unblighted. He was avid of every kind of knowledge, but most eagerly of poetry. Later on, when he was established as the leading orator of Rome, he was also regarded as Rome's best poet. This has caused surprise, because the few lines of his composition that have come down to us are not up to much. In fact, the famous satirist of the first century A.D., Juvenal, quoting one of them, to be cited later, says that if Cicero had written all his output as badly as that he would not have had to fear the daggers of his enemies. But two things must be borne in mind: the first is that if we judge simply by "worst lines," neither Tennyson nor Wordsworth nor Longfellow would stand very high; and that what made Cicero's favourite poems ridiculous was the self-praise to which they were dedicated. In the second place, the great golden age of Latin poetry, that of Catullus and Virgil, was still in the future, so that it is not fair to judge Cicero by their standards. In fact, Cicero's translations from the Greek poets and dramatists were good of their kind, and did much to enlarge and refine Roman taste.

By the age of eighteen, in the year 88, Cicero had decided to do two things: to perfect himself in philosophy, and to enter the political arena. The former was the easier task. We do not nowadays regard Cicero as a great philosopher; but it is worth remembering that it was a philosophical treatise of Cicero's, now alas lost, that first turned St. Augustine's mind to serious studies. Being a Roman and practically inclined, Cicero was eclectic. The system of Epicurus which he had been taught as a boy made no appeal to him. He was repelled by its reliance on the senses, by its physics—why should atoms swerve to form new worlds if there were no gods to direct them? Was chance to dethrone Providence? Finally, how could a philosophy of withdrawal and escape nourish one who was bent on climbing the political heights? Nor did the rival Stoics wholly satisfy him.

In the end it was the Academics, those who perpetuated, according to their lights, the doctrines of Plato, who made the most permanent appeal to Cicero.

To become a statesman was far harder than to become a philosopher. Despite all the upheavals of the last decades, the Senate had contrived to keep the supreme office within its own gift: no democrat had succeeded in becoming consul. Cicero came from outside the charmed circle, he was a *novus homo*, a new man. He felt the disadvantage keenly, not only at the beginning of his career, but to the very end of it, even when he himself had become one of the leading men of Rome. Like other young Italians he made his military début, serving under Sulla in the Social War; but "perceiving the commonwealth running into factions, and from faction all things tending to an absolute monarchy, he betook himself to a retired and contemplative life." His chance of entering the arena soon came. In the year 80, when Cicero was twenty-six, a certain Chrysogonus, a creature of Sulla's, coveting a fine estate, laid an information that its late owner had been proscribed, and so had it knocked down to him at auction for a mere trifle. The dead man's son, who was called Roscius, remonstrated with Sulla and said that the estate was actually worth the equivalent of $400,-000. Sulla was outraged by the young man's presumption in questioning his actions and had him accused of murdering his father, with Chrysogonus faking the evidence. Roscius approached the leaders of the Roman bar, but not one of them would touch his case: they were all afraid of Sulla. Roscius then appealed to Cicero, who had first appeared in court the preceding year. Cicero's friends encouraged him to undertake the defence, saying he would never have a better and more honourable introduction to public life. Cicero accepted the brief, won the case, and so established his forensic reputation.

He now displayed a trait which, like his vanity, was to work to his undoing—timidity. It was, perhaps, prudent to retire to Athens for three years, and he could plead that his health was poor: he was lanky and lean, and suffered so badly from indigestion that he seldom ate anything solid until the evening.

But to run away from Sulla, just when he had shown that he could defy him with success, was unworthy of a budding champion. Unfortunately it was not the last time Cicero would so behave.

Athens was still, despite Sulla's recent ruin of it, a university city. Philosophers abounded, and Cicero resorted to them eagerly. He also studied oratory, both in Greek and Latin. He spent some time in Rhodes, then as now one of the most beautiful and stylish islands in the Aegean, and a great cultural centre. Here, pursuing his studies in philosophy and oratory, he became so proficient in Greek that a leading professor complimented him by saying: "You have my praise and commendation, Cicero, and Greece my pity and commiseration, since those arts and that eloquence which are the only glories that remain to her you will now transfer to Rome." This sentence cited by Plutarch in Greek is of interest, because in its choice of words, its use of balance and contrast, it is an apt example of the models which Cicero had been studying to such effect. It was a true prophecy: that is exactly what Cicero was to do.

Another Greek prophet was not to be so honoured. Cicero had now absorbed the best that Athens, Asia and Rhodes could give him. Meanwhile his friends in Rome had written to him urging him to return. He decided to do so, having perfected "his orator's instrument of rhetoric." On the way, before leaving Greece, he visited Delphi to consult the famous oracle. The priestess, knowing that he was now bent on a political career, "blunted the edge of his inclination" by replying when Cicero had asked how he could attain most glory, "by making your own genius and not the opinion of the people the guide of your life." If only he had followed her advice!

On his return to Rome, he at first lived in retirement. The usual sneers of "high-brow" and "Greek" were levelled at him. But his old father and his friends urged him to resume his practice at the bar. To-day, to be a successful pleader is not seldom the way to political eminence. In ancient Rome, forensic ability was even more important. All communication was oral. There were no journals, no bulletins (until Julius Caesar introduced them). Only by word of mouth could an idea prevail, except in those still limited circles that read books, or indeed were able to read anything at all. In the open-air, gregarious world of Rome, it was "the orator's instrument of rhetoric" that most surely charmed, inflamed and convinced. So it was that Cicero, back at the bar, "made no slow or gentle advance to first place, but shone out in full lustre at once, and far surpassed all the other advocates." He adopted an admittedly theatrical style, modelled on the leading actors of the day, and used to barb his speeches with sarcasms, by which he offended far more than he convinced.

In 75, two years after his homecoming, he started his political career. Being thirty-one, he was now eligible for the quaestorship, and as quaestor he went to Sicily. Here he displayed the integrity which was to be one of the brightest qualities of his being. There was a great scarcity of corn, and it fell to Cicero to requisition it. This naturally caused disaffection; but so fairly did Cicero act, that he soon established himself as the most popular official the Sicilians had ever known—something they were to remember later. He also ingratiated himself with certain noble families in Rome by securing the acquittal of their sons when arraigned before the governor of Sicily in a court martial. In fact, when he returned to Italy at the end of his year of office he was feeling highly pleased with himself. So much so that when he met a leading citizen of Campania on his way up to Rome, he asked him what the Romans were saying and thinking about his actions, as though they were the sole topic of the capital. To which his friend answered: "Tell me, where have you been, Cicero?" To his credit, Cicero used to tell this story of himself.

He now set out to be a walking "Who's Who," to know the names of everybody, in the provinces no less than in Rome, whom they frequented, how much they were worth and where they lived.

Such was the man who in 70, the year of the consulship of Pompey and Crassus, appeared as prosecutor in a *cause célèbre*, which was to prove that this "new man" from Arpinum was more than a match for the embattled corruption of the Senate. In January of 70 B.C. Gaius Verres returned to Rome after having been for three years governor of Sicily. He had been openly, shamelessly rapacious. He lived luxuriously on the fruits of his brigandage. His services of plate were a by-word, and he had even sent to the island of Malta, seventy miles away, for roses with which to stuff his pillows. He was hardly back home before embassies arrived from every city in Sicily, except Syracuse and Messana, all clamouring for his impeachment on the charge of extortion. It was clear from the outset that the indictment was justified. But Verres had powerful friends. The orator Hortensius, Cicero's only real rival and destined to be consul the following year, championed Verres, who was also supported by leading members of the aristocracy, a Scipio and three Metelli, one of whom was to be Hortensius' fellow-consul, the second Verres' successor in Sicily, and the third next year's president of the court before which Verres was now arraigned. The defence tried every trick. They put up a crooked rival of Cicero's to "represent" the Sicilians in collusion with the defence. The Sicilians, remembering Cicero's clemency when he was their quaestor, insisted on his being their advocate. Hortensius, who knew every quirk of the legal labyrinth, did all he could to have the trial postponed until the following year, when as already noted, one of his best friends would be president of the court. But Cicero defeated him, and had the case set down for the very last day of the session. Plutarch says he won the case "not so much by speaking as by holding his tongue." There was not time, in a single day, for the opposing advocates to make their speeches, and the matter brought to an issue. Cicero therefore contented himself with calling witnesses, who adduced such damning evidence that Hortensius virtually threw up his brief. Verres retired to exile. The Sicilians had won. For Cicero it was a triumph. He was now a force to be reckoned with in the world of politics; and Hortensius must yield him place as Rome's leading advocate. Cicero followed up his success by publishing, in the form of five set speeches, all the testimony he had collected. Not only did the case blast Verres' reputation, but it also showed up Rome's utter lack of control over provincial government, and the necessity of putting the courts into clean hands.

Among those who supported the proposal to restore the tribunician power was a young man of thirty-two, called Gaius Julius Caesar. He had already started on an adventurous career. Caesar was a true-blue patrician: as he reminded his audience in one of his first appearances as a speaker, his father was descended on his mother's side from king Ancus Marcius and on his father's from Venus herself, the patron goddess of Rome. This little oration was pronounced in 67 B.C., when he was quaestor, at the funeral of his aunt Julia, the widow of Marius. It was this connection which had first brought young Caesar into jeopardy. As a boy of seventeen, being in the Marian circle, he had married the daughter of Cinna. Sulla ordered him to divorce her. Caesar refused. Sulla wanted to kill him, but was dissuaded by the boy's aristocratic friends. "All right," he said finally, "take him; only bear in mind that the man you are so keen on saving will one day deal the death blow to the cause of the aristocracy, which you have joined me in upholding. *In Caesar there is more than one Marius.*" Caesar made himself scarce. He bribed one of Sulla's officers, who would have arrested him, to let him get away to sea. He made for Asia, and joined the staff of the governor, who sent him on a mission to the king of Bithynia, Nicomedes. The handsome young Roman won the heart of the susceptible monarch, and their relationship was to be a matter for banter, good-natured from his friends, ill-natured from his enemies, till the end of his days. He served for a short time in Cilicia and then, like Cicero, on Sulla's death went back to Rome. Refusing Lepidus' offers of alliance, he indicted Dolabella, a consul who had been honoured with a triumph, for extortion. This was brisk going for a lad of twenty-three. Dolabella was acquitted, and Caesar found it advisable to retire to Rhodes, where he studied rhetoric under Cicero's old master. On his way there he had an adventure which vividly brought out his character. He was captured by some pirates, who demanded a ransom of twenty talents. Caesar laughed in their faces: "Twenty!" he said. "You don't know whom you've caught: I'm worth fifty," and at once sent off his companions to raise the huge sum, about $80,000, required. He spent thirty-eight days with the pirates, with only his doctor and two attendants. Caesar soon showed who was master in the pirates' camp. He joked with them, joined in their sports, recited speeches and poems to them, and called them illiterate barbarians if they did not applaud him. When he wanted to sleep, he sent orders to them to shut up. In fact, he made them, these "most bloodthirsty people in the world," his bodyguard rather than his warders. Finally, when the ransom-money arrived, he jokingly told them that he would come back and crucify them. He did just that. He went off to Miletus, manned a ship, surprised the pirates, captured nearly all of them, and recovered not only his ransom-money but a good deal besides. He delivered the men to prison at Pergamum, the capital, and asked the governor to punish them. This official, with his eye on the money, temporized, whereupon Caesar ordered the pirates, on his own initiative, to be crucified. Plutarch merely records the fact; but his Roman contemporary, Suetonius, in his life of Caesar, has this remarkable sentence: "Even in avenging wrongs he was by nature most merciful, and when he got hold of the pirates who had captured him, he had them crucified, since he had sworn beforehand that he would do so, but ordered that their throats be cut first." So much for Roman mercy.

From Rhodes, Caesar went back to Asia and served in the campaign against Mithradates, and on his return to Rome was appointed a military tribune—his first public appointment. He at once set about courting the people by lavish entertainments, and was so bold as to arrange for the passage of a bill to recall his wife's brother, Cinna's son, and others who having been accomplices of Lentulus in 78–77 had fled to Sertorius in Spain. Such was the young man who now entered Roman politics. He was only thirty; but already "bloody, bold and resolute," and much else besides. A man who knew exactly where he was going and what he wanted. He would get it, too, and neither Cicero, who was the first to see how dangerous he was, nor Pompey, who saw nothing of the sort, would be able to prevent him.

CHAPTER XII

POMPEY AND THE EAST

W E MUST now return to the political stalemate in which we left Rome. The oligarchy had mouldered to decay, Sulla's constitution was a historic curiosity, yet no new hand had so far seized the helm, because neither Crassus nor Pompey would suffer the other to be the pilot. From these doldrums the ship of state was rescued and set upon a new course to a new world by Pompey. The maritime metaphor may perhaps be permitted, for it was by a maritime coup, unprecedented and unrepeated, that Pompey set the new course.

As already mentioned, the Roman empire was a land empire; the Romans never became good sailors, and they avoided the sea whenever they could. Even to reach Spain, as Cicero specifically informs us, it was usual to go by the long land route, rather than by the shorter sea passage; and even had they been so inclined Rome's rulers had had little time to spare for marine affairs, being preoccupied with war at home and abroad, with Sertorius, with Spartacus, with Mithradates, and with the threat to their dominance of the democratic leaders. As a result the pirates had become, in Rice Holmes' words, "the terror of the civilized world." They had, in fact, established a maritime empire, in competition with the land empire of Rome. Cilicia, in what is now south-east Turkey, and the island of Crete provided them with their securest lairs, but they raided as far as the straits of Gibraltar. They were organized in fleets and squadrons under their own admirals; they had their own dockyards, arsenals and signal-stations. The pirate ships were adorned with gilded masts, purple sails and silver-plated oars. "There was nothing but music and dancing, banqueting and revels all along the shore." Even a consul, in command of a flotilla, had been compelled to surrender to them, and when Verres was governor of Sicily, a pirate fleet had defeated a Roman squadron and had entered the harbour of Syracuse. Another plundered Ostia, the port of Rome itself. The pirates were amphibian; they would land, march into the country, pillage estates and hold rich men to ransom (just as they did in Caesar's case). Not even the famous Appian Way was safe where it ran close to the sea. Two praetors, in their purple robes of office, had been snatched with all their suite. Roman troops, on their way to Asia, were delayed because they dared not so much as cross the Adriatic until the winter, when even pirates usually remained in the safety of their harbours. If any of their captives made the proud claim that he was a Roman citizen, and gave his name, the pirates pretended to be very much taken aback: they would kneel and beg for forgiveness. Then having dressed the victim in toga and sandals, "to prevent such a mistake being made another time," they lowered a ship's ladder, told him he was free to go, wished him a pleasant journey—and pushed him overboard. Hardly a temple in Greece was left unrobbed to maintain their fleet of over a thousand sail, with which they had taken four hundred cities. Finally they intercepted the Roman corn-supply, and the city was threatened with famine. Clearly something must be done: equally clearly there was one man and one man only who could do it.

In January 67 one of the tribunes called Aulus Gabinius, a friend of Pompey's, "proffered a law, whereby was granted to him [Pompey] not only the government of the seas as admiral, but in plain language sole sovereignty, answerable to no man, over all men. For the decree gave him absolute power and authority in all the seas within the Pillars of Hercules [the straits of Gibraltar] and in the adjacent mainland for a distance of fifty miles from the sea. Now there were but few regions in the Roman empire out of that compass; and the greatest of the nations and most powerful of the kings were included within the limit. Moreover by this decree he had a power of selecting fifteen lieutenants out of the Senate, and of assigning to each his province in charge; then he might take likewise out of the treasury and out of the hands of the revenue-farmers what moneys he pleased; as also two hundred sail of ships, with power to press and levy what soldiers and seamen he thought fit." The command was to last for three years.

The senators were aghast. Danger there might be, but was this the way to avert it? King Pompey! It was a staggering thought. Here was a tribune proposing to confer on Pompey (he was not named in the bill, but all Rome knew who "the man of consular rank" mentioned in it would be) supreme power such as others before him had wrested from the Roman people by the sword. What a topsy-turvy world! In all the Senate there was only one man who backed the bill, the long-sighted, devil-may-care Julius Caesar. He did so not because he liked Pompey, but because it was his policy to court popular favour, with a view to diverting it to himself later on. A consul who said that if Pompey was setting himself up as a second Romulus he would perish as Romulus had done, narrowly escaped lynching. The Senate tried to gain over other tribunes, and one Trebellius was found to oppose the bill in the Assembly. But in the end Trebellius, threatened with removal from office, withdrew his opposition. Gabinius, realizing that he had acted in the same high-handed fashion as Tiberius Gracchus had against Octavius, thought it prudent to ask the much-respected Catulus to give his opinion. Catulus thought the bill unconstitutional and the meeting was adjourned amid such popular outcry that, says Plutarch, a crow which happened to be flying over the Forum fell down dead. When the assembly met again the bill was passed into law. At once the cost of provisions fell and Pompey's prestige soared.

The debate on the Gabinian law, so keen when it was introduced, has gone on ever since: was it constitutional; did Pompey seek to become king? Cicero, who devoted all his life and talents to the republic, and in the end died for the republic, thought it a wise measure. It was, in fact, the *only* occasion during the decline of the republic when supreme power was *legally granted* to one man, and not usurped by force or fraud, and then used for the salvation of the state, not its enfeeblement;

the only possible exception being Pompey's next command, with powers almost as wide.

The campaign against the pirates was a masterpiece, both in strategy and execution. Pompey spent the winter working out his plan and organizing his forces. He divided the Mediterranean into thirteen regions, allotting a squadron to each, the seamen being, as was usual, Greeks and Asians, and the fighting-men Romans. The idea behind the thirteen zones was that if a pirate fleet escaped one squadron, it would be caught by the next. The straits of Gibraltar and the Dardanelles were sealed. Early in March, operations began. There were to be two grand sweeps, one in the western Mediterranean, the second in the Aegean, converging on Cilicia, the pirate base. The first operation was completed and the seas made safe in forty days. Pompey then sent his fleet round to Brundisium, going overland himself to meet it. On the way he passed through Rome, where he had to deal with a jealous and obstructive consul and was greeted rapturously by the populace, who were now reaping the fruits of his victory in cheap and plentiful provisions. With his usual moderation Pompey restrained Gabinius from proceeding against the consul. From Brundisium he coasted round the Peloponnese and made for Cilicia. He was pressed for time, but managed to visit Athens, where he was cordially received. The pirates were now falling into his hands "by shoals," many of them surrendering because they had heard that he spared those who did so. Indeed, he went further. Instead of crucifying or selling into slavery even those who resisted to the end in their Cilician fortress, he did his best to resettle them, in Asia or Greece, even in Calabria, as far away from the sea and temptation as possible. The pirate strongholds were destroyed. The entire campaign had taken three months. Mommsen is wrong to dismiss it as a mere *razzia:* it was on the contrary one of the most successful naval operations in all Roman history. The only discord in a proceeding which might have produced much of it occurred in Crete, where the governor Metellus questioned Pompey's authority. Pompey was annoyed, but too wise to pursue the issue by force. Besides, he had reason to expect that another command, with even ampler prospects and richer prizes than this one, would shortly come his way. And come it did.

We must now retrace our steps a little. In the year 75, Nicomedes of Bithynia, Julius Caesar's admirer, died, and in his will, so it was alleged, bequeathed his kingdom (perhaps in memory of his young charmer) to Rome. There were it is true the precedents of Pergamum and more recently in 96 of Libya; but the "bequest" was admittedly suspicious. Mithradates, who hated the Romans as keenly as ever and had been making every sort of preparation and alliance with a view to reopening hostilities, saw his chance. He wanted Bithynia for himself, so he now denounced the will as a forgery and championed a putative son of the dead king. His timing was good. Rome was still prostrate from the civil war; the pirates were his allies, Sertorius would make common cause with him; Tigranes (Dhikran) of Armenia, the leading power in eastern Asia, was now his son-in-law. Him he persuaded to invade Cappadocia, whose king Ariobarzanes had already occupied Bithynia. The former realm of Nicomedes was now declared a Roman province. The tax-collectors moved in and made themselves so odious that the inhabitants were ready to welcome Mithradates as a deliverer. He could count too on the interested loyalty of the Greek colonies on the Black Sea. Clearly this tangled threat to Rome must be resisted, and so the two consuls for the year 74 were dispatched to overcome it, Lucullus as general, his colleague Cotta as his admiral.

Lucullus had served with Sulla against Marius and against Mithradates. Sulla dedicated his memoirs to him and made him his son's guardian. He had proved himself an efficient and kindly administrator in Asia, a capable master of the mint, but he had never held an independent command. After initial reverses, of which Cotta bore the brunt, Lucullus forced Mithradates to retire on Cyzicus, an ancient Greek colony, then an island, in the Sea of Marmora, which Cicero called the gate of Asia. Mithradates encamped opposite the city, which was connected with the mainland by a bridge. Lucullus came up with him, and soon had the besiegers besieged. Caught thus between two fires, Mithradates was compelled to fall back on Nicomedia, the seaport capital of

Bithynia, at the north-east end of the Sea of Marmora, and thence via the Bosporus to Heraclea on the coast of Pontus. Lucullus had now forced the king back into his own country, and proceeded to follow him into it. After a dogged campaign which lasted two years, Lucullus had occupied all but the great sea-port of Pontus, and Mithradates was a refugee in Armenia at the court of his son-in-law, who refused to see him for twenty months, during which he kept him under surveillance in a fortress. The Asians were grateful to Lucullus. They had been bled white by the Roman money-lenders, and parents had even been obliged to sell their children as slaves to find the cash for the tax-gatherer. Lucullus reduced all debts by two-thirds and fixed the rate of interest at the Italian legal figure, namely 12 per cent. The grateful inhabitants instituted a yearly festival in his honour; but the financiers of the capital denounced him as a "Greek-lover" and did all they could to undermine his reputation and achievements. Equally dangerous was the underground propaganda of Lucullus' own brother-in-law, Clodius, a man whose vileness of character makes him stand out even in the Rome of his day. Clodius clandestinely fomented discontent and indiscipline, which in the end reduced Lucullus to frustrated immobility. Once more, it must be underlined that a Roman army as then constituted owed no allegiance except to its own cupidity, an allegiance which it would share only with a general who could feed that cupidity; and that a Roman army, to be commanded, must first be cajoled.

Lucullus had meanwhile sent another brother-in-law to demand the surrender of Mithradates. Tigranes was disconcerted by the first plain-speaking he had heard for twenty-five years; but he refused to give up Mithradates, whom he now condescended to see. The two kings drew up a plan designed to compel Lucullus to split his forces. Mithradates would return to Pontus, while Tigranes held Armenia. The old king went back to his Black Sea kingdom, whither Lucullus followed him early in 69. By his capture of Sinope the Roman established himself as master of Pontus. He turned east again, and after a brilliant and arduous campaign, defeated Tigranes and took his capital.

The soldiers were allowed to sack the city; and Lucullus acquired such enormous quantities of treasure that he was able to give the equivalent of two hundred dollars to every man. From the dependent states who then surrendered he recouped the whole expenses of the campaign, without involving the Roman treasury in any expense. But the war was not over, not by any means. Mithradates rejoined his son-in-law and steeled him to continue fighting. Tigranes retreated to Artaxata, in the heart of Armenia, north of Lake Van. Lucullus would have followed him, but his soldiers mutinied, and he had to be content with the capture of Nisibis. Meanwhile Mithradates had temporarily recovered Pontus.

Lucullus' achievement had been considerable. He had not only recovered Asia and Bithynia, but had wrested Pontus as well from Mithradates; he had subdued his army, he had annihilated his navy. He had defeated Tigranes. And all this without the smallest charge on state revenues, and despite the lavish rewards he had showered on his troops. He had, too, won the gratitude of the provincials. And yet he had failed. The reason was one which has led to the disappointment of more than one general in more recent epochs. He lacked, as Plutarch puts it, "that one first and most important requisite of a general," a genius for leadership. In the year 66 he was superseded by Pompey, who by a law introduced by the tribune Manilius had been granted unlimited authority over the entire East, in addition to that conferred by the Gabinian law which had still two years to run. Pompey, it will be remembered, in expectation of his new command, had remained in Asia. He now met Lucullus. Their friends had hoped for a reconciliation; but they were disappointed, and the meeting broke up in an atmosphere of mutual recrimination.

Lucullus returned to Rome, where his enemies tried to deprive him of his well-merited triumph. Once again, we catch a glimpse of the chaotic state of what passed for democracy at Rome. It was not the Senate, but the plebs who had it in their power to grant or withhold the honour; and we see the leading and most responsible men of Rome humbling themselves perforce to beg

the venal and illiterate mob to permit a great Roman to celebrate
the victories which he had won for Rome.

The triumph was magnificent. When it was over, Lucullus
feasted the people and retired into private life. He became famous
for his villas, his gardens (the finest in Rome) and his cuisine
(as he still is). He also founded public libraries and collected
rare manuscripts. For ten years he lived the life of a rich
dilettante. When he died, men remembered the benefits they
had so often disregarded while he lived, and would have buried
him beside Sulla; but his brother laid him to rest on his country
estate near Cicero's favourite retreat at Tusculum.

Pompey started his Eastern campaign with an act of statesmanship. He made a treaty with the king of Parthia, Phraates III.
Parthia was the home of the only other great civilization with
which Rome came in contact which was at the same time a
great power. Carthage had been powerful, but her civilization
had inherited little and bequeathed less. Greece was the begetter
of a great civilization, which she transmitted to posterity, but as
we have seen, she had never been a great power, and by the
time of her first intercourse with Rome was fragmented and feeble. Only Persia, or Parthia, the new power which had arisen
on the débris of the Seleucids as the heir of Persia, possessed
both a culture which was far older and far more splendid than
that of Rome, and a military might which was to prove not only
the equal of Rome but again and again her superior. Before this
narrative is ended, evidence of that superiority will be adduced;
but it may here be said that the opposition of Rome and Parthia,
and later of restored Persia, continued until the very end of
Roman rule in the East, that is until the seventh century A.D.
when both Romans and Persians fell before the Arabs, and that
this opposition did as much as any other one factor to enervate
imperial Rome. It was one of the most disastrous and unnecessary
antagonisms in history, the first global confrontation of East and
West it might almost be called, a phenomenon from which our
own age has suffered so grievously.

Unnecessary it was, because if only Rome, if only Pompey himself had continued as Pompey himself had begun, the whole

history not only of the Levant, which Pompey was to transform, but of Rome itself would have been different. The two nations had everything to gain by co-operation. To start with, Persian culture was deep and august. At the height of the Persian imperial power, in the sixth and fifth centuries B.C., when Persia was mistress of the Levant and of Egypt too, and when the Greeks were trying with varying success to maintain their independence, Hellas herself learned much from Persia, and many a Greek admitted his admiration not only for Persian efficiency, but for Persian standards of conduct as well. Alexander had humbled Persia, and regarded himself as heir to her empire. In his wake, many Greeks had gone east, and a number of Greek colonies had been founded in what had been Persian, and was later to be Parthian, territory.

It was in the year 92 that Rome first had official dealings with Parthia. Sulla was then on the Euphrates, and the Parthian king, Mithradates II, who had already received an embassy from China, sent envoys to the Roman general. The first contacts between the two peoples were consistently friendly, if only because both saw themselves threatened by the growing power of Pontus. In 69 again, Phraates III sought alliance from Lucullus. Lucullus recognized the Euphrates as Parthia's boundary. There are not many natural frontiers in the world, but the Euphrates is one of them. The region to the west of the river can be, and often has been, within the ambit of the Mediterranean; the lands to the east of it have been within it very rarely and only for short periods. More than one Roman emperor was to prove this thesis; and it has been reaffirmed in more recent epochs. Pompey was geographically and politically right, therefore, in adopting the line he did. With his flank thus secure, he moved north against Mithradates of Pontus and routed him at Dasteira in Lesser Armenia, thus preventing him from rejoining his son-in-law and forcing him to take refuge in Dioscurias in Colchis, the many-fabled home of the Golden Fleece and of Medea on the north-eastern shore of the Black Sea. Pompey now turned east again, through the mountains of Armenia, towards Artaxata, the "Armenian Carthage" as it had been called by Lucullus, whose

troops had refused to follow him thither. Pompey was more
fortunate. Not far from the town Pompey was met by Tigranes,
who, led on foot and without his sword into the Roman camp,
prostrated himself before the Roman in token of abject submis-
sion. Pompey raised him up, returned the diadem which Tigranes
had doffed, seated him beside himself and told him that he
might keep his hereditary dominions but must restore his an-
nexations to their rightful rulers. He must also pay six thousand
talents (nine million dollars) as an indemnity. Tigranes was so
delighted to have got off so lightly that he made lavish presents
to every officer and man in Pompey's army.

Pompey now committed a cardinal error. When Phraates,
alerted by the change in Tigranes' fortunes, sent to Pompey to
ask that the Euphrates be formally recognized as the frontier between Rome and Parthia, Pompey answered with the evasive for-
mula that he would delimit the frontier "according to right and
justice." The definition of frontiers in the Levant, where there are
so many racial diversities and economic tensions, has proved a
pitfall for uncandid statesmen down to our own day. But Pompey
aggravated his blunder in the following year. When Phraates
tried to recover from Tigranes Gordyene, or western Kurdistan,
which lies to the east not only of the Euphrates but of the Tigris
as well, Pompey at once sent two lieutenants to occupy the territory. Phraates, acting with great moderation, withdrew his
forces and asked for a new treaty; whereupon Pompey replied
in insulting and provocative terms. The next year, 64, Phraates
attempted to reoccupy Gordyene, whereat Pompey's officers again
ousted him and reinstated Tigranes. This breach of faith was to
have disastrous consequences for Rome. The Persians, and the
Parthians after them, prided themselves on keeping their word.
Phraates could not forgive such double-dealing, nor was he to
allow Rome to forget it.

Pompey meanwhile had once again moved eastward. Marching through Georgia, he rejoined his fleet on the Black Sea coast,
in that delightful country which is now one of the Rivieras of
Russia. For the second time he left to his fleet the task of contain-
ing Mithradates, and devoted the rest of the year 65 to the

occupation of the approaches to the Caspian, his object being to investigate the trade-route to India. He spent the winter in Lesser Armenia, where he mopped up Mithradates' remaining treasure-castles. The old king, who had eluded Pompey's navy and had recovered all his Russian provinces, now had the hardihood to ask that Pompey should restore to him his kingdom of Pontus, as a vassal of Rome. Pompey rejected the proposal and, knowing that Mithradates could not be far off, followed his advance detachments who had already moved down into Syria. That rich land was in chaos. The shadowy Seleucid whom Lucullus had recognized as the rightful ruler had been kidnapped by an emir of Emesa (Homs) called Samsiceramus, a name which in its Aramaic form denoted his connection with the great sun-cult of which that city was the centre; and a still more insubstantial phantom had replaced him in Antioch. Farther south the situation was no less unstable.

Palestine had shaken off the Seleucid yoke after Antioch Epiphanes had tried in 168 B.C. to stamp out the Jewish faith and practice in the very Temple itself. The patriot-priests known as the Maccabees had led the national revolt, and their descendants, known as Hasmoneans, now held sway not only over Judaea, but over certain adjoining regions, among them being Galilee "of the Gentiles," thus ensuring that any child born to Galilean parents would be brought up in the Jewish faith, including, in the fullness of time, Jesus of Nazareth. But the Hasmonean family was now divided by a fraternal feud. Two people profited from this, Aretas (Harith) II, king of the Nabataeans whose capital was Petra, the "rose-red city," and Antipater, a supple and capable Edomite who was chief minister to the legitimate Hasmonean priest-king, called Hyrcanus although he had nothing of the tiger in his disposition. Pompey's deputy, Gabinius, the same who as tribune had promoted Pompey's command, with typical Roman pragmatism, backed the younger brother, Aristobulus, and Harith, who had been besieging Jerusalem, withdrew, leaving Aristobulus in possession of the Holy City. Such was the situation when at the end of 64 Cicero was elected to the consulship for 63, a year which was to be memorable indeed, both at home and abroad.

Pompey quickly restored order in Syria: the roads were made safe, the robber-bands annihilated, the pirate-nests demolished. A region already steeped in history was thus brought into the orbit of Rome, which it was to influence profoundly in the years to come, both for good and evil; so that more than a century later, Juvenal could write in a famous line: "It is a long time now since the Orontes (the Syrian river which rises near Baalbek) flowed into the Tiber." Syrian slaves were so intelligent that they fetched by far the highest prices; and Syria was to give to Rome not only emperors but some of its most eminent jurists, the influence of whose labours is still active to-day. Moreover Antioch remained until the very end of the Roman world a centre of light and learning equal with Alexandria and second only to Rome and later Byzantium, the New Rome, itself.

In the spring of 63, Pompey moved south from Antioch to Damascus. Here he was greeted by Hyrcanus and Aristobulus in person, having postponed a decision on the cases stated by their rival deputations the year before. On this occasion, Aristobulus made a tactical blunder: he brought with him a magnificent vine made of gold, valued at five hundred talents ($750,000). He had misjudged his man. Most Romans, it is true, were ineradicably venal; and most of them neglected no opportunity of enriching themselves. But Pompey was different. Again and again we read that he forbore to touch treasures which he could easily have pocketed, and that he always paid any wealth he acquired by conquest, after satisfying the legitimate demands of his soldiers, into the treasury. He was not the man to be bought by a bribe; and so he decided in favour of Hyrcanus, who was in any case not only the legitimate contender but far more useful, because more pliable, to Roman policy. But he did not announce his decision, being occupied for the present in a campaign against Harith of Petra. This monarch controlled not only the enormously lucrative Eastern spice-trade, but also the outlet to the Red Sea and the terminus of the sea-route (at that period less important, owing to Western ignorance of the monsoon, than the overland trail) to India and China. Aristobulus nevertheless divined Pompey's intentions and decided to defy him. Here again fortune came to Pompey's aid. As he was nearing Petra, and was outriding at the end of the day's march, a group of horsemen appeared carrying javelins crowned with laurel. The soldiers, knowing that they must be the bearers of good news, insisted that Pompey abandon his exercise and read the messages to them from an improvised tribunal made of pack-saddles. Pompey opened the dispatches and announced that Mithradates was dead. The army went wild with joy: the great enemy was dead, the great object for which they and their leader had left Italy was now accomplished. It was time to hurry home.

"The Roman Republic," says the Cambridge Ancient History, "never encountered a stouter adversary in the East than Mithradates." He had lived for sixty-eight years and reigned for fifty-seven, the last twenty-six of which had been devoted to implacable defiance of Rome. In the end it was one of his own discontented children who laid him low. The son besieged him in a fortress at the entrance of the Sea of Azov in the Crimea. Seeing that he was doomed, Mithradates massacred his remaining children, including the young queens of Egypt and Cyprus, and all his concubines. He then tried to poison himself; but having all his life been in the habit of drinking antidotes against the possible attempts of others, he now found himself defeated by his own precaution, and had to seek his quietus from a Celtic mercenary.

Pompey, when the embalmed body of the old king was sent to him by the rebellious son as a token of good faith, forbore to look on it and ordered it to be buried in the royal mausoleum at Sinope.

Pompey was as eager as any of his men to get home, but he could not leave Palestine in turmoil. He abandoned the Petra campaign to a lieutenant called Scaurus. At the prompting of Antipater (who was married to the daughter of a Nabataean nobleman) Harith offered Scaurus a large sum of money to go away—which did not deter Scaurus from issuing coins on which Harith is shown as a suppliant leading his camel and offering an olive-branch to Scaurus.

Aristobulus was summoned to surrender his fortresses, and he promised Pompey, who was then marching down the Jordan valley, to do so. But when Gabinius approached Jerusalem, the gates were closed against him. Pompey arrested Aristobulus and laid siege to the Holy City. He occupied the lower town without resistance, but the great Temple Hill held out against him. Only on the north, where it joins the *massif*, was the plateau vulnerable. Pompey filled in the fosse, and after a desperate struggle, the ramparts fell. Faustus Sulla, son of the dictator, was the first to scale the wall. Pompey, true to his character, respected the inviolability of the sacred treasure; but his forbearance was more than cancelled in Jewish eyes by the sacrilege he committed in entering the Holy of Holies, the empty innermost chamber of the Temple, in which no man might set foot except the High Priest and he only once a year on the Day of Atonement. Cicero was delighted with Pompey: "Our Jerusalemite," he called him, just as earlier he had dubbed him "Arabarch," or hailed him as "Samsiceramus," tickled by the outlandish name.

Leaving the complicated question of Egypt for future settlement, Pompey now set out for home. His achievement had been prodigious. To anyone acquainted with the Levant it appears doubly noteworthy. In the first place, merely to maintain, equip and transport armies in that region of mountains, ravines and deserts, where even to-day communications are far from easy, required the utmost energy and resource. Marches and countermarches, from the borders of Russia to the plains of Parthia, battles fought and won from the shores of the Black Sea to the Mediterranean littoral—it is an unprecedented and astonishing catalogue. Secondly, to lands which have seldom known political cohesion, Pompey brought stability and justice. He was fair to Greek, Armenian, Georgian and Jew alike. To Pompey was due that federation of Greek colonies in Palestine and beyond the Jordan which as the Decapolis (meaning "ten cities"; there were ultimately fourteen) is familiar to readers of the Gospels. To Pompey must also be credited the restoration of many a "client-kingdom" in the area, including that of Judaea, the evolution of which was to be of such import for mankind. For it was owing to Pompey's campaign that Judaea was brought definitely within the orbit of Rome, in such a manner that its religious message must vitally affect the fortunes of Rome.

Financially, the gain to the empire was enormous. After distributing a bounty of 384 million sesterces ($20 million) among his soldiers, he could still remit 480 million ($25 million) to the treasury; and he increased Rome's annual tributary revenue from 200 million to 340 million sesterces. Only in Parthia had Pompey failed; and that failure was to haunt and bedevil Rome for centuries. Everywhere else he had been successful. Nations brought up in the Western tradition are apt to regard the European provinces of the Roman empire as being more important than the Eastern, and to relegate the Levant to a secondary role. That is a great mistake. Spain may at one time have been the richest single province, or pair of provinces; but it was in the East that the bulk of the wealth and the brains and the culture of the empire was to be found. Under the humane emperors of the second century, the whole of the Near East was to enjoy a renaissance to which the remains of cities such as Pergamum, Ephesus, Perga, Attalia and many another still bear eloquent witness. And when the Western empire dissolved before the northern invaders in the fifth and sixth centuries A.D., the Eastern provinces survived for almost another millennium. In the words of the Cambridge Ancient History, "Though Pompey's conquests have little of the glamour of Caesar's Gallic Wars, they will bear comparison with these in their ultimate effects upon the course of ancient history." They will indeed; but we must now return, with Pompey, to Rome.

CHAPTER XIII

POMPEY, CICERO AND CATILINE

POMPEY paid one more visit to Pontus, to ensure that all would be well with the new province, and to reward those who had brought about the death of Mithradates, including his parricide son, who became king of the Bosporus. After ordering the province of Asia to maintain a permanent anti-piracy squadron, Pompey made for Rome. He called at Mytilene, and had a model made of the theatre so that he could have one like it built in Rome, only more splendid, as he afterwards did. His next stop was at Rhodes, where he gave the philosophers a talent each. He did the same at Athens, adding fifty talents ($75,000) for the restoration and adornment of the city.

Rome was on tenter-hooks: what would Pompey do? Would he establish a dictatorship? Would he have himself proclaimed king? What no one expected him to do was what he actually did. Before the troops embarked at Ephesus he distributed to them the handsome bonuses mentioned in the last chapter; when they disembarked at Brundisium, he paraded them, bade them farewell and sent them to their homes, merely asking them to be sure to stand by for the triumph.

This move, or rather the lack of a move, on Pompey's part has puzzled historians, particularly those of the Mommsen school, just as it puzzled Pompey's contemporaries. The latter, reckoning by precedent, took it for granted that an omnipotent general as Pompey now was must of natural necessity seize the city by force and set up a monarchy. Crassus even removed himself and his family and belongings from Rome, either out of fear, or more likely because he wished to prejudice Pompey in men's eyes. We with our hindsight, and knowing what the Romans of the day could not, should fall into no such error. It was not in Pompey's make-up to desire or to plan any such thing. Praise he loved, like Cicero, but for power he had no capacity. Action in the field, practical politics, such as making and remaking maps, bestowing kingdoms, liberating cities, and drawing frontiers—those were Pompey's arts. His inborn hesitancy, his inability to think two moves ahead, these quite unfitted him for the intrigues, the finesse, the combinations and bargainings of the Forum and the Senate-house. Equally inhibiting was his humanity. Not for Pompey the "mercy" of slitting throats before crucifixion: he preferred to make his victims into citizens. Thus Plutarch, who is remarkably fair to Pompey as he is to most of his subjects, can write of Pompey at this point of time: "And well had it been for him had he terminated his life at this date, while he still enjoyed Alexander's fortune, since all his after-time served only either to bring him prosperity that made him odious, or calamities too great to be retrieved. For that great authority which he had gained in the city by his merits he made use of only in patronizing the iniquities of others, so that by advancing their fortunes he detracted from his own glory, till at last he was overthrown even by the force and greatness of his own power." This verdict is precisely true.

Pompey's triumph—it was his third—was of unprecedented splendour. It took two days, the 29th and 30th September, 61, of which the second was Pompey's birthday, his forty-fifth. He had closed his military career at the age of forty-four, the same age as that of both Wellington and Napoleon at Waterloo.

The spectacle was perforce compressed, but was still the most lavish and magnificent that Rome had ever beheld. Banners proclaimed that the conqueror of the world, Pompeius Magnus, had restored to Rome the sovereignty of the seas and had vanquished Asia, Pontus, Armenia, Paphlagonia, Cappadocia, Cilicia, Syria, Albania and Iberia (meaning the territories of those names between the Black Sea and the Caspian Sea), Crete (a snub for Metellus, this, and tactless at that) and other lands, not all of which he had visited in person. Other placards announced that he had overcome Mithradates and Tigranes, had captured a thousand strongholds, nearly nine hundred towns, and eight hundred ships. Thirty-nine cities had he founded, and he had enriched the treasury. A long train of wagons creaked and rattled beneath the load of gold, silver and captured arms. A golden image of Mithradates, twelve feet high, was hauled along, as also one of Pompey, constructed wholly of pearls. (Roman taste would see nothing vulgar in this.) Pictures showed, as in a modern strip-feature, the blockade, flight and death of Mithradates. Then came the captives: Tigranes, son of the Armenian king, with his wife; five sons and daughters of Mithradates who had escaped their father's final slaughtering-bout; the Colchian king, Aristobulus of Judaea, with his son Antigonus; followed by assorted princes, pirates, satraps, soldiers and hostages—to the number of 324. Last of all, Pompey rode down the Sacred Way in his jewel-studded triumphal chariot, attended and followed by his victorious subordinates and troops. Past the Senate-house and the rostra the glittering procession wound its way, and then ascended the slope of the Capitol to the precinct of Great Jupiter himself. Here, Pompey's humanity once again showed itself. According to precedent, the principal captives should now have been slaughtered. Pompey would have none of it: except for the members of royal houses who were retained as hostages, all the others were sent home at public expense. No Roman had ever been so generous before; Caesar in his turn would restore the old barbaric custom.

Pompey now appeared to have reached his zenith, but in fact he had passed it. In order to understand why and how his decline had already set in, it will be necessary briefly to survey events in Rome during his six years' absence. In Sir Frank Adcock's words: "When in 66 B.C. Pompeius took up his command in the East to put an end to Mithradates, he left behind him a military vacuum and widespread discontent." This was just the right breeding-ground for stratagems and plots. At this juncture it must yet again, at the risk of wearisomeness, be emphasized that Roman politics were not comparable to our own systems. Parties, as we understand the term, did not exist. There were no platforms, no machines, no whips, no permanent executives. Politics was simply, as it still is in some Eastern countries, a real-life embodiment of two popular children's games—musical chairs, and follow-my-leader. Stable government is impossible in such conditions. The kaleidoscope is continually turning, and every so often, click! go the brittle chips and a new pattern is formed.

For the period we are about to survey a new and valuable source becomes available, namely the letters and speeches of Cicero, and the notes thereon by his early editors. Plutarch is still at our side, with lives of the younger Cato, Caesar, Cicero, Crassus and Pompey; and his Latin contemporary Suetonius has joined the company with his life of Caesar. The Greek historian Dio is detailed and gives us accurate dates. There are others, including for the Levant the great Jewish historian Josephus. These men all wrote later: Cicero was a contemporary, and his letters provide a month by month, sometimes a day by day, commentary on events such as no other ancient author ever furnished.

No sooner was Pompey on his way to the East than the Senate, with myopic malice, retaliated by attacking his supporters. Gabinius, as we have seen, escaped prosecution by joining Pompey; but a fellow-tribune was indicted on the vague charge of *maiestas*, or contempt of government. Manilius, whose law had procured Pompey's command, was similarly sued for extortion and contempt. This foolish vindictiveness naturally increased the tension in the capital and led to such frequent riots that a special police force had to be enlisted to protect the law-courts. A more serious plot was soon to be hatched—the famous Catilinarian conspiracy. Catiline was that dangerous type, a down-at-heels and disappointed patrician. He had fought in the civil wars as one of Sulla's officers, and had shown himself a brave but ruthless soldier. During the proscriptions he was a busy agent, and rumour said that he had thereby managed to rid himself of superfluous relations. Despite this unpleasant record, he had by the year 68 risen to the praetorship. The next year he went as governor to Africa, where his rapacity was so outrageous that on his return he was set down for prosecution for extortion. Catiline nevertheless put his name forward as a candidate for a consulship in 65. The sitting consul, Volcacius Tullus, rejected his application. Although Catiline had not been formally indicted,

Tullus was within his rights in disqualifying him. But Catiline felt himself aggrieved. So did two other candidates, Autronius Paetus and a nephew of Sulla's called Publius Cornelius Sulla. These two headed the poll, but were convicted of bribery under a new law of 67 B.C. The three disappointed men—and a pretty trio they were—decided to claim their rights by the simple expedient of murdering the two successful rivals, and a few other obnoxious persons such as Volcacius. The idea was to pounce upon their victims on the 1st January, 65 B.C. (when the consuls would meet the Senate on the Capitol), seize the insignia of office for Autronius and Sulla, who would thus become consuls for the year, and obstruct the prosecution of Catiline so that he could be nicely in the running for a consulship in 64. The whole scheme sounds so silly that we may wonder how even in the corrupted currents of the Roman world it could ever have been seriously entertained. Even so, the conspirators blabbed. The Senate enlisted a bodyguard, the conspirators were foiled and the consuls lived out their year of office unscathed. Unscathed too were the conspirators. One of their principal subordinates, Piso, was actually rewarded with a quaestorship in Spain, the reason being, Sallust affirms, that Crassus was behind him. There is little doubt that Crassus did put pressure on the Senate, many members of which were in his pay, to hush up the plot and to send to Spain one of his own creatures through whom he could keep an eye on that opulent province. This was typical of Crassus' methods. He had not originated the plot, nor had he backed it; but once it had failed the opportunity for a little double blackmail was too good to miss. Unfortunately for Crassus it did not pay off. Piso was so arrogantly insulting to the Castilians that he soon forfeited his life, and so lost Spain for Crassus. That enterprising financier must now look elsewhere; and where better than Egypt? Egypt was even richer than Spain, and its affairs were in a sorry mess. The reigning king, Ptolemy XI, surnamed Auletes, or "the Piper," held his throne by a very shaky title; because it was alleged that his predecessor, Ptolemy Alexander, had "bequeathed" his kingdom to Rome. The will was presumably spurious, because Alexander had been monarch of Egypt for only a few days; before that he had been joint ruler with his queen, Berenice, whose rights he could not extinguish. The Senate had taken no steps to claim their "inheritance"; they had simply disregarded the will; and it may be presumed that its validity had lapsed. To annex Egypt, a country with which Rome had no quarrel, would indeed have been inexcusable. What Crassus was apparently angling for, as Adcock says, was a commission to go to Egypt and "regularize" the Piper's position vis-à-vis the Senate. There would be some nice pickings there. But the Senate, nerved to opposition by Catulus, would have none of it. The Piper turned to Pompey, whose good will he won by sending him a body of cavalry for his Syrian campaigns. Catulus had led the opposition, but it was Cicero who had animated it; and the rejection of the Egyptian bill was the first and perhaps most important victory which Cicero gained over Crassus in these three years before Pompey's return.

Crassus was now, in 65, to put the seal of respectability on himself by becoming one of the censors. In this exalted capacity he tried to have the dwellers beyond the Po made full citizens. As they were so far from Rome, it was most unlikely that many of them could ever have voted; but the region was one of Rome's most fertile recruiting-grounds, and Crassus thought it would be as well to have its men beholden to him. His proposal that they should be enfranchised by a mere stroke of the censors' pens met with opposition from his colleague, who was none other than the stern, unbending tory, Catulus. Both censors resigned. Crassus, twice balked by Catulus, who was supported by Cicero, now turned to Catiline. This desperate rip had been kept waiting two years before he could again be nominated for the consulship. The trial for extortion which had seemed too imminent to admit of his standing in 66 only came on in 65, and did not end in time for him to stand for the 64 consulship. Catiline was defended by the very man he had intended to murder; the jury had been rigged; Clodius, the prosecutor, was complaisant if not collusive; and Catiline was acquitted. (Of all races who have ever practised Roman law, the Romans had the least respect for it.) Now at last, in the summer of 64, Catiline, the newly-washed lamb, could stand for the consulship for the following year. According to accepted practice, Catiline chose his own running-mate, Gaius Antonius, uncle of the famous Mark. He had been expelled from the Senate in 70 as one of Sulla's agents at the instance of the young Caesar, but had stood for a second praetor-ship and thus was once again qualified to become consul. Apart from that act of resolution, Antonius was notorious only for rapacity and licence.

But a third candidate was now in the field—Marcus Tullius Cicero. He was by far the best qualified of the three competitors, except in one respect—his birth. While all their other privileges had been eroded by the rising democratic tide, the aristocracy had maintained its hold on the consulate. Not since the consulate had been last held by Marius in 86 had it been attained to by anyone outside aristocratic ranks. So keenly was Cicero aware of his disability in being, as Catiline called him, a mere "immigrant" whose father was not even a senator, that he had at first offered to defend Catiline and so secure him as his partner, an offer which Catiline insultingly refused. The campaign was hectic. Cicero's rivals used bribery on a massive scale; and such was the menace to security of their intimidation that a special measure was passed dissolving all clubs, except *bona fide* trade guilds. The Senate would have tightened the law against corrupt practices, but the proposal was cynically vetoed by a tribune who supported Catiline. Something of the fetid climate of Roman politics is conveyed to us in two contemporary documents. The first is the *Candidate's Handbook*, generally ascribed to Cicero's brother Quintus. Cicero must spare no pains, he says. The equestrian order, it was true, was on his side, and so were many eminent men whose goods or reputations had been saved by Cicero's advocacy. (He had been Verres' prosecutor, but shone most brightly in defence.) Every artifice must be employed. "A flattering manner is essential. It may be wrong and dishonourable in other walks of life, but when seeking office it is indispensable." Another brutally modern injunction is: he must not be over-scrupulous. He must not refuse his services to people who ask for them merely because he knows he cannot keep his promises. Human nature being what it is, "all men prefer a false promise to a flat refusal." It was important that he should let everyone know that he had the support of Pompey, and that his success would be acceptable to the great general. Finally, he should get some new scandal going against his rivals—some crime or immorality or corruption. Here Catiline and Antonius were playing into his hands. Which brings us to the second document. Aspirants for high office were required to conduct their electioneering wearing a toga whitened with chalk—*candidata* as it was called, whence our word "candidate"—and parts of Cicero's speech to the Senate *in the whitened toga* have come down to us. Taking his cue from the tribune's veto, he heaps every sort of vilification on Catiline—murderer, he calls him, tyrant, corrupter, adulterer, married to his own daughter by an adulterous mistress, a man who attempted incest and intended massacre. Broad hints of a hidden hand behind Catiline incriminated Crassus.

The effect produced by this speech, combined with Catiline's reckless indecency, swung the voters in Cicero's favour, and he was returned at the head of the poll, with Antonius second and Catiline a good third.

Cicero was forty-three. Having reached the summit of his ambition he might have expected that he would be suffered to rest awhile. This was not to be. Trouble started on the first day of his consulate, indeed even before it. And now Caesar gave the first evidence of his subversive ambitions. Catiline was by no means quelled: Cicero was convinced (or said he was) that Catiline had tried more than once to have him assassinated before he had entered office. He was up again before the end of the year, charged with having committed murder during the Sullan proscription; but as good luck would have it Caesar was president of the standing commission which heard capital cases. To others who had been arraigned on the same charge Caesar showed no mercy—he treated them as murderers. Catiline was acquitted: he could be useful.

Caesar had already done much to conciliate the populace. As aedile in 65 he had flattered them with lavish shows, and had collected so many gladiators that his opponents, fearing that they might be the intended victims, rushed through a bill to limit the number of gladiators that could be kept within the city. This shows what suspicions Caesar had already aroused. Rumours were rife not only that he had backed Catiline for the consulship, but had also, with Crassus, been behind the conspiracy against Volcacius and his colleague. It was even said and believed that he was to have taken an active part in it. He now, with the far-sighted subtlety that Pompey lacked and he himself possessed so amply, contrived a master-stroke. Towards the end of the year 64 the pontifex maximus, the high priest of Rome, died. This office was not only august, but extremely influential, and was tenable for life. Centuries later and down to our own day Christian Popes would use the title, so venerable was it. Caesar was determined to have it. But he stood no chance against his two rivals because under existing regulations it was the pontifical college which made the appointment. Caesar, nothing daunted, induced a tribune, Titus Labienus, who had been on his staff in Asia, to carry a measure in the popular assembly whereby the election of the supreme pontiff was given back to a tribal college, from which it had been removed by Sulla. Caesar spent his last borrowed farthing on bribery. When he left home on the morning of the election he told his mother not to expect him back—except as high priest. So well had he laid out the money that he secured more votes in the tribes of his competitors than they did in all the others, and was duly elected. His status was now assured, but his solvency was not. Here again Crassus was of the greatest help to Caesar—and to himself.

Crassus and Caesar, now linked by a golden chain, at the end of 64 induced a tribune, called Rullus, to introduce a measure which would have placed in their hands, financially speaking, more power than even Pompey wielded. It was, as Cicero saw, aimed against Pompey, and designed to confront him with a *fait accompli* when he returned. On the surface, though, it looked beneficial enough, indeed a piece of philanthropy. It was to be an agrarian law on an empire-wide scale. Land was to be bought from those who were willing to sell, and the last remaining public land in Italy, in Campania, was to be distributed to needy citizens and veteran soldiers—which meant rewarding Pompey's soldiers without their being beholden to Pompey. In the provinces, leases on confiscated municipal lands were to be called in—in Sicily, in Greece, in Spain, in Africa and above all in the East, where besides domains in Bithynia, Macedonia and Cilicia, the vast estates of the Attalids of Pergamum, of Mithradates and of the Ptolemies of Egypt were to be brought into the scheme. All this dazzling opulence was to be administered (or manipulated) by a board of ten commissioners, to be appointed by a minority of seventeen tribes—who would be so much more easily, and cheaply, "directed" than the full thirty-five. The commissioners' decision on all matters of title and compensation was to be final, and to provide a purchase fund they were to be empowered to call in public debts, to employ the proceeds of Sulla's confiscations and recent war-booty, and—another blow at Pompey—to anticipate revenues to be expected from Pompey's conquests. Cicero saw through the scheme at once. On the very first day of his consulate he inveighed against it in the Senate. "Are you going to give them Alexandria?" he asked, a shrewd reference to Crassus' alleged design on the Piper, with Caesar as his abettor, of two years before. The Senate was easily convinced: the popular assembly required more florid treatment. Cicero gave it to them. His speech is extant, a magnificent example of mob-oratory at its best. What was it that this beatnik tribune, with his long hair, shaggy beard and grubby clothes, wanted the Roman people to enact? Nothing less than the creation not of one king, but ten. And Pompey, the one man the Quirites would have chosen, was not even to be included. The so-called agricultural settlements of veterans would really be so many garrisons, to rob citizens of their liberty; they might even plant one on the Janiculum, the hill on the right bank of the Tiber, and overawe the city. And much more in the same vein. Specious? Sophistical? Yes, it was; but that is less the fault of Cicero than of the Roman political system which committed the safety, honour and welfare of Rome and half the known world to the whims and appetites of a fickle and largely illiterate mob. Better a Cicero to charm them, than a Catiline to inflame them. Cicero was not only successful in winning the people, he also detached his colleague Antonius from Crassus by offering him, in place of a seat on the board of ten, the first choice of a lucrative province to govern when he ceased to be consul. With opinion now running so strong against him, Rullus could only admit defeat. He withdrew the bill.

The next move of the so-called democrats ended in farce. Caesar brought an accusation against an old man called Rabirius, who was alleged to have killed Saturninus in 100 B.C. For the trial, he revived an antique court of *perduellio*, or high treason, which went back to the days of the kings and had been abandoned soon after. The two judges chosen "by lot" happened, to nobody's surprise, to be Caesar and a distant relative of his who had been consul the year before. Caesar's object was to test the validity of the ultimate decree of the Senate, which had led to the overthrow of Saturninus; he feared that it might one day be used against him and his. He now assumed the guilt of Rabirius, and in accordance with the archaic law, ordered that he be "scourged and tied to a cross in the Field of Mars," expecting that Rabirius would appeal to the people. Here Cicero intervened. He denounced the "unpopular" sentence of crucifixion, and represented the proceedings as an attack not only on the ultimate decree, but also by implication on the consul for the year 100, that is on Marius, Caesar's uncle.

He induced the Senate to declare the whole proceedings invalid, and vetoed their continuance on his own authority. Caesar was determined to press the case. He persuaded his jackal, Labienus, to hail Rabirius before the Concilium Plebis, and then arranged for the urban praetor to transfer the hearing to the Comitia Centuriata. Cicero reappeared for the defence of the poor old man. Before the vote could be taken the Assembly was dispersed by Labienus, no doubt in collusion either with Cicero or with Caesar, because a red flag had been lowered on the Janiculum—a signal which in the dim and distant past had meant "Fall in, everybody, the Etruscans are coming." Caesar gained nothing by this vindictive and ridiculous prosecution; but that did not deter him from keeping up his pin-pricks on Cicero. Through a tribune he proposed that the sons of Sulla's victims should be reinstated in their political rights. Cicero had the measure thrown out, on the ground that Sulla's legislation must stand or fall *in toto*, and that the present was no time for dangerous innovations. Next came the prosecution of Gaius Piso for extortion and violence in the region beyond the Po, a district in which Caesar, like Crassus, had good reasons for courting popularity. Cicero defended the officer and secured his acquittal.

The real trial of strength was still to come. By his last defeat at the elections of 64 Catiline lost not only the consulate but the support of Crassus as well; he was nevertheless determined to try again. By way of laying ground-bait, he announced that if he were returned he would institute *novae tabulae*, that is "a clean slate," meaning that the bribe he offered—for he could no longer use Crassus' cash—was a general cancelling of debts. This proposal made a wide appeal—to impoverished nobles, of whom there was no lack in Rome, veterans of Sulla's armies, who had frittered their war-gratuities away, hooligans, toughs, bums and larrikins of every sort. As polling-day drew near Catiline strutted about with growing confidence. "What harm," he would say, "when I see two bodies, the one lean and consumptive with a head [meaning the Senate, with Cicero] and the other great and strong without one, if I put a head to that body which wants one?"

"If my fortunes catch fire," he boasted, "I'll quench it, not with water, but by pulling the house down." A gang of his supporters arrived from Etruria. Once again, Cicero was a match for Catiline. He knew exactly how to exploit the growing alarm. He asked the Senate for a bodyguard, and that the day of the elections be postponed. The bodyguard was refused him, and the election deferred for a few days only. But the younger knights rallied to him, and on polling-day he went down to the city— he lived on the Oppian hill—surrounded by his protectors and took care to let his toga slip from his shoulders, to show the polished cuirass which he was wearing beneath it to save him from Catiline's daggers. This, unlike Caesar's *opera buffa*, was really good theatre, to which the Romans have always been sympathetic. Catiline was again rejected, Murena and Silanus being returned as consuls for the year 62.

Catiline was now desperate. Three times, so it seemed to him, he had been defrauded of the supreme office to which his birth entitled him. What had been denied him by legal means he must therefore seize by force. He assembled his conspirators, and set about enrolling his commandos. Cicero was soon informed of his intention, the first inkling coming from a popular lady called Fulvia, before whom one of her conspirator-clients had spoken too freely; for even in those days such dames were employed as intelligence agents. Next came a mysterious incident.

About midnight on the 20th October, Cicero was roused from sleep to receive Crassus and two other gentlemen. Crassus explained that after supper an unknown man had delivered to his porter some letters, most of them addressed to others, but one to Crassus himself. This he had opened, and found that it was an anonymous warning to leave Rome, so as to avoid the intended massacre. He now handed the other letters to Cicero, to whom he had come, he said, to give the consul warning—it was also a tactful way of showing Cicero that he had no hand in the conspiracy. Crassus' information confirmed what Cicero had learned from Fulvia. He called the Senate together the next morning—Rome was still a small city, or at least that part of it fit for senators to live in—took the letters with him, delivered them to their addressees, and bade them read them out. Each missive contained the same warning. The Senate, bewildered by this sudden summons and the strange purport of the letters, bade Cicero make further inquiries; but when the fathers met a day or two later, Cicero told them that Manlius, one of Catiline's accomplices, was on the move and would resort to arms on the 27th.

A senator called Arrius, who was in Caesar's confidence, announced that troops were assembling in Etruria. The Senate now realized the true proportions of the danger and passed the ultimate decree. Cicero had his plans ready. He sent all the gladiators in Rome back to their "schools" at Capua. He called out the municipal militias and sent the praetor Metellus Celer to raise fresh levies in the north. Marcius Rex, who was encamped outside the walls, waiting with his troops for a triumph for his share in the Mithradatic War, was sent to patrol Etruria. An isolated band did try to break into Praeneste (Palestrina) but was repulsed by the local defence-force. Catiline had been foiled at every point. Once again Cicero had shown that he was master; yet once again Catiline got off scot-free, because there still was not enough evidence to establish his guilt beyond all reasonable doubt. This evidence Catiline was soon to furnish. Caesar, long-sighted as usual, seeing that sooner rather than later Catiline must overreach himself, and the plot be discovered, decided like Crassus that a little "insurance" would do him no harm, and (according to Suetonius) himself related to Cicero certain details of it.

On the night of November 6th, Catiline assembled the conspirators to replan his campaign. In addition to murdering leading senators, he now proposed to start fires in various parts of the city, to invite the slaves to loot it, and to organize wide-spread revolts throughout Italy—in a word, anarchy. The gladiators from Capua were to be enlisted (how wise Cicero had been to banish them from Rome) together with the armed ranch-patrols from Apulia—Antonius had extensive estates here—and the deep south. Catiline himself was to head a march on Rome from Etruria. It was, on the face of it, a hare-brained scheme, which is no doubt why Crassus and Caesar would have none of it. And as before, the accomplices talked; hardly had the meeting dispersed when Fulvia had news of it and at once went and told Cicero, bidding him not to admit two knights who were to call on him the very next morning in order to pay their respects— with stilettos. When they found the consul's door barred to them, they banged on it and shouted, thereby exciting all the more suspicion. But Cicero still could not lay hands on Catiline. Next day, the 8th November, he summoned the Senate, and there bluffing it out was Catiline himself. In his speech—one of his most famous, which we can still read in the published version—Cicero made great play with his knowledge of Catiline's plans, and recounted the latter's criminal career in lurid detail. But he concluded lamely, merely inviting the convicted traitor to quit Rome and leave him in peace: he still dared not send him to his just reward for fear of being accused of exceeding his authority, and being caught by the patrician back-lash—Cicero's perpetual anxiety. Catiline did leave Rome, and set out to join Manlius, whose camp he reached (preceded as though he were a consul by twelve lictors) a few days later. Cicero, meanwhile, had addressed a mass meeting in the Forum, to which he explained how affairs stood. The Senate then declared Catiline and Manlius public enemies, at the same time offering an amnesty to their followers if they laid down their arms by a certain day, an offer which brought no response. Towards the end of November, Cicero found time to defend the consul-elect Murena against a charge of bribery. The case was brought under a severe law which Cicero himself had promoted that very year. Murena was undoubtedly guilty, and the prosecutor was the redoubtable Marcus Porcius Cato. Despite these three disadvantages, Cicero won the case, chiefly by ridicule. All Cato could say was: "What a witty consul we have." The victory was politically important to Cicero, besides being personally gratifying, because he relied on Murena to maintain the struggle against Catiline in case the conspiracy dragged on into the following year. It certainly looked as though it would, with the rebel forces swollen from two thousand to ten thousand, when suddenly, by a circumstance which would be considered inadmissible if introduced into a work of fiction, the catastrophe came.

It happened in November of 63. A group of envoys came to Rome from a Gaulish tribe called the Allobroges, to make the now only too common complaints against Roman tyranny and extortion by Roman money-lenders. They were about to return, unsatisfied, when one of the conspirators approached them, with a view to enlisting some of their famous cavalry in the rebel army. The tribesmen very sensibly sold their information to the government; whereupon Cicero bade them to obtain a signed and sworn agreement from the five principal plotters. This they did, and on the night of December 2nd they set out for the north, taking with them not only one of the conspirators but also a highly incriminating dispatch to Catiline from his chief aide. When the party reached the first bridge over the Tiber, they allowed themselves to be held up by an armed patrol which brought the whole party and its papers back to Rome.

Now at last Cicero could act, and act he did. He arrested the four of the five signatories who were still in Rome, all of them senators, together with a fifth accomplice. The Senate ordered their detention, but in deference to their rank they were allowed to live in private houses, including those of Crassus and Caesar.

The great plot was unmasked, but what was to be done with the plotters?

On December 5th, Cicero summoned the Senate and had the proceedings recorded, apparently for the first time, in shorthand. All the earlier speakers recommended the death-penalty, sixteen of them; but then Caesar, now not only high priest but praetor-elect as well, delivered a carefully prepared oration, in which he proposed that the malefactors should be interned for life in various provincial towns, and their property escheated to the state. This was a typically clever move; it would ease the consciences and salve the pride of the senators by thus dealing with their fellows, and would at the same time conciliate the rebels. Other members supported Caesar, and some of the earlier speakers now retracted their former words. Such was Caesar's magnetism that although many including Cicero himself strongly suspected his complicity in the plot, it was just as well he was not directly accused, because, as Plutarch puts it: "if Caesar was accused with the conspirators, they were more likely to be saved with him, than he to be punished with them." As it was he nearly carried the day—even Cicero's friends thought it would be to the consul's advantage that he should—but Cato "so vehemently urged in his speech the strong suspicion against Caesar himself and so filled the Senate with anger and resolution, that a decree was passed for the execution of the conspirators." One by one they were led to death, the first by Cicero himself. The processions passed down the Sacred Way, past Caesar's official residence as high priest, past the Senate-house and the rostra, to the great dungeon at the foot of the Capitol. "The people affrighted at what was doing, passed along in silence, especially the young men; as if, with fear and trembling, they were undergoing a rite of initiation into some ancient sacred mysteries of aristocratic power"—in such language does Plutarch conjure up for us the ambivalent atmosphere in the Forum that evening. Relief there was, but by no means universal sympathy or approval. Cicero himself announced that the prisoners were beyond hope of rescue. *"Vixerunt,"* he said: "They have lived."

The plot was over. Cicero was hailed as the Father of His Country: he had saved Rome; but he had also put Roman citizens, and senators at that, to death without formal trial, for which one day he would be called to account.

Catiline himself died early in the new year, in a battle near Pistorium in the basin of the Arno. Ironically, the first casualty was Antonius. Catiline died, as he had lived, recklessly: he charged single-handed into opposing ranks. As the *Handbook* put it: "Catiline was afraid of nothing, Antonius trembled at his own shadow."

Had Cicero retired at the end of his year of office, turning for a time to his philosophical pursuits, had he even been content to resume his lucrative and brilliant career at the bar, he might have escaped obloquy; but this he could not do. His pathological vanity—overcompensation for his obscure origin—goaded him into damaging extravagances. Everywhere, in season and out of season, orally and in verse, he lauded and extolled his own virtues and achievements. He advertised himself as a conqueror "in a toga" of the same standing as Pompey, a comparison which Pompey did not relish. He wrote verses which contained the line—the one which Juvenal was to ridicule:

> O Rome, how fortunate!
> Born in my consulate!

In the spiteful, jealous world of Rome, this campaign of self-exaltation, coupled with Cicero's gift for wounding by his wit, soon brought its nemesis. Early in 62, one of the tribunes introduced a bill in the popular assembly calling on Pompey to rescue Rome from Cicero's "autocracy." Caesar supported him, but Cato stood by Cicero. Riots broke out again, and again the Senate passed its ultimate decree. The incident showed what the alignment of forces would be when Pompey returned. Cicero's ideal of a "Concord of the Orders" was never to be realized. One other event of the year 62 must be mentioned, not because of any intrinsic importance, but because it has a bearing on the political line-up. In December 62 the ineffable Clodius, dressed as a girl, broke into the official residence of the high priest, Caesar, where the ladies were celebrating the rites of an ancient goddess, the Bona Dea, at which no man might assist. Clodius was discovered, and the Senate, in view of the insult to the state religion and to the home of the high priest, took the matter up with vigour and secured the appointment by the Comitia Centuriata of a special court to investigate the matter; but the jury was to be drawn from the ordinary panels, which meant that Crassus could, and did, bribe it as usual. Cicero gave evidence against Clodius, in order to invalidate his alibi: Clodius said he had been out of town that evening; Cicero testified that Clodius had been to see him three hours before he was discovered in Caesar's house. Caesar was curiously non-committal, as Crassus wished him to be. He refused to give evidence against Clodius, and when asked why, in that case, he had divorced his wife (she was his third: there was one more to come), made his famous answer that "Caesar's wife must be above suspicion" —a remark that must have made Rome snigger, for Caesar was notorious for his extra-marital amusements. With Crassus and Caesar thus allied, the jury felt it would be only right to acquit Clodius, which it did. When the gloating Clodius next met Cicero he thought to bait him by saying that the jury had evidently not believed his testimony, to which Cicero replied: "Twenty-five of them believed me, and condemned you: the other thirty didn't believe you, because they didn't acquit you until they'd got your money."

This was in June of 61. Pompey had arrived at Brundisium six months before; and it was to a Rome thus divided and distressed that he came back.

CHAPTER XIV

THE FIRST TRIUMVIRATE

IN NORMAL times Clodius' escapade need not have had any political *sequelae;* but just as a scratch on a diseased body may lead to distempers which a robust one will resist, so in the ailing body politic of Rome, the affair of the Bona Dea was to generate a running sore.

The trial had dire results. Clodius, who had been humiliated not only by Cicero's evidence but by the personal gibes Cicero could never resist, now swore to be avenged on the man whom he considered an upstart. This, added to the antagonism between Caesar and Cato which the conspiracy had crystallized, destroyed almost the last hope of maintaining anything like a *Concordia Ordinum,* or alliance of all good men in defence of the constitution, to attain what Cicero had striven for so valiantly. That hope was extinguished altogether by two more incidents. Before the end of the year 62, the Senate, disgusted by the flagrant venality of the jury which acquitted Clodius, and urged on by Cato, sought to abolish a strange immunity from prosecution for corruption which had been conferred on non-senatorial jurymen by Gaius Gracchus sixty years before. Then at the end of 61 a syndicate of tax-gatherers who had contracted to collect the revenues for the province of Asia, finding that they would lose by their bargain, asked for a rebate. Crassus was behind the syndicate; but Cato opposed any concession. In this matter as in that of the non-senatorial jurors' privilege, Cicero counselled the senators to make concessions to the equites, but without success in either case.

Cicero had at one time undoubtedly looked to Pompey as the possible bulwark of the state; but he had, as already related, mishandled Pompey. The latter was not uncorrupted by power, and to be patronized by a Cicero who for ever vaunted his own virtues and courage was too much for him. Crafty Crassus was more adroit: he had slipped over to Asia during the year 62 and had met Pompey. He had pretended to be afraid of what Pompey would do when he came back, but that, as Adcock points out, "concealed his characteristic purpose, to be first in the field when there was a bargain to be struck." The terms of that bargain were not disclosed, and Pompey and Crassus returned to Italy separately and by different routes.

Meanwhile Caesar, who had made Rome rather too hot for him, decided that it would be prudent to absent himself for a season. He accordingly went as propraetor to Spain. Here he gave the first solid evidence of his abilities both as administrator and general. In Spain, as elsewhere, the bugbear of debt was always present, no doubt aggravated by the aftermath of the Sertorian War. Like Lucullus in Asia, Caesar made a compromise settlement, whereby the debtors paid two-thirds of their incomes to the creditors.

Caesar was already well-known in the country from the time of his quaestorship, and he had a number of Spanish friends: it was but natural that he should want to see the Spaniards honestly done by. He also wanted to make a little money both for his soldiers and himself. He therefore undertook a campaign in the far west, supported by a naval expedition, which swept up the Atlantic coast of the peninsula all the way from Cadiz to Corunna. This combined operation was a brilliant success and added the greater part of what was to become the province of Lusitania to the Roman realm. Caesar, fighting in the country which was later to be the scene of Wellington's great achievements, proved himself a good general. His troops hailed him as Imperator; he enriched both himself and them, and could now go back to Rome with every expectation of being awarded both a triumph and a consulship. In Cicero's words, "the wind was now fairly behind him."

He arrived before Rome on the eve of polling-day. It was forbidden that a general should enter the city before his triumph, and if he did so he forfeited his right to it. Caesar therefore asked that he might secure his nomination by proxy. The Senate were inclined to grant this wholly reasonable request; but they allowed Cato to stage a filibuster whereby the motion was talked out.

Caesar, presenting himself in person, easily headed the poll. As his colleague he was allotted a certain Marcus Calpurnius Bibulus, a former friend of Caesar's who was now his opponent. Bibulus' rival for the office, Lucceius, was a very rich man, and the combination of Caesar and Lucceius would have been formidable indeed. Caesar's die-hard enemies therefore clubbed together to enable Bibulus to offer the same price for votes as Lucceius. Even Cato subscribed. To such lengths were the conservatives prepared to go to thwart Caesar, just as they had thwarted Pompey. Their stupidity recoiled on them, however, for in the end it was the Senate that was humbled.

An ancient historian of the impending war recorded that its seeds were sown "in the consulship of Metellus," that is in 60 B.C. with the formation of what we call the First Triumvirate. The poet Horace expressed the same view. Caesar and Pompey inevitably now coalesced, with Crassus to back them. It was simply a matter of political chemistry. Caesar had approached Cicero—more as a matter of form than anything else. He knew that the author of the "Concord of the Orders," the man whose motto was *Otium cum dignitate*, "Peace with honour," would never be a party to the very combination which was to destroy both. Even Cato saw, too late, what had happened. When people said that the rivalry between Pompey and Caesar was the origin of all Rome's troubles, he replied that it was not their enmity but their unanimity "which gave the first and greatest blow to the commonwealth." Crassus was, from Caesar's point of view, a convenience. Despite his Spanish year, he was still in need of cash; and Crassus owed the Senate a grudge over the affair of the Asian tax-syndicate, whose burden they had refused to lighten.

It was, as might be expected, Caesar who made the running. Pompey's star was now on the wane. He had never been a politician, and had no head for the calculations of the closet and the cabal. "His position," says Mommsen, "was an awkward one and vacillated with so much uncertainty between the parties that people gave him the nickname of Gnaeus Cicero. As Cicero himself saw, he had in fact lost favour with all. The anarchists saw in him an adversary, the democrats an inconvenient friend, Marcus Crassus a rival, the wealthy class an untrustworthy protector, the aristocracy a declared foe." The Senate did all they could to humiliate him. They bluntly refused him a second consulate. The very first request the victor made to the Senate, that the election of the consuls for 61 might be postponed until after his entry into the capital, so that he could canvass for a protégé, was rejected. Pompey then asked for a general confirmation of all the dispositions he had made in the East; but Lucullus carried a proposal that each be discussed clause by clause—a ruse which led to endless delay and confusion. Nor were his soldiers granted their allotments of land, in those days the only practicable form of pension. Rome's greatest general was now reduced to negligible frustration: he had fallen into political paralysis. Thus did Pompey's extremity become Caesar's opportunity.

Having once made the pact, Caesar kept his word. The year of his consulate, 59, saw a greater output of legislation than any one year since the days of Sulla's dictatorship. First, as Caesar rightly saw, for he was now the soldier-politician he would remain until his death, must come the satisfaction of Pompey's veterans. He therefore brought forward an agrarian bill which would not only provide for them but would also rid Rome of a number of its superfluous citizens. Any such scheme was bound by its very nature to run into difficulties and opposition. In our own, post-mediaeval world, congestion, disaffection or resentment has for more than four centuries found a lasting remedy in migration to new lands, to the Americas, to the Antipodes; it still does. The Roman world had no such resource.

The East was crowded already, the north was savage and hostile, and such small footholds as the Inland Sea afforded had been occupied, generally by Greeks. Indeed, far from Rome being able to direct an "overspill" to other lands, it was the overspill from abroad that flooded Rome.

Nevertheless, Caesar tackled the problem with characteristic boldness. Very little public domain now remained in Italy; and so to find the necessary acres private land was to be expropriated at the price entered in the censors' records. To avoid speculation, the plots were to be inalienable for twenty years. The whole project was to be directed by a board of twenty from which Caesar and all office-holders were specifically excluded. There was also to be a small management committee, on which Cicero was offered a place; he declined it.

This bill was far less open to objection than that of Rullus: Caesar and Crassus had profited by that fiasco. But having done so they were calmly and cynically determined to stamp on any opposition that their milder measure might encounter. Unlike Gracchus, who had sought to by-pass the Senate and appeal directly to the people, Caesar, posing as the constitutional democrat, submitted his bill to the Senate for discussion, even inviting them to amend it if they saw fit. Caesar knew quite well what the attitude of the Fathers would be. They had already insulted him by ordaining that at the end of his year of office he should be allotted not a provincial governorship but the care of the forests and field-tracks of Italy. Caesar, on the other hand, had shown equally clearly what he thought of the Senate. His very first act as consul had been to arrange for the daily publication of a gazette of their proceedings, and those of the popular assemblies, so that all could read, and criticize, the deliberations of persons who had hitherto considered themselves above the cognizance of the vulgar. When the land bill was introduced, Cato denounced it. Caesar hauled him from the platform and threatened him with imprisonment. When the Senate persisted in their obstruction, Caesar appealed to the Comitia, adding a provision which required all senators to swear that they would not resist the measure, on pain of exile. Bibulus, asked for his opinion, merely replied that he would fight Caesar and everyone else. It was a silly boast; for when finally the bill was put to the vote, and three tribunes vetoed it while Bibulus announced that he proposed to "watch the heavens" so as to suspend business, Caesar simply unleashed a pack of Pompey's unsatisfied soldiers. Bibulus had a bucket of dung emptied over him, and his *fasces* were smashed. The Forum was soon empty and the law was passed. Even Cato had taken the oath, persuaded by Cicero, who had realized that "Caesar, weak as he then was, was stronger than the whole state." His colleagues had been less astute: the union of Pompey and Caesar (which their own folly had made inevitable) took them by surprise. Bibulus shut himself up in his house for the rest of the year, so that wags pretended to date documents "in the consulate of Julius and Caesar." Caesar's first agrarian law was supplemented by another towards the end of May, which called in the leases of the state domain in Campania, in the reassignment of which Pompey's veterans had first choice, the most favoured civilians being those with three or more children. There was less opposition this time. One senator did prefer exile, and Cato had twice to be hauled off the platform and led away still haranguing all and sundry; but the rest confirmed the bill on oath.

Caesar had conducted his two agrarian laws himself: he wanted to show Pompey that he was a loyal colleague, and the rest of Rome that he was its master. That done, he relegated his subsequent legislation to a handy-man, the tribune Vatinius. In accordance with the terms of the triple compact, Vatinius introduced a short law ratifying all Pompey's Eastern settlements *en bloc*. This was a wise step for two reasons: first, because Pompey's dispositions were, as we have seen, admirable in themselves, and secondly, because it would in any case have been impossible to alter them. The concord between the two men was sealed by Pompey's marrying Caesar's only child, Julia, to whom her elderly husband remained devoted until her death five years later.

Pompey's claims were now satisfied, and it was Crassus' turn. The obliging Vatinius at once secured an easing of their contract for the Asian tax-collectors. Vatinius got his commission on the deal, as he did on the formal agreements drawn up with various client-kings of Asia confirming the rights Pompey had granted them. Ptolemy the Piper had to part with the equivalent of ten million dollars for the privilege of keeping his crown. Crassus had reaped his Egyptian harvest at last. Things were going splendidly for the two junior partners; but what was Caesar to get out of it? Caesar knew, as always, just what he wanted. No forests and cattle-tracks for him! His tribune had the popular assembly set aside, in May or June, the Senate's allocation of consular provinces for the following year, 58, and grant to Caesar the province of Cisalpine Gaul (i.e. Italy between the Po and the Alps), together with Illyricum, which usually went with Macedonia but was a fertile recruiting-ground for soldiers such as Caesar would soon be needing. The real "teeth" of the grant lay in its duration; it was to be not the normal one or two years, but five; five whole years in which to consolidate power. Whoever held such power for five years held it permanently; for with three legions and the authority to raise another, the power to choose his own subordinates and to found colonies where he would, Caesar was already on the high road to sovereignty. Pompey had won prestige and power in the East, Caesar would do it in the north, but he would know how to use it, as poor Pompey did not. Shortly after, the governorship of Gaul beyond the Alps, *the* province *par excellence* and known to this day as Provence, fell vacant. Caesar had this given to him as well, thereby acquiring yet another legion. It was to serve as the ideal base for his conquest of the rest of Gaul.

The Triumvirate was not popular. The Senate did its bidding for fear of faring worse. Caesar's most salutary measure was one which consolidated the laws against extortion and closed several loop-holes in them. Not every senator could have relished that, nor yet a measure which required that in criminal cases each class of juror, senators, knights and *tribuni aerarii*, should vote separately, so that it might be known whether they were for conviction or acquittal; but beyond pamphleteering against "the three-headed monster," there was little that the senators could do.

Caesar, looking ahead as usual, knew that the moment his back was turned, and himself on the way to Gaul, his legislation would be challenged. It was essential that he leave behind him not only pliant consuls—that was easy: Pompey's old henchman

Gabinius and Caesar's new father-in-law Piso would, and did, serve—but some agent with a bit more edge to him and no scruples, who would maintain Caesar's interests by hook or by crook. There was one man who met the requirements, and that was Clodius. Clodius should be a tribune and work for Caesar. The Bona Dea scandal was forgotten: it had served its turn. It had frightened Clodius and made him beholden to Caesar for his freedom. Besides, Caesar had a new wife now.

There was one obstacle though: tribunes must be plebeians, and Clodius was a patrician. When in 60 Clodius had tried to stand for the tribuneship, the consul Metellus Celer had ruled that his adoption was invalid. No such trouble arose now: Caesar had him enrolled as a plebeian, at the very end of a day on which Cicero had been speaking a little too freely in court about the deplorable state of affairs. It was a warning of what was to come.

On the first day of the year 58, while Caesar was still in the suburbs, Clodius proposed four bills. The first was a bribe, but at the expense of the state (so much more satisfactory than private purchase), designed to put the people in a responsive mood: corn was henceforth to be distributed free to all who asked for it. Already 320,000 citizens were drawing a monthly ration of five pecks at half the market price. Now everyone could live for nothing. That the cost to the treasury absorbed more than half of the new revenues accruing from Pompey's conquests meant little to Clodius.

The second law prohibited censors from expelling senators except after a judicial enquiry. This was intended to secure Clodius' own position in an assembly which was still supposed to embody the old Roman virtues. The third measure was a real reform. It curtailed the antique idiocy whereby magistrates could suspend business (as Bibulus had tried to do) by "watching the heavens." Even Clodius dared not abolish this venerable mumbo-jumbo altogether; he could only restrict it to augurs and tribunes.

The fourth law was the worst and to him the most necessary of the lot. It restored the political clubs which had been disbanded in 64. This simply meant that gangs were now legalized, and that Clodius was to be head gangster.

Clodius was now lord of Rome. As such he could proceed against the two pillars of the Senate whom he and his master Caesar most feared, namely Cicero and Cato. Caesar as we have seen had tried to conciliate Cicero. He had renewed the attempt, had offered him a staff appointment, or some foreign mission on Cicero's own terms. Not that Caesar valued Cicero for himself; it was merely that his oratory could be useful to him. But if Cicero declined to put his gifts at Caesar's disposal, then Cicero must go.

The case needed a subtle approach; Clodius' usual strong-arm methods would never do against Cicero. For one thing, although Cicero's vanity and his sharp tongue had won him many enemies, he still had many friends. Above all, against open violence Cicero was bound to appeal to Caesar, and Caesar would be bound to come to his help, unless he was to unmask his own dynastic designs, which he was not yet prepared or equipped to do. Clodius hit on a plan which had the double advantage of appealing to prejudice and justice at one and the same time. Five years before, as consul, Cicero, morally warranted by the ultimate decree, had executed the Catilinarian conspirators. The Senate had approved the action by the spirit of their resolution, but *not by legal process of trial before a court*, thereby infringing the ancient law. Clodius now introduced a bill to outlaw "anyone who had condemned a Roman citizen to death without trial." No names were mentioned, but everyone knew that it was aimed at Cicero. Not everyone was sorry, by any means. Cicero, wrapped in his cloak of vanity, had not realized how cold the atmosphere had become: now that it was torn from him, he shivered. After the most undignified vacillation, now vaunting, now imploring, he faced the inevitable and left Italy, sped by skirmishers from Clodius' private army. Spurned by some, but loyally aided by others, Cicero, finding himself excluded from Sicily, crossed from Brundisium to Epirus, to pass a year of honourable exile in Greece. His beautiful new home on the Palatine was burned, and two of his country-houses destroyed.

That left Cato. He was, unfortunately, although very tiresome, one of the few honest men in Rome (a little straightforward bribery was no longer accounted dishonest in Rome), and could not conveniently be prosecuted. Clearly some diplomatic arm-twisting was indicated. Cato was "offered" the commission to restore the refugees from Byzantium, who had been displaced by the Mithradatic wars, and then to liquidate the estate of Ptolemy, brother of the Piper and last king of Cyprus, which like Egypt was deemed to have been bequeathed to Rome by the late king. The king of Cyprus, less enlightened than his brother of Egypt, had not even come up with the appropriate bribe, and so Clodius solved the question by having Cyprus declared a province. Ptolemy was to have been compensated with the high priesthood of Venus at Paphos, but he conveniently poisoned himself. Cato perforce accepted the offer. He took with him as adjutant his son-in-law, Marcus Brutus. If Clodius and Caesar thought they had entrapped Cato, and that he would come back with a tarnished reputation, they were mistaken. Cato was an expert accountant. He made exact inventories of the whole treasure, personally supervising the auctions to prevent collusion and the forming of "rings," much to the disgust of his greedy compatriots. The proceeds amounted to seven thousand talents (some ten million dollars). Lest any of the money should be lost on the return voyage, Cato had it packed in two hundred little boxes, to each of which was attached a long rope with a piece of cork on the other end. In case of shipwreck the floats would show where the treasure had sunk. In the event, only one of the ships miscarried, bearing one of Cato's duplicate ledgers, the other of which was accidentally destroyed by fire while Cato was in camp at Corfu. Despite this loss, when he came sailing up the Tiber he was given a royal welcome, like a triumph. He took no notice of the consuls and praetors, nor would he accept any honour from the Senate. This time, Cato had won.

Meanwhile Crassus and Pompey had not been idle. If they could not get their fingers on the Cyprus treasure or besmirch the man who had obtained it for Rome, they could at least put the squeeze on the Piper. In order to find the money for his first payment Ptolemy had imposed heavy taxes. His people had revolted; he had been compelled to flee and was now a suppliant at Rome. What an opportunity! The citizens of Alexandria had, it is true, sent a counter-embassage to plead their cause against Ptolemy; but they were easily disposed of by gold, or when that did not work, by steel. Of course Ptolemy must be "restored": there was money in it. Ptolemy clearly thought that Pompey was to escort him back in triumph. The Senate commissioned the consul Spinther, who was to be governor of Syria in 56, to undertake the task. But at the beginning of that year a flash of lightning struck a much-venerated statue of Jupiter. The Sibylline books, on being consulted for a means of expiation, were found to contain an oracle which forbade the restoration of an Egyptian king "by a multitude," i.e. an army. The plan was abandoned; and Pompey was once more foiled. Crassus now tried to worm his way into the embroglio, but he too failed. In the end Pompey could do no more than counsel Ptolemy to apply to Gabinius, who in 55 was governor of Syria. Even this plan proved a failure.

Gabinius was just about to invade Parthia, and had already crossed the Euphrates when the news arrived that the Piper, on Pompey's recommendation, would be grateful if Gabinius would help him to regain his throne for a consideration of ten thousand talents. Gabinius at once abandoned the Euphrates for the Nile. He had committed a double breach of the law, first in accepting the bribe, and then in waging war outside his province. He was recalled and arraigned on both charges, acquitted of the latter, but condemned to repay the money. Never having received the full sum, he was unable to refund it, and so went into exile in Dalmatia, where he died ten years afterwards.

Pompey's dissatisfaction was a threat to the Triumvirate itself. Clodius was now losing ground. Pompey had found, in a tough called Milo, tribune for 57, a counter-weight to Clodius. Milo soon had his rival gang in being. Thus fortified, Pompey took up the cause of Cicero, to such good effect that, after desperate and bloody gangster warfare in the Forum itself, the Senate finally voted to recall Cicero by 416 against Clodius' solitary "no."

On 9th September 57 Cicero returned to Rome amid the most flattering manifestations of sympathy and regard.

Caesar, although engaged in arduous campaign in Gallia Comata, the "Long-haired" Gaul beyond the Alps, kept in close touch with affairs in Rome, where he maintained a network of agents and informers in all ranks of society. In the early months of 56 B.C., he was wintering as usual in northern Italy, at Ravenna, in his Cisalpine province. Here he received alarming news. That Crassus had been intriguing against Pompey there can be no doubt, using Clodius as his tool. Pompey, losing patience, accused Crassus before the Senate of plotting his death. Cicero took his cue from Pompey, and in March of that year, while defending a benefactor in court, made an eloquent on-slaught against Clodius. A little later he reopened the question of Caesar's land law. Cicero's tactics were plain: he hoped to divide Caesar and Pompey, and so to destroy the Triumvirate, which he loathed as the negation of all he regarded as right and Roman. Finally, a candidate for the consulship of 55 openly said that if elected he would have Caesar deprived of his provinces.

Caesar saw that he must act, and quickly. A lesser man might have decided that the compact had failed, and that he must at once assert his own supreme and undivided authority, backed by his army in being. Not so Caesar: his army was not yet the finely forged weapon he intended it to be, nor was his ambition of conquest in the north yet sated. He decided on compromise. He called his partners to a conference. Crassus at once went north and was soon followed by Pompey, who had been appointed to reorganize the city's food-supply and was about to cross into Sardinia (one of Rome's granaries) from Pisa. To suit Pompey's convenience the neighbouring town of Lucca was chosen as the meeting-place. A host of expectant senators hung around the closed doors of the council-chamber. The conference was brief. Caesar went back to Gaul: he had made his wishes clear. Pompey and Crassus were to be consuls for the ensuing year. Despite violence and shameless "rigging" they were elected, and Cato was prevented from becoming praetor. Cicero's last hope was shattered. He abandoned the Forum for the study.

The two consuls made some mild efforts at administrative reform; but the year 55 is chiefly to be remembered as that of the dedication of Rome's first permanent stone-built theatre, modeled on that of Mytilene. To avoid criticism from the ultra-conservatives, such as had cut short a similar project in the preceding century, Pompey cleverly combined his theatre with a splendid portico, a meeting-place for the Senate, of which the actual auditorium could be represented as merely an annex. By a happy chance, we can reconstruct the lay-out of the building, because it is shown in a surviving portion of a great map of Rome which was engraved in the second century A.D., and a few of the arches which supported the tiers of seats still house a restaurant in the modern Via di Grotta Pinta. The theatre was inaugurated with games involving the slaughter of five hundred lions and seventeen elephants; which moved Cicero to write: "What pleasure can it give a civilized man to see a feeble human creature torn by a powerful wild beast or a splendid animal transfixed by a hunting spear?" What indeed; but the games were to continue to the very end of the Roman world, and survive to this day in the carnage of the bull-ring.

At the end of their year of office, it had been arranged that Pompey should proceed to Spain and Crassus to Syria. Pompey had no desire to leave Italy, where he was happy enough touring the country with the young wife to whom he was devoted. Crassus had his own designs. He was now sixty, and enormously rich, his coffers having been copiously replenished by the sale of the thousands of prisoners which Caesar had sent back from Gaul, or by their employment in working his vast country estates. But one thing he still craved—military renown. If he went to Syria he could win it, and perhaps make a bit on the side as well. He would invade Parthia. Where Lucullus and Pompey had failed he would succeed.

There was no cause, or even excuse, for the war, which was

one of wanton aggression. Caesar, who was doing a little aggression of his own in the north, wrote to urge Crassus on: whether he perished or came back happy and even richer, Caesar would be the gainer. The people of Rome took a different view of the expedition: it was only by Pompey's intervention that Crassus was allowed to leave the city, after being solemnly cursed at the very gate by an outraged tribune.

Nevertheless it was with high hopes that Crassus set out for Syria. He ran into difficulties at once. Rome's best troops were with Caesar in Gaul. There was also an army in Spain, now under Pompey's control. Gabinius, the outgoing governor of Syria, delayed handing over his own troops. Crassus' levies, in Adcock's words, were "a second-class" army, and Crassus hardly more than a "second-class general." He had with him, though, some competent subordinates.

During his first campaign in 54, Crassus was busy in northern Mesopotamia, ostensibly "working up" his troops, but in reality engaged in wholesale temple-robbery, which embraced the sacred treasure of Jerusalem that Pompey had spared. The Parthian king, Orodes, now sent an embassy to enquire whether the war was Crassus' private enterprise or officially waged by Rome. If the former, he said, he would let Crassus off lightly, because he was an old man. Crassus replied that he would give his answer at Seleucia, that is in the heart of Mesopotamia, near modern Baghdad; at which the envoy held out his hand and said: "Hair will grow on my palm, Crassus, before you see Seleucia."

Mesopotamia, as Pompey had already discovered, and as many a Roman was to confirm in the centuries to come, is an extremely hazardous country for an invader. Two rivers, the Tigris and the Euphrates, intersect great wastes of desert so flat that an Arab geographer would be able to calculate a degree of the earth's circumference on them. Except upon the banks of the rivers and the narrow hinterland which they irrigate the country is barren, bitterly cold in winter and unbearably hot in summer. Only by keeping to the rivers is it possible for an army to survive, and not always then, as the British were one day to learn.

It was not only the terrain that was against Crassus: he found opposed to him a wholly new kind of army led by a brilliant young general. The military mind has been throughout the ages notoriously and often disastrously conservative. Roman soldiers were no exception to this melancholy rule. Ever since the legion had overthrown the up till then invincible phalanx, it had been regarded as an axiom that the legion, specially as rearmed by Marius, was the ultimate ideal of military efficiency. Parthia was to shatter this proud illusion.

In the words of the late Sir William Tarn—the foremost authority on both Alexander the Great and Parthia—"It was his [Crassus'] misfortune to meet late in life an opponent who had all the imagination which he lacked. Surenas—his personal name is unknown—was a tall young man, not yet thirty, who dressed elaborately and painted his face like a girl; but he feared nothing and had an idea, a dangerous combination. It had occurred to him that archers were useless without arrows: this does not seem to have occurred to anyone before. As he was the second man in the empire, and very wealthy, the number of his retainers was limited only by his wishes; and from them he formed a body of 10,000 horse-archers, the largest force he thought he could munition. They 'always accompanied him,' that is, they had constant training; but the vital matter was his corps of 1,000 Arabian camels, one to every ten men, who were an integral part of his army and carried a huge reserve of arrows." Horsemanship and archery, together with truthfulness, had always been cardinal virtues among the Persians; but here they were united in a new synthesis. "For the first time in history, so far as is known, there had appeared a trained professional force depending solely on long range weapons and with enough ammunition for a protracted fight."

The Parthians also had heavy cavalry, clad like their horses in scaled armor, called cataphracts. They thus possessed the ancient equivalents of both the aeroplane and the tank. Crassus possessed neither. The result was inevitable. Crassus allowed himself to be misdirected and lured by Surenas onto ground of the latter's own choosing, namely Carrhae, the Haran of the Old Testament, in what is now eastern Turkey. Here he and his seven legions were utterly defeated. His son was killed. He himself surrendered and met his death, no one knew how, as he was on his way to the Parthian camp. Of Crassus' seven legions numbering forty-four thousand men, ten thousand ultimately reached Syria under the leadership of Cassius. Ten thousand were made prisoner. The rest were dead. All the standards were lost. It was one of the worst disasters in all Roman history. The tragedy was to have a macabre epilogue. Surenas, having gloated over the defeated invaders, sent Crassus' head and hand to king Orodes, who was at the Armenian capital of Artaxata for the celebration of his son's marriage to the king of Armenia's sister. After the banquet a travelling company of Greek actors (for the Armenian king was a cultivated philhellene) came on to perform the last act of Euripides' *Bacchae*, the death of the hero Pentheus at the hand of his frenzied mother Agave. The part of Pentheus was being played by Jason of Tralles, a city of Asia lately plundered by a Roman tax-collector. Suddenly a messenger arrived and flung the head of Crassus down in the crowded hall. At once Jason changed his role from Pentheus to Agave, picked up the severed head and played the rest of the scene with this gruesome "property" in his hands.

Surenas did not long survive Crassus; his king killed him out of jealousy, to be himself strangled by his son shortly afterwards.

CHAPTER XV

CAESAR VS. POMPEY

THE death of Crassus not only put an end to the Triumvirate, it also made the confrontation of Caesar and Pompey inevitable. Caesar had foreseen this, and was determined that when the tug of war occurred, he himself should be the victor. But that time, in his view, was yet to come: for he was still engaged on his vast career of conquest in the north. This was essential to him, first because it gave unlimited opportunities for loot, and secondly because he must at all costs, both for his self-esteem and in order to impress the people, prove that he was at least Pompey's equal in the field, besides being his superior in the Forum. At an age when Pompey had completed his triumphs, Caesar had hardly begun his. It was time he began to excel.

In retrospect, Caesar's campaigns in the north have generally been allowed to outshine Pompey's in the East, just as Caesar intended that they should. This is due to two causes. The first is curiously fortuitous. In the making of modern European civilization, France has played an outstanding role, and still does. Since in that civilization there is so much that can be traced back to Rome, and since French is a predominantly Latin tongue, it is easy to suppose that what is now France was always the cradle of civilization and that it owes that civilization to Caesar. This is in fact very wide of the truth. Provence, the old Mediterranean province, Roman since 120 B.C., was to bear witness to its *Romanitas* until the end of the Roman world, and never more so than in the world's last days. But the rest of Gaul remained largely untouched by Roman civilization. The names of cities so familiar to us, such as Chartres, Rheims, or Paris itself, are in origin the names not of cities, but of the tribes whose centres they were. Archaeology, so eloquent in the East, is silent in the north. Professor A. H. M. Jones, whose *Later Roman Empire* is already an established classic, points out therein that it is hard to find a single Roman column surviving in northern France.

Literary sources point to the same conclusion. Ausonius, a native of Bordeaux who lived in the latter part of the fourth century A.D., wrote a poem in which he gives us a catalogue of twenty famous cities. Being a native of Gaul, he might be expected to include a few Gallic towns in his list. Together with his southern birthplace, of which he was extremely proud, he mentions Arles "the little Rome," Narbonne and Toulouse, but not one in Gaul north of the Loire; there was none worth mentioning.

The second and more prevailing reason is Caesar himself. Among his many accomplishments was an ability to write in a clear, simple style, which Cicero eulogizes as "bare, direct and charming." Thus equipped he compiled among other works now lost to us his famous *Commentaries,* in seven books, on his Gallic campaigns. It was published in 51. Because this slice of biography is so clearly written, it has served as a "first reader" to countless generations of schoolchildren, who from the outset of their acquaintance with Rome have been brought up to see Caesar as he saw himself. To quote the Cambridge Ancient History: "Beneath the artist in simplicity of style, the *Commentaries* have a purpose as artfully concealed. Caesar was writing not so much for his admirers as for those who feared that the Gallic Wars were only a stage towards his complete conquest of Rome. In particular, he had to defend himself against the charge of waging war *sua sponte,* without the Senate's permission; and his chief concern was therefore to prove that his wars were inevitable." In fact, his wars were almost wholly aggressive, particularly his invasion of Britain; but for English-speaking students it is not unnaturally a high-light of the Caesar saga. It is as such that a schoolboy reads it and Caesar thus becomes his first military hero.

Caesar's wars were not only aggressive, they were waged with a ruthless brutality that shocked even Romans. Captives had their right hands chopped off to deter others, faith was broken with chieftains, whole tribes dispossessed and massacred, or left to starve, their lands laid waste, their crops and houses burned. This was done, as similar crimes have been committed since, in the name of "security." Caesar himself says of one such operation that when a tribe from beyond the Rhine had attacked his cavalry, their chieftains called next day to explain why they had done so: the cavalry had provoked them by coming too near their camp. Caesar arrested them and at once set out for their camp. The men, taken by surprise, were either slaughtered or drowned in the Rhine. As for the rest, "the remaining multitude of children and women," says Caesar, "started to flee in all directions," so Caesar sent horsemen to track them down. The whole tribe perished. The arrest of the envoys was pure treachery. Cato even suggested that Caesar be handed over to the Germans as a punishment for it.

It is not necessary, in this study, to give a detailed account of Caesar's Gallic campaigns. They were waged against tribes who, like all nomads, were always on the move. It was thus possible to represent their movements as threats to Rome's interests, as some of them may have been. Since some of them, too, like the unfortunates just mentioned, came from beyond the Rhine, Caesar could pose as the defender of civilization against barbarism. It will be sufficient here to quote the earliest extant account of his campaigns, (apart from his own commentaries) that of Suetonius: "During the nine years (58–49 B.C.) of his command this is in substance what he did. All that part of Gaul which is bounded by the Pyrenees, the Alps and the Cévennes, and by the Rhine and Rhone rivers, a circuit of some three thousand miles, with the exception of some allied states that had rendered him good service, he reduced to the form of a province; and imposed upon it a tribute of 40,000,000 sesterces ($1,200,000). He was the first Roman to build a bridge and attack the Germans beyond the Rhine; and he inflicted heavy losses upon them. He invaded the Britons too, a people unknown before"—some people, says Plutarch, doubted whether they really existed at all—"vanquished them and exacted money and hostages. Amid all these successes he met with adverse fortune but three times in all: in Britain, where his fleet narrowly escaped destruction in a violent storm; in Gaul, when one of his legions was routed at Gergovia; and on the borders of Germany, when his lieutenants Titurius and Arunculeius were ambushed and slain."

His men adored him. He could lead them anywhere. The sight of this pale-faced, tall man, his black eyes flashing here and there to match the restlessness of his soul, so beautifully, almost foppishly dressed, sharing all the hardships and perils of war with his legionaries, inspired them to deeds of daring and to unwavering loyalty. He was an expert horseman who would ride at a gallop with his hands behind his back. He could even dictate to two secretaries at once while on horseback. And he could move from place to place with astonishing speed. He would drive a hundred miles in a day. He once went from Rome to the Rhone in eight days.

The people of Rome were enraptured by the exploits of their general. The material benefits which many of them received in the form of slaves and bribes were reinforced by the feeling of relief, carefully fostered by Caesar, that once again Rome had been saved from the hereditary enemy. Few, if any of the citizens, knew or cared about the Eastern world, but not one was ignorant of the story of the German invasion of 390 B.C., which remained a traumatic memory until the last days of Rome, and many could actually remember how in 100 B.C. Marius had averted a similar disaster. For the mass of the Roman populace Caesar was the great deliverer. No wonder that, before the Lucca conference, the Senate had ordered that thanksgiving celebrations should last for a fortnight. In 54 Caesar put in hand the construction in the Forum of the basilica bearing his name, of which the foundations remain.

While Caesar was thus daily increasing his power and authority, Pompey was sinking into incompetence and eclipse. Although he had preferred to remain in Italy, committing his proconsular duties in Spain to subordinates, he had utterly failed to control the city. Rioting was now endemic. Milo and Clodius and their gangs harried each other in the streets no less than in the lawcourts, until finally, early in 52, Clodius was wounded in a scuffle on the Appian Way just outside the walls, and dispatched by

Milo himself. Clodius' retainers burnt down the Senate-house to provide a funeral pyre for their dead leader. Milo inevitably had to face prosecution for his death.

That Pompey and Caesar should clash, and that the victor would become king of Rome, was now evident; the death of Crassus had knocked the linch-pin from the creaking mechanism of the Triumvirate. Even before that the personal link which bound the two rivals had been broken by the death of Julia, soon followed by that of her only child. The people gave her a magnificent funeral, and Caesar celebrated lavish games in her memory. He then with the callousness that was to become a family characteristic proposed to repair the rift by offering his great-niece Octavia, now his nearest relative, in marriage to Pompey, at the same time asking that Pompey should give him his only daughter to wife. That both these ladies were already married seemed to be no obstacle to Caesar, to whom the marriage bond was merely a convenience, or more often, an inconvenience. Pompey declined such a cold-blooded composition and married the daughter of Q. Mettellus Scipio.

After the death of Clodius, and before the trial of Milo, so great were the daily threats to any semblance of public order that the Senate appointed Pompey, not dictator—that would make him a second Sulla—but sole consul.

Pompey now roused himself and acted with all his old vigour. Were the trial of Milo to be conducted in the usual form it was bound to occasion yet more disorders. With the approval of the Senate he promulgated two laws, one to restrain violence, in which was mentioned not only the murder of Clodius but also the riots which had followed it; the second to check the wholesale bribery which had preceded the murder. When the trial came on, it was held before a jury composed of honest men, and in a court-house surrounded not only by Clodius' thugs, but by Pompey's soldiers. Despite Cicero's, admittedly timid, advocacy, Milo was condemned and forced to go into exile at Marseilles. From that pleasant resort he sent Cicero a polite note thanking him for the copy of the speech which he would have delivered—if he had not been overawed by the soldiers: the mullets, he said, were excel-

lent. Other hangers-on of both Clodius and Milo were prosecuted. Cicero, greatly daring, successfully defended two of Milo's
men; but four of Clodius' were condemned. Pompey half-way
through the year associated his father-in-law with himself as consul, thus removing at least the appearance of dictatorship.

Pompey had now made a come-back. He was the champion of
stability, and therefore of the Senate. He was both consul and
proconsul in one. Caesar was the darling of the people, but his
status was delicate. His original five years' tenure of his command in the north had been renewed for the same period in
54, which meant that in March 49 he would become a private
citizen. He could stand for office later on in the year, but meanwhile he would be, to say the least of it, vulnerable.

Meanwhile Pompey passed a measure which required that five
years must elapse before a consul or praetor could proceed to a
provincial command—which meant that for the next four years
following the enactment, governors would be nominated by Pompey and his friends, and that by the end of five years there would
be plenty of candidates in addition to Caesar, capable of holding office. There would, in fact, be no excuse for prolonging his
term of office yet again. It was in accordance with this law that
Cicero found himself "drafted" to go as governor to Cilicia, a
charge that, being the honest and capable man he was, he carried out with distinction and justice. His province included the
neighbouring island of Cyprus; and it was as governor of Cilicia
that Cicero refused the request of the "noble" Brutus that he
exact by force the repayment of a loan which Brutus had made
to some luckless Cypriots at the rate of 48 per cent interest.

Pompey now passed an ordinance which re-enacted the requirement that candidates for office must attend in person. It
was the original law that had robbed Caesar of his triumph; and
at Lucca a personal dispensation from its provisions had been
granted to Caesar. Unfortunately, in drafting the new law, Pompey forgot this exception, and had to write it into the law after
it had been promulgated and engraved on the customary bronze
tablet in the record office. This "forgetfulness"—whether it was

genuine or not, we do not know—naturally aroused Caesar's suspicions.

The threat to Caesar's ambition soon moved from the hypothetical to the practical. He redoubled his bribery, but could not silence the opposition. Early in 51, he asked for a brief prolongation of his command. The Senate refused it, which encouraged one of the consuls, Claudius Marcellus, to move that the house discuss the termination of Caesar's command and the appointment of a successor. This made Pompey uneasy, but his uneasiness sharpened to alarm when Marcellus had a councillor of one of Caesar's new colonies whipped there in Rome, to show what he thought of Caesar's authority. Pompey saw the danger of Caesar's pretensions, but he was not the man to take the first step in disloyalty to an old colleague. He therefore postponed the debate until March of the following year.

Cato meanwhile openly announced his intention of prosecuting Caesar. Cicero still hoped that Caesar would give way, and that a compromise might be reached. Caesar would tolerate no such abatement of his claims; *aut Caesar, aut nullus,* Caesar or nothing, that was his aim. It always had been, and now at last he was strong enough to achieve it. He was secure in Cisalpine Gaul, the "Acropolis of Italy" as Appian called it, whence he could keep an eye on events in the capital; but he needed an active and unscrupulous agent in Rome. He therefore purchased for the enormous sum of sixty million sesterces (two million dollars), the sum of the creature's debts, a young profligate called Curio, a man who as Velleius puts it "had a real gift for wickedness." Caesar could have had him cheaper before, but had rejected Curio's offer. Curio had then turned to the opposition, which was why he was so expensive now. He was to be a tribune, Caesar's tribune. To be on the safe side, Caesar also bought one of the consuls, Aemilius Paullus. He, being a consul, naturally put a still higher price on his honour, and asked an extra quarter million dollars.

Curio was worth the money. When the matter of the provinces came up for discussion in March 50, he interposed his veto. He maintained it when Pompey and the Senate together insisted that Caesar should quit his province on the 1st November. Curio's year of office expired on 9th December; whereupon Caesar chose as his successor a young man of thirty-three called Marcus Antonius, destined to fame as Mark Antony, who hurried down to Rome to be in good time for the election. He also intended to stand for the post of augur, a vacancy in the college having been caused by the death of the orator Hortensius. Antony was duly elected to both offices, but the consuls-elect for 49 were both declared enemies of Caesar.

Slowly, inexorably, the tension increased, the danger grew. Pompey was lying sick in Campania. Curio now proposed that both Caesar and Pompey should disband their armies. This was ingeniously subtle: Pompey and the opponents of Caesar suspected a trap, and yet to block the proposal would put them technically in the wrong. All the same, when on 1st December the question was put to the vote, it was carried by 370 to 22. A veto was overruled and so the desperate die-hards insisted that Pompey should assume command of the forces in Italy. Caesar had won first round: Pompey could be regarded, on paper, as the aggressor. In fact, Caesar never intended to disband his forces: he had spent the previous months in seeing them all disposed in comfortable winter quarters not too far from the frontier, and yet not provocatively near. He knew perfectly well that despite the efforts of Curio he could not escape prosecution if he returned to Rome as a private citizen. Had not Cato repeatedly sworn to impeach him? Asinius Pollio recorded that at Pharsalus when the enemy were routed, Caesar said "word for word": "They would have it so. Even I, Gaius Caesar, after so many great deeds, would have been found guilty, if I had not turned to my army for help." Suetonius, who preserves this quotation for us, also reminds us that Cicero in his book *On Duty* says that Caesar constantly had on his lips some lines from Euripides: "if wrong may ere be right, for a throne's sake were wrong most right." Caesar still hoped to reap the fruits of war without war. He sent an envoy, Hirtius, to Rome on 6th December; but hearing that Pompey had been appointed to protect Italy, Hirtius assumed that the time for negotiation was passed and went back to Caesar without seeing him, from which Pompey deduced that war was now inevitable. Caesar shared this view, and began to concentrate his forces. "Curio made one more effort. He went to Ravenna and received from Caesar an ultimatum with which he posted back to Rome in time to deliver it to the consuls before the meeting of the Senate on the first of January." It was Curio's earlier proposal, backed by a threat: let the Senate make good the proposal they had voted by such a large majority a month ago that *both* commanders should lay down their arms. The consuls temporized, and refusing to have a vote taken on this precise issue, started to discuss the general state of affairs. Pompey, who being in command of an armed force might not enter the city, sent a blunt message to say that unless the Senate stood firm they would have to look elsewhere for a leader. After much debate, the fatal decision was taken: that unless Caesar laid down his arms by a certain date he should be declared a public enemy. Antony and his colleagues at once vetoed the measure. They were chased from the house and had to seek safety in fleeing from the city disguised as slaves. This gave Caesar an excuse, gossamer thin though it might be, that he was "upholding the rights of the people" against a conservative usurpation. The Senate now passed the ultimate decree; but Caesar had already made up his mind. The fugitive tribunes reached Ravenna late on the night of the 10th, to find that Caesar, on hearing the report of their defeat, had assembled the one legion he had with him and had explained to them how matters stood. Orders had also been given for the rest of his troops to come southwards over the Alps. For his first bold step Caesar counted, with all the resolution of his astonishing character, on surprise, backed by Caesar, his genius, his fortune. He spent his last day at Ravenna in watching gladiators at training, and inspecting the plans for their new school. He then dressed for supper, and chatted affably with his guests. As soon as it was dark, Caesar asked to be excused, bidding the company stay until he came back. This created no surprise, because Caesar besides having so much to attend to was well-known for his scanty appetite for either food or drink. He had already instructed a few chosen friends to meet him, some going one way and some another, on the bank of the little river—it is not more than a creek—which divided his province from his homeland. It is called the Rubicon, and like the Jordan, is more famous, and always will be, than many mightier streams. Caesar himself made the journey in a hired carriage, drawn by mules borrowed from a neighbouring bakery. He reached the river by a roundabout route and there in the chill night came up with his friends.

Only now, and only this once, did Caesar appear to be irresolute. As well he might be. For on his decision hung not only his own future, that bright summit of fortune for which he had striven so long, so hard, but equally the fate of his fatherland. He realized what he was doing if he crossed that river: he would be sacrificing Rome to Caesar, liberty to monarchy. Such was the disturbance of his mind, that the night before he had had a terrifyingly revealing nightmare: he dreamed that he had violated his own mother. He discussed the pros and cons of his bold resolve with Asinius Pollio and the others, trying to reckon "what tribulation his action would bring on mankind, and how posterity would think of it." Suddenly he broke off. As though stung to passion he said, in Greek, "The die is cast," and strode across the little bridge.

CHAPTER XVI

KING CAESAR

CAESAR'S crossing of the Rubicon has come to be regarded as one of the great divides of history, a synonym for a long-debated, irrevocable decision. And rightly; for when after an absence of nine years Caesar returned to Italy, a new era of history opened, or rather was opened by Caesar himself, who had planned it and knew just what shape he intended to give it, namely monarchy, the rule of one man. Cicero had already said that the republic was dead, and that only the semblance of it remained. Pompey, too, had realized Caesar's ambitions, but had lacked the wit to counter them.

"Politics is the science of the attainable," as a great Italian was to say when, nineteen hundred years after Caesar, Italy was once again undergoing political transformation. Caesar understood this truth as few men have done. So long as he could prevail by gold, he would do so. He had, Plutarch tells us, used it lavishly not only, as we have seen, in Rome itself, but in conducting his own foreign and intelligence services. It was now clear to him that gold could do no more—already the law of diminishing returns was setting in. Steel must now be substituted for it. Rome and Rome's empire must be taken by force. This being granted, it is easier to understand why events from the year 49 B.C. to the year 30 B.C., which saw Octavian (Augustus) sole and undisputed master of the Roman world, are regulated almost wholly on the battle-field. The great contest lasted for three rounds, which may for convenience be tabulated as follows:

Round 1: Caesar against Pompey, won by Caesar at the battle of Pharsalus, 48 B.C.

Round II: After murder of Caesar (in 44), Octavian and

Antony against republicans, won by Octavian and Antony at the battle of Philippi, 42 B.C.

Round III: Octavian against Antony and Cleopatra, won by Octavian at the battle of Actium, 31 B.C.

Having crossed the Rubicon, Caesar pressed on through the night and was at Ariminum (Rimini) by dawn the next morning. He had with him five thousand men, that is one legion. Ten others would soon be on the march from Gaul, including one called "the Larks" which Caesar had himself raised there. Everything depended on his moving rapidly. It was still early winter, because although the dates are given us according to the calendar as then in force, it was seven weeks in advance of the season, so that 10th January 49 was, or should have been, 22nd November 50. Caesar had had a long time, literally years, to mature both his military and psychological plans. He had gradually and deliberately created a man in his own image—himself —an invincible general who was destined to overthrow all his adversaries. He reckoned therefore that the news that he was moving no longer north but south, and that Rome, not the Rhine, was now his goal, would create havoc and consternation. He was right. The whole country was aghast. It seemed, says Plutarch, as though not individuals merely were on the run, but whole towns. The chaos in Rome was complete. Refugees from the countryside were pouring into the city while others, equally terrified, were hurrying out of it. Pompey was the target of recriminations which hampered such action as he was able to take. He could not, be it remembered, enter the city itself, being the holder of a military command, a restriction which must have made it well nigh impossible to organize any logical plan of action. Instead therefore of putting Rome in a state of defence he declared it to be in a state of anarchy and decided to leave it, bidding the consuls and all true patriots to do the same. This (as Napoleon and some later critics have held) was Pompey's first and fatal blunder, the fountain-head, in fact, of the utter disaster which soon engulfed him. He now had no permanent base; he was on the run, continually improvising. He had not even Rome to bargain with: he simply abandoned the capital of the empire to his rival. And by abandoning Rome he appeared to his compatriots to have abandoned them, too. Pompey did not realize this. He thought that he could retire to the East, the scene of his great triumphs of fifteen years before, that he could there raise large and loyal armies, and that in the meantime Spain and Africa would be his bastions in the west. His fleet would maintain communications: Caesar had no fleet. Pompey saw himself as victor, and so did many others, including Caesar's own trusted lieutenant, Labienus. He deserted Caesar, who contemptuously sent his money and baggage after him. The Pompeians continued to play into Caesar's hands. Jealousy even prevented the adoption of Cato's sensible proposal that Pompey be named commander-in-chief. They then sent two envoys to treat with Caesar, which gave him the opportunity of making the specious "propaganda" point that he was still prepared to disband his army if Pompey would do the same; and that if Pompey would countermand his military preparations and proceed to his province, that is to Spain, he was ready to hand over his own provinces to his successor and to present himself in person as a candidate for the consulship. This proposal would, if accepted, have meant that Pompey would be *limogé* in Spain, and separated from his troops, whereas Caesar would be the "man in possession" in Rome, in supreme control at the centre, and able to recall his own armies at a moment's notice. He clearly did not expect Pompey to agree, and continued to improve his military position. Caesar and his army were one splendid machine, tested and tuned by long years of expert handling. Pompey had seen no service for fifteen years, which meant that not only was he himself rusty, but that his reputation was too. Soldiering is a young man's job. Thousands of young men, besides others who had grown old in his service, looked upon Caesar as their god, the giver of all good things. There were none, now, in Italy who regarded Pompey in that light. The only "inspired" or "committed" soldiers in the country were not among Pompey's levies, but two legions which Caesar, during the squalid negotiations previously described, had agreed to return to Pompey, ostensibly for a Parthian campaign. They had never got any farther than Italy, and could hardly be expected to turn their arms against their adored Caesar.

Never was Caesar to display to more advantage his versatile brilliance than during his return. While pretending to parley with Pompey, he moved down the east coast of Italy, occupying the towns as far as Ancona. Pompey's makeshift garrisons simply melted away before the thrusting Caesarians, and Caesar was now master of the Great North Road of Italy, the Via Flaminia. He also dispatched Antony with five cohorts—something over two thousand men—across the Apennines to occupy Arretium (Arezzo) on the Via Cassia, a branch of the Flaminia which still runs up into Tuscany. His routes to Rome were now assured. Meanwhile Pompey and the consuls had withdrawn, by the Via Appia, to Capua, en route for Brundisium, and Cicero was in charge of Campania. This left Domitius, Caesar's phantom "successor" as governor of Transalpine Gaul, out on a limb at Corfinium, which lay east of Rome and right in the path of the swelling Caesarian torrent. Domitius had thirty cohorts with him. Towards the end of December he received urgent orders from Pompey to retreat before he was cut off. Domitius disregarded these orders and was, inevitably, surrounded. At this point he became hysterical and asked his doctor for some poison. After drinking it he changed his mind, having heard with what clemency Caesar treated his captives. His doctor then informed him that what he had swallowed was not poison at all, but a sleeping draught, whereat the neurotic proconsul jumped out of bed and ran off to surrender to Caesar. Domitius was pardoned (which did not prevent his opposing Caesar again later) and those of his troops who had not already been mopped up and enrolled in Caesar's forces now joined them. The report of this "peaceful penetration" had a calming effect in Rome, and many of the refugees returned.

There was now no obstacle to Caesar's pursuit of Pompey, who had by this time reached Brundisium, together with all his available troops. If Caesar could overtake him before he escaped to Greece, the war might be brought to an end there and then. Twice Caesar sent a messenger ahead to offer some form of composition—what, we do not know—as he hurried by forced marches of twenty miles a day down the east coast. He was just five days too late. He reached Brundisium on the 17th January. Pompey and ten thousand men were still in Italy, but the consuls and more than half the army had crossed to Dyrrhachium on the 12th. Dyrrhachium (later Durazzo, now Durrës in Albania) was not only a port, it was the terminus of the Via Egnatia, the Great High Road to the East, which ran right across nothern Greece to Thessalonica and Byzantium. Its possession, therefore, was of great value—indeed, it was essential— to a general planning a campaign in Greece as Pompey now was. Caesar, having arrived before the closed gates of Brundisium made yet a third effort to interview Pompey, at the same time trying to block the harbour to prevent Pompey's escape. Both moves were in vain. As Caesar himself tells us in his account of the war (for as in the case of the Gallic campaigns we possess his own story of what happened), Pompey returned the correct reply that he could not negotiate without the consuls. Then, having constructed an ingenious network of booby-traps which effectively delayed his pursuers, he slipped away across the Adriatic.

All hope of a speedy peace had faded: it was to be war to the knife. Caesar by his astonishing advance had made himself master of Italy in sixty-five days, and that without shedding a drop of blood. His generosity was politic. It was all right to butcher "natives" up in Gaul, but it would never do to kill Roman citizens—at least, not if it could be avoided. There might be exceptions, of course. When Caesar, seeing that he could not immediately follow Pompey for lack of shipping, returned to Rome, his first care was to loot the treasury.

Metellus, a tribune, protested at this seizure as being contrary to law. "Laws and arms have each their own time," said Caesar: "If you don't like what I'm doing, get out: war doesn't permit of free speech. When I've finished the war, and made peace, come back and talk as much as you like." Reminding the courageous tribune that he was in his, Caesar's, power, he strode off to the treasury, and finding the doors locked, sent for smiths to break them open. When Metellus again protested, Caesar raised his voice and said he would kill him if he continued his resistance. "And," he added, "that, you know, young man, is more disagreeable for me to say than to do." By such means did Caesar acquire 15,000 bars of gold, 30,000 bars of silver, and 30,000,000 sesterces ($1 million). His immediate financial worries were thus disposed of. Not that his troops were as yet clamouring for money. On the contrary, Suetonius tells us, such was their devotion to Caesar that they not only offered to serve without pay or rations, but every centurion of every legion proposed to furnish a horseman from his own savings.

Caesar now realized that despite the speed and resolution with which he had occupied Italy, he must plan a full-scale war against his elusive enemy. He controlled the capital and the homeland; his hold on the peninsula in its entirety had already been secured by a pliant praetor, who in the absence of the consuls had proposed and passed a bill which conferred full Roman citizenship on the population of Cisalpine Gaul, thus rounding off the total enfranchisement of Italy below the Alps. Caesar would once again have liked to win over Cicero, but once again he failed. He must now consider his strategy. As against Caesar's control of Italy, Pompey and the Senate held not only Greece but Spain and Africa and the seas as well. Whichever way he moved, Caesar would need transports, and so orders were sent to all maritime towns to commandeer all suitable vessels and to send them round to Brundisium.

But before tackling Pompey, Caesar determined to stamp out any possible danger from Spain, which was still technically Pompey's province. It was perilously near Italy: what Hannibal had done, a Pompeian successor might at least attempt. Moreover, it was essential to secure Rome's food supply. Curio was therefore dispatched to make sure of Sardinia and Sicily. He was then to cross to Africa, where King Juba might make common cause with the Pompeians. The Spanish campaign would call for all Caesar's brilliance as a strategist. The Pompeians disposed of seven legions in that country, divided into three commands, two of which were held by highly competent officers. Knowing

Spain as they did, their aim was to avoid a pitched battle, to wear down Caesar's army by guerrilla tactics, and finally to come to grips with what remained of it on ground of their own choosing. Caesar's plan was the exact opposite of this—to force his foes to give battle and to destroy them. This he achieved. Leaving three legions to besiege Massilia, which had declared for Pompey, Caesar pushed on with six others and a small contingent of cavalry. The principal Pompeian force had occupied Ilerda, a town on a hill above the river Segre, a tributary of the Ebro. The town could be reached only by one stone bridge, which was in the hands of the defenders. Exposure and privation had weakened Caesar's army, when he decided on a novel plan. The stone bridge was impregnable. Two temporary bridges which Caesar had constructed some twenty miles upstream were swept away as soon as the snows began to melt. The position appeared hopeless, but Caesar remembered something he had seen in Britain —the coracles, fishing-skiffs made of wicker, which were used (as they still are) on certain streams of that rude island. The coracles were built, the river was crossed, a new bridge built, and the swollen stream rendered fordable by the diversion of part of its volume. The hill itself also seemed impregnable, but as a future historian was to write of an assault on another hill in another Peninsular War, "nothing could stop that astonishing infantry." The Pompeians tried to escape, but Caesar's veterans insisted on fording the river, which reached their shoulders, and set off in pursuit of their adversaries. After a week of manoeuvre the Pompeians were surrounded and forced to capitulate. The generals were pardoned and the army disbanded. The remaining Pompeians abandoned resistance, and within two months the whole of Spain was in Caesar's hands. This dashing campaign, one of Caesar's most scintillating exploits, had shown two things: that not even the best Pompeian generals were a match for their rival, and that, even against fellow-Romans, Caesar and Caesar's army were a welded unity that must prevail.

The conqueror now turned for home, and was just in time to receive the capitulation of Massilia on the way. He treated the inhabitants magnanimously. His troops wanted to massacre all the males, and loot the city. Caesar would permit neither. The city might be stiff-necked, but it was also extremely venerable, a beacon of Hellenism in the uncouth north which must not be extinguished.

Meanwhile a disaster had occurred in Africa. At first Curio, enterprising and high-spirited, had carried all before him; but King Juba overcame him in a battle in which Curio himself was killed. The loss of two legions was the price of defeat— that and the fact that Africa could still be used, and would be used, as a rallying-point for the forlorn hope of the Pompeians.

Worse was to come. Pompey was firmly established at Dyr-rhachium. When he had organized his forces, it was to be expected that he would attack Italy both from the sea, which he commanded, and by land, that is by moving northward through Caesar's province of Illyricum. The young Caesarian ad-miral, Dolabella, Cicero's son-in-law, whose task it was to mask the Pompeian navy and preserve Italy and Illyricum from in-vasion, was defeated by Pompey's fleet off the Dalmatian coast and forced to fall back on the northern province, where he hoped to be protected by Caesar's army, part of which had been stationed on the island of Veglia, south of Trieste. Dol-abella was again forced to retreat and the troops on the island were besieged. Some escaped on rafts but a contingent of Gauls killed themselves rather than give in.

The remainder, no less than fifteen cohorts strong, were com-pelled by hunger to surrender. They were broken up and in-corporated into Pompey's army. Caesar still held the coast of Illyricum, but it was now a liability.

What was Caesar's legal status? While he was in Spain, he had taken steps to regularize it. Finding that he could not be elected consul *in absentia*, he had himself proclaimed dic-tator. In that capacity he passed an edict for the relief of debtors and the discouragement of hoarding, for the civil war had upset the finances. He also had all the descendants of Sulla's victims reinstated in their civil rights. When he returned to Rome he was duly elected consul for the year 48. He could now once again turn his attention to the war. Pompey had not been idle. He was in command of nine legions. But whereas Caesar was alone, supreme and adored by his men, Pompey had to contend with a motley host of malcontents, backbiters, intriguers and hypocrites. Cato was there, Cicero too, whom Cato reproached for leaving Italy, where he could have been a neutral go-between. Cicero, as usual, made himself unpopular by his ill-timed facetiousness. Nevertheless, Caesar saw that given time Pompey would become stronger. He must strike at once. He arrived at Brundisium on the last day of the year. Although it was winter he was determined to attempt the crossing, even though through lack of transport it would mean dividing his army into two contingents. The first corps, consisting of some two thousand men, landed safely near the Acroceraunian promontory, midway between Corfu and Dyrrhachium. The remainder, under the command of Antony, was unable to follow because its ships were either sunk at sea or blockaded in Brundisium. Caesar could only rage and wait: he dare not attack Dyrrhachium, towards which Pompey was now hurrying from Macedonia. In this first heat of the race, Pompey was victor. He entered Dyrrhachium. Caesar could only form a camp some thirty miles south of the town, where the two armies faced each other across the river Apsus. To hasten the arrival of his reinforcements, Caesar even attempted the foolhardy exploit of going back to Italy in a rowing-boat, but was forced to abandon it by foul weather. At last, in late February, the transports were sighted. The wind carried them north in full view of both armies. After a very narrow escape from Pompey's cruisers they managed to reach the shore —some distance to the north. Caesar at once made a detour inland, marched round Pompey's position, effected the long-awaited union of his army, and marched south again, hoping to bring Pompey to action and thus to end the war. Pompey could not face an engagement with so efficient an army, so dazzlingly led. He contented himself with seizing a height overlooking the Adriatic six miles south of Dyrrhachium. He was relying on lack of supplies to waste Caesar's forces, while he himself could revictual by sea. Caesar's reply was to construct a line of works fifteen miles long, almost wholly enveloping the

Pompeian-held terrain. This circumvallation may seem extravagantly arduous and of limited efficacy—Napoleon was to criticize it—but it was in fact the standard manoeuvre of ancient warfare. It had been used for instance during the famous and fatal siege of Syracuse by the Athenians four hundred years earlier and would be employed by Vespasian and Titus at the siege of Jerusalem in the next century. Pompey decided to break the fetters. Having drawn Caesar away from his camp by a feigned report that Dyrrhachium was ready to surrender, Pompey attacked Caesar's lines in his absence. The assault very nearly succeeded, and Caesar himself very nearly fell in an ambush; but the affair ended in stalemate once more. Pompey's second plan was simpler and surer. At the southern end of Caesar's lines there was a gap where they approached the sea. Through this gap Pompey mounted a surprise night attack, with sea-borne forces bearing fascines for filling up the ditch before Caesar's main lines and wearing wicker masks to protect their faces against missiles. He simultaneously ordered a second attack on the thinly-held circumvallation. This time his success was complete. After desperate fighting, he was able to lead his troops out into the open country, leaving behind him the defeated Caesarians; upon which their leader commented: "The victory would have to-day been on the enemies' side if they had had a general who knew how to gain it," meaning that Pompey, by disengaging, had missed his chance of ending the war. Caesar was now in a very different situation. It was harder than ever for him to obtain supplies, because the inhabitants regarded him as already beaten. Pompey came to his succour. Turning north again, he marched away from Caesar. He was still, Plutarch tells us, perplexed and cast down: his heart was not really in this distasteful and to him futile war. His companions taunted him with being lukewarm—all except Cato, who still hoped that Roman might spare Roman.

Pompey gave as his reason for thus increasing the distance between himself and Caesar the need for meeting a Caesarian force under Calvinus which was preventing the arrival of Pompeian reinforcements from Macedonia. Pompey set out along the

Egnatian Way to fight Calvinus, to rescue whom Caesar also moved east, taking a more southerly route. This brought him into Thessaly, where he effected a junction with Calvinus. The broad plain of Thessaly, the most fertile in Greece, sufficed to refresh his troops, even though the corn was not yet ripe. The final battle was now inevitable, if only because neither side could move without having first crippled the other.

Just how the ultimate confrontation was brought about we are not told; but the two armies came face to face at the little town of Pharsalus, not far below the fantastic peaks which now sustain the monasteries of the Meteora. On the 9th August the armies engaged. Caesar's forces numbered only twenty-two thousand men, his eight legions being by this time much depleted. Pompey's army was about twice as large. It was on his cavalry that he chiefly relied, and Caesar had devised a simple but most effective way of dealing with them. He told eight specially selected cohorts not to hurl their spears at the horsemen and then charge in the usual way, but to stand their ground until the mounted men were near enough and then to jab the weapons upwards into their faces. The cavalry were completely demoralized by this novel tactic. They broke and fled, whereupon Caesar's reserves, thrown in to complete the havoc which the right cohorts were already wreaking, chased them to their fortified camp and stormed it.

Doffing his general's uniform and decorations, Pompey slunk out of his tent, a ruined fugitive. Caesar, after uttering the disclaimer quoted earlier, pardoned his surviving opponents, including the Brutus who was to be his assassin, and incorporated them in his own forces.

Pompey made for the coast, pausing in the stifling heat to slake his thirst in the famous and lovely vale of Tempe. What a reverse, what a theme for a Greek tragedy, that this man to whom all Greece had once been obedient should now be leaving Greece like a runaway slave! On reaching the coast he embarked in a little ship and crossed to Mytilene where he met his young wife Cornelia. She fainted when she heard the awful news, for like so many others, she had been confident of a Pompeian victory:

people had even been buying houses in Rome so as to be near the restored hub of things. Whither could Pompey turn? There were only two choices, either Roman "Africa" or Egypt. Perhaps feeling that it would be too humiliating even now to be protected—and possibly betrayed—by King Juba, Pompey made for Egypt. The Piper was dead now. He had named as his heirs his eldest surviving daughter and his elder son, a lad of eight or nine. The daughter was twenty-two, and her name was Cleopatra. Brother and sister were at war, the boy having become the dupe of a clique of sordid adventurers who had compelled Cleopatra to quit Alexandria. Cleopatra had raised her own army and now faced her brother at Pelusium, the port of the opposite, or eastern, side of the Delta. Pompey sent a messenger ahead to tell the lad, Ptolemy XII, that he was on his way, and to seek his protection. Pothinus, the eunuch who headed the disreputable cabal, summoned a council to decide what should be done. It was on the deliberations of Pothinus, of a Greek schoolmaster called Theodotus and an Egyptian schemer called Achillas that the fate of Pompey the Great now hung, while he himself was kept waiting in the roads off the sandy shore. Opinion was divided, until Theodotus pointed out that whether they harboured Pompey or allowed him to escape they would be equally obnoxious to Caesar. Best kill him, he said, because that way they would please Caesar and have no reason to fear Pompey: "Dead men don't bite," he added with a smile. Achillas, with two Romans who had once served under Pompey, now put off in a boat to bring him ashore. Pompey's companions, who had divined from the delay that something was amiss, urged him to put to sea again. It was too late; the strand was alive with troops, and several warships were being manned. Pompey bade farewell to Cornelia and set off for the beach. The boat's crew were sullen and silent, as Pompey conned the little address in Greek he intended to make to the king. When they came near the shore Pompey took the hand of his freedman Philip to help him stand up so as to salute those who had come to greet him. As he did so, first one of Achillas' Roman companions, then the other, then Achillas, stabbed him in the back. He said nothing, but covering his face with his cloak sank down and died. Cornelia, who had been anxiously watching from the ship, uttered a shriek which was heard on shore. The assassins cut off Pompey's head and left his body there on the beach. Philip the freedman later wrapped it in a shirt of his own and managed to collect a few planks from an old fishing-boat, "not much, but yet enough to make up a funeral pile for a naked body and that not quite entire."

Such was the end of Pompey, in the fifty-ninth year of his age, and on the very anniversary, the 28th September, of his triumph thirteen years before over the pirates and Mithradates. In death he was to enjoy a devotion that few had shown him in life. Two emperors would win honour by repairing the sepulchre, there in Pelusium, of so great, so gentle, a Roman. He had done much for Rome, and what he had done would endure. Pompey's East would be Roman when Caesar's West was Roman no more. It was his limitations, not his vices, that undid Pompey. In the words of Myres: "Pompey was the last upright and moral citizen, the last loyal servant of the Republic who had also the genius to conquer and administer an empire."

Three days after Pompey's death Caesar arrived in pursuit of him. When Theodotus showed him the embalmed head of his rival and his signet-ring with the lion's paw holding the sword engraven on it, he turned away in disgust.

Caesar now had to plan for the future. He must subdue Africa; but first he must restore his finances, which were as so often at a low ebb. The sum the late Piper had promised had not been fully paid up, and Caesar now determined to collect it. He also fell a victim to Cleopatra. Both as debt-collector and as lover he made himself odious to Pothinus and his accomplices. They easily excited the mob of Alexandria—one of the most vicious in all the ancient world—to show hostility to this alien who gave himself such airs in their capital. The return of Ptolemy's army from Pelusium resulted in Caesar's being blockaded in the palace. It was here that Cleopatra visited him by having herself wrapped up in a carpet, which her Sicilian confidant, rowing across the harbour, boldly carried into his apartments. Caesar was delighted. He was her slave, and it was impossible that he should leave Egypt before she was firmly established as its sovereign. All winter the rioting went on in the streets and havens of Alexandria. Caesar had some narrow escapes; the great library, says Plutarch, was burned. But reinforcements arrived, and in the end Caesar was once more the victor (27th March, 47). Pothinus had been killed, so had Achillas; so had king Ptolemy. Caesar had presumably collected what money he could. After a short trip up the Nile with Cleopatra in the reviving spring sunshine, it was time for him to be off. First of all there was a small insurrection in Asia to be quelled, where one of the sons of Mithradates, taking advantage of the disjointed times, had invaded Pontus and Cappadocia. Caesar said good-bye to Cleopatra for the time being, hoping to see her and the son she was soon to bear him in Rome. He left Alexandria with three legions early in June 47, and by the middle of the month was at Akko (Acre) in Phoenicia. Here he settled the affairs of Judaea to the satisfaction of the Jews, who always held him in high regard for his favour to them. They were exempted from military service and the payment of tribute. Antipater was of the greatest help. Caesar granted him Roman citizenship and appointed him procurator of Judaea. Pressing on through Syria, Caesar pounced upon Pharnaces. The man who had murdered his father was spreading devastation. He plundered far and wide, and with all his father's anti-Roman viciousness castrated those Roman youths whose good looks stimulated his lust. Caesar met him at Zela, and routed him.

It was the outcome of this campaign that Caesar reported to the Senate in the three words "*Veni, vidi, vici*—I came, I saw, I conquered." It was only a little later than midsummer when he reached Rome again, after an absence of eighteen months.

The absence was some months too long. When the news of Caesar's victory was confirmed in Rome, everybody naturally posed as his supporter. The Senate appointed him consul for five successive years, and dictator for an unlimited period. He was, in fact, king. He was to nominate the governors of the praetorian provinces. Antony, though not constitutionally eligible,

never having served as praetor, was to be his Master of the
Horse: it was enough that Caesar willed it, for he was now above
the constitution.

A little later, in what was to be the last years of his life, his
portrait even appeared on the coins, wearing the veil of the
high priest or the laurel of the triumphator, it is true, but in
token of his regal status for all that.

Unfortunately Antony was the last man to be charged with the
restoration of order in an Italy still rent by faction and civil
strife. While Caesar was dallying with Cleopatra, Antony was
having his fun too. He was welcomed at Brundisium by his
mistress, an actress called Cytheris; and Cicero in a famous
diatribe, which was to cost him his life, describes his debauches,
his lawlessness and his craving for low company. The soldiers
whom he billeted on the citizens copied their master and treated
Italian burgesses as though they were Asian provincials. More
serious trouble followed. Milo had returned from exile while
Caesar was in Greece, and had tried to resuscitate the Pompeian
cause in Campania. He soon met his death. Then Dolabella,
always in debt, tried to have Caesar's recent enactment annulled.
He was a tribune now, by the same subterfuge as had availed
Clodious; his colleague Trebellius was on the side of the creditors,
and the city was once again given over to riot and arson. Even
the Vestal virgins felt insecure and dispatched the treasures of
their temple in the Forum to a safe distance. Worst of all, the
legions quartered in Campania were mutinous. Antony visited
them, but they scorned his attempts at pacification. Poor Cicero,
Dolabella's father-in-law, was distracted—but to our advantage.
Caesar had allowed him to remain in Italy despite his adhesion
to Pompey, and it is from his quavering pen alone that we gain
our knowledge of these troubled months. At last Caesar
arrived, and with Caesar tranquillity. The tribunes forbore to
wrangle, Dolabella was brought to heel and Antony too. They
had both bid high prices for the confiscated estates of fallen or
exiled Pompeians, hoping that they would never be called upon
to pay. Caesar insisted that they do so.

The quelling of mutinous soldiers had become a commonplace

for Caesar's magnetic dominance. He first sent an officer to assure them that they would be given four years' pay and more after the end of the coming African campaign. The men, as Caesar might have foreseen, replied that what they wanted was cash down and their discharge. One legion actually stoned the officer, and then the whole army moved on Rome, camping in the Field of Mars itself. Caesar, after posting guards on his own house and on the city gates, went down to meet them. Ascending the platform, he told them that since they asked for their discharge they should have it—there and then. He addressed them no longer as "fellow soldiers" but as "citizens" and informed them they would be excused participation in his triumph. At once they were his again. Even the tenth legion, his *corps d'élite* whose defection hurt him most keenly, were taken back into favour—apparently: Caesar saw he could not humble them at that particular moment, but he would, and did, penalize them later on. That was Caesar's way. The men were also to have their gratuities and their grants of land.

Caesar could now set out for Africa, where the wreckage of the Pompeians had rallied. Chief among them were Cato and Scipio. Cato had landed at Berenice (Benghazi) in Cyrenaica with about ten thousand men in time to hear of the disaster at Pharsalus. Allowing those who wished to leave him, he set out to join Scipio and Juba. His journey on foot from Cyrenaica, right round the gulf of Syrtis, through a waterless desert and amid the chills of winter, up into Tripolitania and on to Utica in what is now Tunisia, is one of the most remarkable marches in military history.

He was enabled by it to make a junction with Scipio and King Juba. Caesar landed some miles south of Utica at the end of 47, but could do little until his veterans arrived refreshed and rested in the spring. He was then able to lure Scipio down to the town of Thapsus, on the seashore of southern Tunisia, and there utterly to defeat him. A few Pompeians escaped to Spain. Cato was at Utica, where he boldly withstood the arrogance and cruelty of Juba. When the news came that all was lost, he calmly assembled his little senate of Roman expatriates and bade them trust Caesar's clemency, and again allowed those to embark who wished to. He restrained the demoralized Pompeians who would have massacred the luckless civilians. He then retired to his house and, after reading Plato's discourse on the soul, put an end to his life.

Cato was, in a sense, the Last of the Romans. He was a patriot of the old, rigid school, prickly, prim and prudish; but inflexibly honest. He was a puritan, and like all puritans made the second best of both worlds; but that was an achievement in an age when few men were able to make anything of either. He lives in history as Cato Uticensis, more renowned for his death than for his life. A Latin poet of the next century, Lucan, was to bestow upon him one of the noblest epitaphs of all time: *Victix causa deis placuit sed victa Catoni*: The vanquishing cause pleased the gods; the vanquished, Cato.

Africa was now Caesar's. Numidia (Juba had committed suicide) was split into two, one part being given to a Roman collaborator, the other becoming a province. Caesar could now return to Rome for his triumph. Pompey's final triumph had lasted for three days, Caesar's should take four. The civil aspect of his conquests was to be played down by emphasis on his foreign conquests: Gaul, Egypt, Pontus, Africa, these were to be the themes, with the usual lavish assembly of treasure, bullion, pictures, placards (*Veni, vidi, vici* included), and with a princess of Egypt (Cleopatra's sister) and a prince of Numidia (Juba's son) and Vercingetorix the Gaul as the actors. Caesar himself was followed by his unconquerable legions, singing bawdy songs about their lecherous and bald-headed general. Lavish donations were made to officers, troops and spectators alike. When it was all over Vercingetorix, who had been a captive for six whole years, was ruthlessly strangled in the prison below the Capitol; for when it came to "sparing the fallen" Caesar was no Pompey: it was not to him that Virgil's grand motto could ever be applied. The citizenry were feasted at twenty-two thousand tables (Crassus had provided less than half that number) and Caesar was escorted home through the dusk by torch-bearers mounted on elephants. His late daughter Julia, Pompey's wife, was commemorated by games which included plays, a mock naval battle, fights between prisoners of war and criminals, and a hunt for four hundred lions and giraffes. Caesar's forum and basilica were solemnly dedicated, though they were completed only by Augustus, and a temple to Venus, the patroness not only of Rome but of Caesar's family—a delicate hint at its identity—was inaugurated. On each day of the triumph Caesar had mounted the steps of the temple of Jupiter on his knees and had deposited his laurel wreath on the altar. But he was empowered by the Senate to wear it whenever he liked. This gave him a double satisfaction: it concealed his baldness; it concealed, too, any ambition he may have been fostering to wear a more durable diadem.

Magnificent as the triumph was, Caesar had one more campaign still to win. In the winter of this year, 46, he was compelled to revisit Spain where, as indicated above, the very last Pompeian fugitives had sought asylum. Pompey's sons, Gnaeus and Sextus, were there, so was the renegade Labienus. Caesar left Rome early in November and reached southern Spain in twenty-seven days. The rest of the winter was spent in inconclusive manoeuvres; but on March 17th, 45 B.C., Caesar brought the Pompeians to action at Munda, near Córdoba. It was a very close-run thing. Caesar said afterwards that he had often fought for victory, but that this was the first time he had ever fought for his life. In the end he utterly routed the enemy. Among the dead were Labienus and Pompey's younger son.

Caesar was now master of the whole world of Greece and Rome, the first man ever to be so. He had won what was to be his last victory and could now address himself to the arts of peace. Once again he celebrated a triumph, once again he entertained the populace with lavish and expensive displays. But by no means everyone was pleased at his glorying in the overthrow and death of fellow-citizens, including the children of one of Rome's greatest sons. A king perhaps they could tolerate, but a tyrant? The answer was soon to be given.

CHAPTER XVII

"IMPERIOUS CAESAR, DEAD AND TURNED TO CLAY"

WHEN Caesar was young and unknown, Plutarch says, during his first appointment in Spain, he surprised his friends one day by sitting silent and pensive for some time and then bursting into tears. When they asked him why, he showed them the life of Alexander he had been reading and said: "Haven't I every reason to weep, when I consider that Alexander at my age had conquered so many nations and all this time I've done nothing worth remembering?"

Now, at the age of fifty-six, he had equalled Alexander, being sole sovereign of the entire world of Greece and Rome. Caesar had always been vain of his appearance, had always loved power and money without being too scrupulous as to how he acquired them. His vanity now became swollen into megalomania. In addition to being consul for a decade and dictator in perpetuity, he was to be known as Imperator. This title had hitherto been conferred only in the field, where it was bestowed as a reward by a grateful army on a successful general. It was now to be given as a prefix like that of Emperor to Caesar and, although he had no legitimate son, it was to descend to his children's children. He was out to found a dynasty. His proconsular authority gave him supreme command of all the armies of Rome, which now amounted to thirty-eight legions. All magistracies, at home and abroad, were in his sole gift; and by virtue of his office of censor he could and did pack the Senate, now increased to nine hundred, with his own nominees, centurions, legionaries, diviners, sons of freedmen and even Gauls among them. He went further: he was to be a god. A statue of him, carved in ivory, was to be borne in the procession which preceded the chariot races in the hippodrome, in company with the statues of the deities of Rome. Another statue was set up in the

Capitol, among those of the seven kings, yet a third in the temple of Quirinus, as the deified Romulus was called; this one bore the inscription "to the unconquerable god." In public Caesar was to sit on a gilded chair, clad in purple, as a perpetual reminder that he was not as other men.

Even his house was to be dignified with a special gable, like that of a temple.

He seems, in these last months of his life, to have thrown all caution, all discretion, to the winds. In 46 he had even entertained Cleopatra, installing her in his suburban villa on the Janiculum together with her boy-husband and the little Caesarion. Cleopatra was enrolled among the friends and allies of the Roman people. Her statue was placed within the temple of Venus Genetrix by the side of that of the goddess. That the censor, the guardian of Rome's morals, should thus establish his mistress and his illegitimate son in Rome must have shocked many, even in that epoch; but what disgusted all was the elevation of a foreign queen, specially one so brilliant and so attractive as this Greek sovereign of Egypt. Cicero was appalled at the woman's arrogance. Poor Cicero! He had fallen on evil days. His beloved republic was dead. So was his adored daughter, Tullia, who had been the light of his life. He had at last divorced his shrewish wife and had then married a rich young heiress, but she too soon died. He spent much of his time now in writing philosophical treatises. He found time, too, to compose an encomium on Cato, to which Caesar was moved to reply in a violent and vindictive effusion called *Anti-Cato* which did nothing to enhance his reputation.

Caesar scoffed at the tribunes and insulted the Senate. When they came to acquaint him with their latest decrees in his honour, he received them sitting down, on his golden chair outside the temple of Venus Genetrix. There was, in fact, hardly any grade of official society which had not some cause for resentment against the sovereign dictator.

But before we come to the inevitable sequel, it is only fair to look at the bright, the constructive, side of Caesar's rule.

First, Caesar sincerely wanted an end of party strife. He de-

clared an amnesty. Statues of Pompey which had been thrown
down after Pharsalus were restored, even those of Sulla. Personal
enemies were pardoned.

The veterans were rewarded with their allotments in Italy
and in the provinces as well. And not only the veterans. Caesar
was determined to stimulate migration. Eighty thousand citizens
were taken overseas to people new colonies, among which were
Hispalis (Seville), Carthage, now refounded, and Corinth. This
last, once the commercial capital of Greece, had lain a deserted
ruin since Mummius had sacked it just a century ago. In recent
years the site has been excavated by American skill and munif-
icence, and now affords an outstanding example of what Caesar's
colonies, as embellished by his successors, looked like. The broad,
paved streets, the colonnades, the market-square, the shops,
the fountains and official buildings and temples—all the amenities
of the Graeco-Roman city in its hey-day—may there be contem-
plated. As an additional stimulus to migration Caesar drastically
reduced the bread-dole. The number of recipients was cut from
320,000 to 150,000, the figure being based on a house-to-house
census. A police force was introduced, the maintenance of roads
and streets provided for, traffic regulated. Municipal councils
were instituted. In case his policy of colonization and the re-
duction of urban pauperism might result in a general depopulation of the city and the homeland in general, Caesar sought to
maintain the balance by two enactments. The first required that
all owners of sheep-runs must employ at least one free shepherd
for every two slaves (thus also lessening the danger of slave
revolts); and the second forbade any citizens between the ages
of twenty and forty to be absent from Italy for more than three
years (which should suffice for his university education in
Greece) unless he were in the army. Senators' sons might go
abroad only as cadets on the staff of a general or magistrate.
Citizenship was granted to doctors and artists, most of whom
were aliens by birth.

Customs duties on imports, abolished in 60 B.C. after Pompey's
enriching campaigns, were reimposed.

A vast program of public works was drawn up. In addition to

the new basilica and forum, there was to be a new Senate-house, a temple to Mars, a theatre on the flank of the Tarpeian rock, an open space on the site of the lake which had been excavated near the Circus for the sea-fight which had taken place at his triumph, a grand colonnade leading from the Forum, round the foot of the Capitol, to the Field of Mars, with an assembly-hall for the Comitia. The Tiber was to be controlled and diverted. The harbour of Ostia was to be strengthened and enlarged, a ship-canal constructed. The Lucrine Lake was to be drained, the Pontine marshes reclaimed. The isthmus of Corinth was to be pierced with a canal. Of this admirable program some items, including the harbour improvements at Ostia, were carried out by later emperors; others, such as the control of the Tiber, had to wait until the nineteenth century. Nero tried to pierce the isthmus of Corinth, but only in the 1880s was the canal finally constructed. The Lucrine Lake was drained by Claudius in the first century A.D., the Pontine marshes by Mussolini in the twentieth.

Provincial governors were to be strictly supervised, and so were the tax-gatherers. We have seen that Caesar had assessed Gaul beyond the Alps at a definite sum (a low one, too—no more than the fortune of ten knights). He now did the same for Asia, and probably Sicily as well. Before the new system could be applied to the whole empire, a census would be necessary. It was planned by Caesar, and carried out by Augustus, as we know from the Gospel of St. Luke. To secure the frontiers, Caesar projected campaigns against the Dacians, who had been raiding Pontus and Thrace; and he was determined to humble the Parthians and wipe out the stain of Carrhae. No doubt with the great foundation of Alexandria in mind, Caesar ordained that public libraries for both Greek and Latin works should be established and fostered.

When it came to sumptuary legislation, control of finery, riding in litters, the cost of sepulchral monuments, and even certain expensive foods, Caesar was no more successful than Sulla had been before him. He was after all well known to every citizen as an extravagant lecher, and even though his lictors invaded private dining-rooms, they were powerless to change the national habits.

Apart from that one exception Caesar's program of reform must be accounted admirable; although the amount of work that still remained to be done in the transformation of Rome from a rambling and insecure riverside town to an ordered and secure world capital is shown by the myriad tasks which Augustus later undertook. But then Augustus had more than forty years in which to shape his new state, Caesar but two.

Caesar's most enduring achievement—it has lasted to our own day—was the reform of the calendar. The old Roman calendar consisted of 355 days. There was therefore between it and the true solar calendar a discrepancy of ten and a quarter days. This meant that times and seasons became hopelessly confused, harvest festivals might fall in winter and the new year was unpredictable.

Every so often, to remedy matters, the pontiffs intercalated an extra month to bridge the gap. This was simply a haphazard makeshift and was constantly being neglected. For instance, since the year 52 B.C. there had been only one intercalation, so that by the year 45 the calendar was two whole months in advance of the season. The blame really lay with Caesar himself, the pontifex maximus; but he now decided to be done with mere tinkering and to adopt a scientific calendar based on scientific observation. While he was in Egypt Caesar had discussed the problem with members of the famous museum, or university, of Alexandria, and a Greek astronomer called Sosigenes had advised him to adopt a scheme which, as we know from an inscription preserved in Cairo, had been in use in Egypt for nearly two hundred years. It was based on the calculation, only a little more than eleven minutes out, that the length of the solar year is 365 days and a quarter. There was in existence in the library at Alexandria a still more accurate computation made in the second century B.C. by Hipparchus of Samos, the greatest of all ancient astronomers, who had fixed the length of the solar year as 365 days, 5 hours, 55 minutes and 12 seconds—and that without any such instruments as even Galileo or Newton possessed. But Hipparchus' calculation was ignored or forgotten, and Sosigenes' adopted. The months were constituted as they are now, with a "leap year" every fourth year, the extra day being inserted after 23rd February, the last day of the primitive Roman year. The new year was reckoned as starting from the 1st January. In Caesar's honour, the fifth month, reckoning from the old first month of March, was henceforth called the "Julian," our July. The calendar as thus adjusted has lasted to our own day with only one amendment, put into affect by Pope Gregory XIII in 1582, by which time the Julian calendar was ten days behind the solar year. Even this would have been unnecessary if the Hipparchan scheme had been realized. Pope Gregory's calendar was generally adopted in Europe, and even by old-fashioned England in 1752, to the accompaniment of demonstrations by workmen who protested at being deprived of eleven days! The only successful stand against the new system was made (as we should expect) by the tax-gatherer. Even now in England the income tax year starts on April 6th, which in 1752 was the new date assigned to the 25th March, i.e. Lady Day, the traditional beginning of the financial year. The Julian calendar is still used by the Orthodox and Armenian churches in Jerusalem.

With the die-hard republicans even this salutary reform found no favour. Cicero himself sneered at it, which shows how far Caesar-hatred had gone, how deeply it had taken root. Caesar himself was alone to blame for this; which is why to this day his tragedy lays a spell on old and young alike. At this juncture we enter one of the most brilliantly-lighted periods of all history; for it has been recorded, dramatized and adorned by William Shakespeare.

The closing scenes of Caesar's life are known, in Shakespeare's telling of them, to millions who have never read Plutarch or heard of Suetonius. To many, also, Antony and Cleopatra are the Great Lovers of all time because Shakespeare has so immortalized them. Shakespeare, we are told, had "small Latin and less Greek," but he had Plutarch in the translation of Sir Thomas North. That he should have found in the pages of the retiring priest of Delphi the raw material of his dramas is one of the greatest tributes ever paid by genius to talent. It is even possible, as it were, to peer over Shakespeare's shoulder and see him at work, specially in one famous passage which will be quoted in its place. As to how Shakespeare saw his Romans, in what light he wished to represent them, the argument, as in most matters concerning Shakespare, still proceeds. In Professor Coghill's view it seems that, so far as Caesar is concerned, Shakespeare intended to represent him as a great man, foully assassinated, whose perfection was marred by minor faults, such as arrogance. Brutus in the play makes an agonizingly wrong choice. Caesar's faults, as described by Plutarch, are played down. At the same time, our sympathy is aroused on behalf of Brutus. Perhaps we shall be right in saying with Samuel Johnson (a penetrating critic) that Shakespeare did not have heroes and knew that kings were men. *Julius Caesar* (1599) and *Antony and Cleopatra* (1606–7?) are, with his other Roman play, *Coriolanus* (1607–8?), Shakespeare's deepest studies of political life, as shown in an epoch about which he could be detached, as he could not wholly be in his English histories. They concern the great dilemma, the tug between public duty and private motive, and the structure of a state as affected by these two in great men. Through all three Roman plays there runs Shakespeare's constant preoccupation with the question: Who, and what, is the truly great, magnanimous man? And this is seconded by his other preoccupation: How, if at all, can the overturning of Order and hierarchy be justified? What sort of people do it? How is Order to be restored? We may add a third preoccupation: A man must be what he seems.

These great themes underlie others of Shakespeare's plays, *Hamlet* and *Macbeth* among them; but in none is the picture so vivid, the light so fierce, as in *Julius Caesar;* because the situation in Rome, after more than half a century of strife, violence and fraud, showed up all these very preoccupations in the most lurid light and shade.

We must now attempt to set down in cold prose the elements which the dramatist's genius was to transmute to drama. Just when the conspiracy was formed we do not know. At the very outset, we are arrested by two remarkable facts. The first is that the conspirators never seem to have had any long-term plan of action, no program of reform or restoration. They provided for nothing beyond the murder itself, lacking wholly their victim's far-sightedness. The second is that Caesar never got wind of the plot. To quote the Cambridge Ancient History: "Cicero's letters show that the Roman aristocracy was a whispering gallery, and yet, though more than sixty men were in the plot, the deadly secret was kept." Compare this with the conspiracy of Catiline eighteen years before. Two explanations for this secrecy may be advanced. One was the arrogance of Caesar himself. The Senate had sworn to protect him, so he dismissed his body-guard. When his friends warned him that his life was in peril his reply was that it was of more value to Rome than to him. He was urged to recall his guards, but refused: better to die, he said, than to live in fear of death. Clearly, it would not be easy to convince such a man that a plot was in existence to murder him: he was insulated by vanity. Secondly, we must remember that the plot was hatched and the murder executed with great rapidity—and by a group of men which, as Seneca points out, contained more "friends" of Caesar than open enemies. The lead was taken by Gaius Cassius, the capable general who had saved Syria from the Parthians after Carrhae, had been one of Pompey's admirals and had been pardoned by Caesar, whom he once referred to in a letter to Cicero as "our old and merciful master." Brutus was a man of a wholly different stamp, a doctrinaire intellectual brought up on Greek philosophy. He was a convinced Platonist. He was conscious, too, of being a descendant of the Great Liberator Junius Brutus, who had ex-pelled the Tarquins and whose statue stood on the Capitol. Brutus' mother was Servilia, Cato's daughter, for whom Caesar had at one time had so extreme a fondness that many thought him to be the father of Brutus. Certain it is that Caesar treated him like a son. He had nevertheless taken the side of Pompey out of conviction, although Pompey had put his father to death, and joined him at Pharsalus. He spent the night before the battle in his tent, writing an epitome of Polybius. Caesar, know-ing where he was, gave orders that he was on no account to be killed: either he was to be brought to Caesar, or allowed to escape. After the battle, Brutus joined Caesar, and it was Brutus' guess that Pompey would make for Egypt which sent Caesar there. Brutus meanwhile obtained Caesar's pardon for Cassius, his brother-in-law. On setting out for the African campaign, Caesar made Brutus governor of Cisalpine Gaul and then preferred him to Cassius (who he admitted had the stronger claim) in the appointment to the city praetorship, which caused a rift between the two men.

Plutarch records that Caesar had his suspicions of Brutus, and of Cassius. When someone told him that Antony and Dolabella were up to some mischief, Caesar replied: "It is not sleek, long-haired fellows that I fear, but the pale and lean," meaning Brutus and Cassius. Nevertheless, "secure in his moral disposition" he could not believe that Brutus would actually attempt to precipitate matters by murder. Brutus might well have risen to be the first man in the state "if he had had patience for a little time to be second to Caesar." But Cassius, fierce and malicious, continually egged Brutus on out of personal spite. In Plutarch's phrase, "Brutus felt the rule an oppression, but Cassius hated the ruler." Cassius hated all tyrants: had he not as a boy boxed the ears of young Faustus Sulla for boasting about his father? Brutus was further stimulated by anonymous letters and inscriptions scrawled on the pedestal of his great ancestor's statue: "O that we had a Brutus now!" and "O that Brutus were alive!" His praetorian chair was filled each morning with notes such as "You are asleep, Brutus!" or "You are no Brutus!" This was the people's counter to the growing fear that Caesar was to be another Tarquin, another king. Cassius, exploiting the prevailing mood, started to enlist his friends in his design against Caesar. They all consented, but on one and the same condition, that Brutus should head it; for only thus would it be accepted as being honourable and in the public interest, and as possessing "the first religious sanction." Cassius thereupon resolved to make it up with Brutus. He called on him and was reconciled. He then asked Brutus whether he intended to be in the Senate-house on the first of March when, it was said, Caesar's friends were going to move that he be made king.

Brutus replied that he would not be there. "But what if they send for us?" asked Cassius. "In that case," answered Brutus, "I should regard it as my duty not to hold my peace, but to stand up boldly and die for the liberty of my country." Cassius with some emotion replied: "Die? No Roman will suffer you to die. Don't you know yourself, Brutus? Who do you think put those writings in your praetor's seat? Weavers and shopkeepers? No, they were the first and most powerful men in Rome. From other praetors they expect largesses and shows, but from you they claim, as an hereditary debt, the extirpation of tyranny." Cassius added more to the same effect, until in the end they embraced and each went off to sound his friends. The timing of this conversation, which may be taken to have set the actual plot afoot (as distinct from vague ideas or threats), is of great interest. It must have taken place only a little before the first of March, because the Senate had already been summoned for that day; so that the whole plot, from conception to execution, took little more than a fortnight.

Brutus' name soon assembled a determined group. It did not include Cicero, "though he was very much trusted and as well beloved by them all, lest, to his own disposition, which was naturally timorous, adding now the weariness and caution of old age, by his weighing, as he would do, every particular, that he might not make one step without the greatest security, he should blunt the edge of their forwardness and resolution in a business which required all the dispatch imaginable." (As perfect a little sketch of Cicero's character as even Plutarch ever penned.)

The final stimulus to the conspiracy had been given, as indicated above, by Caesar himself. On the 26th January of 44 B.C. while Caesar was riding back from the celebration of the Latin Festival on the Alban Mount, some of the throng which lined the Appian Way hailed him as king, to which Caesar replied, with an off-hand jest, that his name was not Rex but Caesar. Two tribunes arrested the man who had first uttered the fatal name. Caesar did nothing at the time; but a little later when the tribunes published a manifesto complaining that they had no freedom of action, Caesar had them brought before the Senate (of which they were, of course, members) and declared that they were scheming to bring him into disrepute. He demanded that they be punished; and they were accordingly expelled from the Senate and on the motion of another tribune removed from office. Since Tiberius Gracchus had illegally deposed Octavius no tribune had been thus humiliated. The whole city rang with indignation.

Three weeks later, on the 15th February, the Lupercalia, or Wolf-Festival, was held. Caesar, who had just been declared Dictator for life, took his seat on his gilded chair on the rostra, wearing his purple robe and his laurel wreath. Down the Forum came running the Luperci, half-naked according to ritual and touching with their hide whips every woman they passed a piece of antique magic which was supposed to promote fecundity. With the Luperci was Mark Antony, as priest of the Juliani, who had recently been joined to the Luperci. He too, although one of the consuls for that year, the other being Caesar, was almost naked and carried in his hand a diadem wreathed with bay. When he came to the rostra, he made his way through the crowd, and ascending the rostra, held out the diadem to Caesar with the words "The Roman people offer you this through me" and tried to place it on his head. The crowd roared its disapproval, and a shout of relief went up when Caesar waved Antony away. A second attempt was similarly received. Caesar then ordered that the crown be placed upon the statue of Jupiter on the Capitol and an official entry made in the public records: "Mark Antony by order of the people offered royalty to Gaius Caesar the Dictator who refused to accept it." It is beyond all reasonable doubt that Mark Antony would never have acted as he did unless Caesar had given him leave beforehand. It was this public hint of Caesar's inner ambitions that touched off the conspiracy.

Caesar was now actively preparing for his Parthian campaign. He would soon be gone, so the conspirators must act swiftly. The Senate was to meet on the 15th March, the fatal Ides; and by one of history's great ironies it was to meet not in the Senate-

house in the Forum, but half a mile away in the portico attached
to Pompey's theatre where stood the statue of Pompey erected
by a grateful Rome. Caesar was to be there, and so there the
deed must be done, because only in the Senate could so many
senators assemble without arousing the slightest suspicion. As
soon as it was day—and Romans of every class were early
risers, if only because their artificial lighting was primitive—
Brutus left his house, bearing a dagger which only his wife, the
devoted and courageous Porcia, was aware of. The other conspirators met at Cassius' house, and brought out with them, as
though they had assembled for that purpose, Cassius' son, who
was on that day to assume the toga of manhood. They carried
daggers too, concealed in their stylus-cases. The rest of the Senate
would be unarmed, but in the neighbouring theatre a troop of
gladiators was to be in readiness in case of emergencies. Caesar
did not arrive, and the conspirators became anxious. Whether it
was his wife's dream, or the unfavourable omens, or that he just
was not feeling well, he sent for Antony and told him to dismiss
the Senators. The evening before he had been dining with Lepidus, taking with him the very Decimus Brutus who was supply-
ing the gladiators, an old and trusted officer. After dinner when
he was signing letters a discussion arose about death, and someone asked what death was best. Caesar, before anyone else could
speak, said, "A sudden one."

Decimus Brutus was now sent to persuade Caesar to attend
the House; and so, a little before noon Caesar stepped into his
litter and was carried down past the rostra, round the northern
flank of the Capitol and into the Field of Mars. On the way he
met a soothsayer—there were many such in superstitious Rome—
who had bade him beware the Ides of March. "The Ides of
March are come," said Caesar lightly. "Yes, come but not past,"
replied the man calmly.

As the procession reached Pompey's theatre someone thrust
into Caesar's hand a paper which gave information of the plot.
Caesar would have read it, but the jostling of the crowd prevented him. He entered the chamber actually holding the paper.
Meanwhile the plotters had some anxious moments. First, a

senator with the honoured name of Popillius Laenas came up to Brutus and Cassius and whispered: "I hope you will succeed; but hurry up, the thing is no longer a secret." Then a man came up to Casca, one of the conspirators, and shook his hand, saying: "You kept the secret from us, but Brutus has told me everything." Casca was taken aback and might have given the plot away but that the man at once went on to make it clear that he was merely referring to an election to the aedileship. Then came news, fortunately false, that Brutus' wife was dying: the strain of waiting had in fact made her swoon. Finally, as Caesar stepped from the litter Popillius Laenas went up to him and was seen to be in earnest conversation with him. What was he saying? The conspirators were on tenter-hooks, and were ready to take their own lives. Some actually had their hands on their daggers under their togas, when Brutus, realizing that Laenas was asking Caesar for something, not informing him of anything, gave a sign to Cassius (he dared not use words with so many around him who were not in the plot) that all was well. Laenas kissed Caesar's hand and went away, and Caesar entered the House, which rose to salute him. He took his seat in a recess at the end of the portico, beneath Pompey's statue.

As soon as Caesar was seated, the conspirators crowded round him, as though in deference, and put up one of their number called Tillius Cimber to intercede with the Dictator on behalf of a banished brother. He took Caesar by the hand and kissed him on the head and breast. Caesar refused the petition: the associates pressed it. Caesar brusquely started to his feet, whereupon Cimber caught hold of his toga and pulled it off his shoulders. "Why this is violence," cried Caesar. Casca, who was standing behind Caesar, at once drew his dagger and struck him from behind just below the throat. Caesar caught Casca's arm and ran it through with his stylus—the sharp writing-instrument used for writing on wax tablets. As Caesar tried to rise to his feet again, Casca called out to his brother in Greek to come to his aid. By this time all the conspirators were crowding so close about their victim, and striking him with such fury, that they wounded each other. Caesar, after being struck twenty-three times without uttering a cry, was still grasping Casca's hand as he looked round desperately for some way of escape—until he saw Marcus Brutus coming at him with drawn dagger. Then he dropped Casca's arm, and saying to Brutus in Greek: "You, too, my child?" covered his head with his toga and so died.

The senators, including Cicero, fled, jostling each other at the door though no one was pursuing them. Brutus called them back, but in vain. Then the conspirators, too, left the hall. But a short while before the scene of uproar and violence, it was now deserted and still. Only, at the foot of Pompey's statue lay Caesar, dead and covered with blood. A little later three slaves ventured into the chamber, placed Caesar's body on a litter and carried it home, "with one arm hanging down."

The conspirators, as already stated, had no plan. Moreover they had already committed a cardinal blunder—judged by their own standards, that is. One of the most poignant aspects of the whole drama, clearly brought out by Plutarch and by Shakespeare, is that good men should not undertake to do bad deeds. Brutus was a good man, who even when planning murder thought he was doing good. He would kill, he said, what was bad, namely tyranny in the person of the tyrant, but no one else. Such was his authority that when all the others were for murdering Antony as well, Brutus succeeded in saving his life at the cost, as it turned out, of his own and of those of most of his associates. That is why Shakespeare argues that Brutus was too noble for the dirty work he had helped to do, and that he should have kept with his like. Antony had been prevented, by a ruse, from entering the House; but when he heard the uproar he made off, changed his robes—he was, be it remembered, consul—for a slave's garb and hid.

Meanwhile the conspirators ascended to the Capitol, quite at a loss: their "Freedom Rally," as they strode with bared weapons through the streets, had been a complete failure. A little later Brutus and Cassius, who from the Capitol had been able to watch the return of Caesar's corpse to his house in the Forum and to witness the tears and groans with which the populace had greeted the pathetic cortège, ventured down into the Forum and addressed the people. They were greeted with hostile silence, and again ascended the hill. Towards evening they were visited by Cicero and others. After the murder, Brutus had particularly singled out Cicero, and had congratulated him on the restoration of liberty. Cicero now strongly pressed for an emergency meeting of the Senate there in the temple on the hill, because he was convinced that all true republicans were rejoicing at Caesar's death, and that it was essential to keep the initiative.

On this occasion at least Cicero was beyond question right; but his counsel was rejected. Instead the conspirators asked him to go and see Antony and call on him, as consul, to defend the state. Cicero refused, saying, again perfectly truly, that Antony would promise anything so long as he thought he was in danger and that when he saw he was not he would be what he always had been. In fact, Antony was already master of the situation and of Rome. The conspirators had no armed force except the gladiators of Decimus Brutus; Antony had a whole legion commanded by his Master of the Horse, Lepidus. He had something else, too: Calpurnia, Caesar's wife, had handed over to him the keys of Caesar's money-boxes and all his papers, including his will. Thus armed, he started to play a very subtle game. First he sent his son up to the Capitol as a hostage, and asked Brutus and Cassius to come down. They did so—there was nothing else they could do. That evening Cassius supped with Antony and Brutus with Lepidus. Next morning in accordance with what looked like an agreed line of action but was in reality Antony's opening move, Antony convened the Senate having repressed Lepidus' rash proposal to use force. The House met in the temple of Tellus, that is as far away as possible from Pompey's portico, and conveniently near to Antony's own home.

Professional republicans at once called for extreme measures: Caesar's corpse must be thrown into the Tiber, the "liberators" must be rewarded from public funds. Poor souls, they did not understand—such characters never do—that rivers do not flow backwards: the torrent of revolution was now in full spate; clever navigators would ride it, not try to stem it. Cicero, with daring timidity, called for a general amnesty. Other moderates supported him, and finally the house decided illogically but prudently that Caesar's assassins should be immune from prosecution, while at the same time all Caesar's own acts should be validated (for were they to be cancelled many of the senators would find themselves deprived of position and prospects), and not only those of his plans which had already been published, but also those which might be found among his papers. And Caesar was to have a public funeral.

Antony had played for the highest stakes, and he appeared to have won. He was no statesman, but a *coup d'état* calls not for statesmanship but for nerve. And that he possessed. He was in the prime of life, not yet forty. He had been brought up as a fashionable rip in the corrupt Rome of the dying republic. He was handsome, with a broad forehead and an aquiline nose, which people said made him look like Hercules. Liberal and lecherous, he was just the man for Caesar, to whom he was related on his mother's side. He had been with Caesar in Gaul in 54, and it was through Caesar's influence that he had become quaestor, augur and tribune. He had shown himself a good soldier in the East, where he had become the firm friend and patron of Herod of Judaea, son of Antipater and soon to be Rome's essential buttress in the Levant. After the battle of Munda, Caesar had chosen his kinsman to ride back through Italy with him. He was Caesar's most trusted colleague and had shared the consulate with him. Antony had, in fact, every hope of being named heir to the childless Dictator, and according to Cicero had boasted of the prospect. Who therefore more eager than he to have all Caesar's *acta* and will confirmed? From the Senate Antony went home. He opened the will. The document, far from advancing him to the supreme status which he had expected and which his enemies had foretold, proved—though he did not then know it—to be his death-warrant. For not Antony but the obscure Octavian (Caesar's great-nephew) was named heir, Antony being relegated to the category of "second heir," which in the Rome of the day was little more than a way of paying a posthumous tribute to friends at no cost to the testator. Thus before the second act of the great Roman drama had been played out the third and last had begun. But no man except perhaps Octavian, studying obscurely in Apollonia, knew it as yet.

In death as in life, Caesar had known how to captivate the people: he left his gardens beyond the Tiber to the public, and a dole of three hundred sesterces (ten dollars) to each citizen; so that by 20th March, five days after his death, as the stately cortège left Caesar's house to enter the Forum, on which it abutted, it was halted almost at his door by the emotional mob. His honours were recited, together with the oath which the whole Senate had taken to protect him. At once, as Appian tells us, the onlookers seized such wooden furniture as they could find to hand and there and then built his pyre. The famous speeches with which Shakespeare has embellished the scene are his own creation, based merely on indications in Plutarch of the contrasting oratorical styles of Brutus and Antony. When Shakespare takes wing without Plutarch to guide him, he goes astray. The familiar lines:

> "You all do know this mantle: I remember
> The first time ever Caesar put it on:
> 'Twas on a summer's evening in his tent,
> That day he overcame the Nervii"

ignore the fact that on that particular day Antony was some thousand miles distant from Caesar. But they catch perfectly the temper of Rome during Caesar's funeral and Antony did make play with the blood-stained and dagger-rent clothes. Men said that the soul of Caesar was seen to mount to heaven from the pyre in the form of an eagle. And among those who mourned him, none were more assiduous than the Jews of Rome for whom he had done so much. The houses of the conspirators narrowly escaped burning.

Within a month Brutus and Cassius were compelled to leave the city. Antony willingly arranged that Brutus, who was urban praetor, be granted leave of absence. He was equally complacent to Dolabella when he claimed the reversion of Caesar's consulship. Lepidus was made pontifex maximus in Caesar's

room, and so master of the official house by the Forum, which
had so lately sheltered Caesar. Antony conciliated the senators
by proposing a motion for ever abolishing dictatorships such as
those of Sulla and Caesar. Lepidus, about to set out for southern
Gaul and Spain, was authorized to negotiate with young Pompey, who still commanded the six legions in Spain. Cicero was
fed on flattery. Everyone seemed to be content, and the grateful
Senate voted the province of Macedonia to Antony and that of
Syria to Dolabella. Within two months of the murder, the site
of Caesar's pyre had become a place of pilgrimage and Caesar's
lieutenant, Antony, was master of Rome. The tyrant was dead,
Cicero lamented, but despotism still lived. Cicero could do nothing: the challenge was to be taken up by a boy of eighteen,
who for the next sixty years was to be the guiding force of Rome
and her destiny.

CHAPTER XVIII

THE SECOND TRIUMVIRATE

THE boy who now presumed to claim three quarters of Julius Caesar's enormous fortune and the whole of his glory and destiny was born of obscure parents in 63 B.C., the year of Cicero's consulate. His grandfather, a plebeian of the Octavian clan, was a banker—a profession little regarded by the snobbish Romans —at Velitrae, in the Volscian country. His father had raised the family status to that of the official classes; having served as quaestor, aedile and praetor, the established *cursus*, he then governed Macedonia with ability and honesty. More important for the prospects of his children, he had (like Marius before him) married into the great Julian house. His wife Atia was the daughter of a citizen of Velitrae called Marcus Atius Balbus and Julia, Julius Caesar's sister. Atia became a widow before her husband could serve as consul, in the year 58 when her son was only five. She was married again, to one L. Marius Philippus, a friend of Cicero; but she devoted her attention not to the fashionable world of Rome, but to the education of her son. His full name was Gaius Octavius Thurinus, but he never used the cognomen, which was given him in memory of his father's victory over some runaway slaves at Thurii in Sicily, an association which Caesar's great-nephew preferred to forget.

Gaius was born at Rome in a house at the eastern end of the Palatine, but he was brought up in the country, mostly at Velitrae but also in the other country villas of his family. He was seldom allowed to visit the city, but kept to his tutors and his books. He was an "old Roman," calm, careful and studious. His features were Roman too. He was five foot seven in height, with a broad forehead and a high-bridged nose. A certain softness in his face was more than compensated for by the penetrating gaze of his almost hypnotic grey eyes. Before he became a youth he was a man, mature and steadfast. Wine he seldom tasted, and his delicate constitution restricted him to a Spartan diet. From his mother he had learned that respect and veneration for the traditions and religion of Rome which was to characterize him to the end of his days.

As a boy, his early promise, his nobility of bearing and his remarkable beauty had commended him to his great-uncle. At the age of twelve he was allowed to deliver the funeral oration for his grandmother Julia, and so to enter public life as a scion of that famous family. He was made a member of the pontifical college. Fired with the glories of the *gens Julia*, he was eager to accompany his great-uncle to Africa, but his mother forbade it on the ground of his poor health. He nevertheless rode in the triumph of 46 B.C. Next year again illness almost prevented him from going to Spain, but he arrived in time to accompany the victor of Munda back to Italy. In the autumn of the same year, 45, Caesar (having, unknown to Gaius, decided to make him his heir) sent him across the Adriatic to Apollonia to finish his education. With him went a few chosen friends, of whom two were to be his ministers in after years, Gaius Cilnius Maecenas, who claimed descent from the Etruscan kings, and, closest of all, his exact coeval Marcus Vipsanius Agrippa, "the supreme example in history," in John Buchan's words, "of a man of the first order whom loyalty constrained to take the second place." Naturally enough the distinguished young man, already known to be the protégé and favourite of a relative who was the first man in Rome, was a centre of interest in the military society of Apollonia where a portion of the army destined for the Parthian campaign was quartered: it would be wise to keep in with one who it now appeared was reserved for so high a destiny.

Then in March came the dreadful news: his great-uncle had been murdered in the midst of the very senators who had sworn to protect him, and by men whom he had protected, pardoned and promoted. Some of the officers wanted to march on Rome at once, with Gaius at their head; the rank and file would certainly have followed him. The future Augustus was more prudent: he thanked the soldiers for their loyalty and then set off in a hardly

seaworthy ship for an obscure port on the Calabrian coast. On
landing he was welcomed by the garrison of Brundisium; and
it was here that he learned that Caesar had left him three
quarters of his fortune and had adopted him as his son. His
cautious mother, who understood only too well what the inheritance involved, tried to dissuade him from accepting it; but
Octavius answered the mother he trusted so well with the famous
words which Homer makes Achilles address to his mother
Thetis: "Now go I forth that I may light on the destroyer of
him I loved: then will I accept my death whensoever Zeus
and the other immortals will to accomplish it." He was to live
for another fifty-eight years; but many were destined to die before him.

The other strain in Octavius' heredity, that of the banker, now
opportunely showed itself. Despite the embarrassing assurances
of loyalty on the part of colonists and soldiers, Octavius was determined to take no risk which might bring him into open conflict with his enemies. His mother and stepfather were at Puteoli
(Pozzuoli). So were Cicero and a group of Caesarians. Them
he must first consult. Then he must go to Rome, give formal
notice to the urban praetor that he had accepted the inheritance,
make a public declaration of his plans for administering the
will, and have the adoption officially ratified. He also took another sensible step. Caesar, with an eye to the Parthian campaign, had sent ahead into Asia a large imprest of treasure. This
his heir ordered to be returned to him in Italy. Cicero, now
sixty-two, "a philosopher who had lost all philosophic balance,"
in Buchan's words, welcomed the lad of nineteen, who had
already profited from reading the master's works. Addressing him
as "father," Octavian sought his counsel. Despite his entourage
of Caesarians he made a good impression. "He is devoted to me,"
the vain old man wrote to his friend Atticus, though he found
it hard to see how anyone with such heredity could be a good
citizen. The lad seemed harmless enough; but it was galling indeed that this stripling could go to Rome in safety, while the
"liberators," Brutus and Cassius, dare not be seen there. Cicero
added, with a certain waspish malice, that there was bound to be

"a terrible row between him and Antony" before he could come by his inheritance. Here again Cicero was right.

As Octavius entered Rome at the end of April, there was a halo round the sun, a sure token of divine favour. He was eagerly greeted by the mob, who looked to him for the payment of the dole promised them in Caesar's will, and by former partisans of Caesar. Mark Antony was consul, his brother Gaius praetor and a third brother, Lucius, tribune. To Gaius, Octavius announced his formal acceptance of his adoption; Lucius introduced him to the statutory public meeting, at which he made a tactful speech, promising to pay the citizens at once the money Caesar had bequeathed to them and to celebrate, at his own expense if need be, the games to be held in July in honour of Caesar's victories. He said nothing of any amnesty for the murderers, thereby disappointing Cicero. Republican sentiment was still strong. One day in the theatre Octavius sought to use Caesar's gilded chair. When a tribune forbade him, the spectators applauded. Lucius had proved unfriendly and dilatory in the matter of the law necessary to ratify the adoption. But it was Mark Antony who now showed the hostility which was to ruin him. It was natural that the advent of this unknown young man, legally entitled to despoil him of his illegally acquired reversion of Caesar's power and wealth, should annoy Antony. A wise man would have exploited the inevitable and come to terms with Octavius, using what he could not destroy. But Antony was not a wise man. So far, it is true, he had behaved with moderation. He was the obvious leader of the Caesarians, yet he had not by extreme measures against the republicans caused any division in the state. Now he was to be not only challenged but—far harder to bear—impoverished by a youth half his age (Antony was just on forty). His "quick spirit" precipitated him into the tragedy of errors which was to end only with Actium. Instead of greeting Octavius, whom he had often met in the intimate circle of Caesar's "family," he left Rome. Using Octavius' money he recruited a bodyguard down in Campania from among Caesar's veterans. By the same means he bought the adherence of Dolabella, Cicero's gangster son-in-law.

As soon as Antony returned to Rome, Octavius called on him, in Pompey's old house which Antony had annexed. Antony kept his visitor waiting in an ante-room and during a short interview was studiously rude to him. He made no effort to conceal his contempt for "the boy" as he called him, a mere money-lender's grandson. He declined to hand over Caesar's fortune, so that Octavius had to pay the legatees from his own funds. He blocked Octavius' candidature for the tribunate. Octavius was not the man to take this lying down. He organized his own band of veterans and openly denounced Antony as a traitor who had done nothing to avenge Caesar and had then stolen the money which should have been given to the people. Octavius would pay it himself, he said, if it cost him his last sestertius. He wrote to his soldier friends across the water, telling them how shabbily Antony was treating him. In July the games in Caesar's honour were celebrated. Octavius again tried to claim the right to be seated in Caesar's gilded chair, and again Antony forbade him, but this time the people were on Octavius' side. Then on the last day of the celebration a comet appeared, which was recognized as being the Julian Star, which meant that Caesar was now safely installed among the gods—a splendid omen for his adopted son, as everyone at once acknowledged. Antony at last realized that he must take Octavius seriously, that he must fortify his own position. He therefore contrived that a plebiscite should confer on him, for a period of five years, the province of Cisalpine Gaul. He thus ousted Decimus Brutus, who was appointed to Macedonia, which had been formerly, as already noted, assigned to Antony; but Antony kept command of the Macedonian legions. Dolabella was to have Syria, and the two consuls alone were to decide which of Caesar's unpublished "intentions" should become law. With Italy's security and practically unfettered legislative initiative at his sole disposal Antony could afford to be liberal. He was formally reconciled to Octavius, or Octavian as he was now called by virtue of his adoption. Brutus and Cassius were got rid of by having them appointed supervisors of the corn-supply from Asia and Sicily, with the governorships of unnamed provinces later on—Crete for Brutus and Cyrene for Cassius, as it turned out. But when they set sail in August, it was to Macedonia and to Syria that they went.

Cicero meanwhile had returned to Rome, and in August he delivered the first of his tirades against Antony called, after Demosthenes' famous orations opposing Philip of Macedon, Philippics. They were to cost Cicero his life, as we shall shortly see. Antony was nettled, and countered with a ridiculous allegation that his life had been in danger as the result of a plot in which Octavian had been implicated. "Caesar [that is Octavian] explained," says Plutarch, "but was not believed, so that the breach was now as wide as ever; each of them hurried about all through Italy to engage, by great offers, the old soldiers that lay scattered in their settlements, and to be the first to secure the troops that still remained undischarged." The remainder of the year was passed by both sides in manoeuvring for position. Octavian—or Caesar as Cicero was now calling him —behaved with great adroitness. He had to conciliate the soldiers, to whom he must appear as his "father's" avenger and successor, while at the same time keeping in with the conservatives who had backed the "liberators." Cicero was now wholly on his side; but Octavian found it impossible to remain in Rome. His caution was losing him the confidence of the Caesarians, and the opposition refused to regard this boy of nineteen as a political factor. Moreover, Antony was approaching with an army. Octavian retired to Etruria, enlisting more troops on the way. In Rome Cicero's eloquence had done its work. Four more Philippics had followed the first. In the fourth he issued an overt challenge to Antony. In the fifth, delivered on the 1st January, 43 B.C., he made himself surety for Octavian's loyalty to the republic. The Senate resolved to send an embassy to negotiate with Antony before declaring him a public enemy, but continued their military preparations.

One of the new consuls, either Hirtius or Pansa, was to command the army. Octavian was given senatorial rank, and the state was to pay the bounties (or bribes) which he had promised to the two Macedonian legions which had come over to him. He was to be allowed to stand for the consulship ten years before the statutory age; he was joined with the consuls as co-commander with the authority of a propraetor. As the year wore on, it became clear that no one in Rome wanted to rekindle civil war, and that neither protagonist could count on the unquestioned loyalty of either troops or citizens. Brutus and Cassius had now been officially assigned Macedonia and Syria, which meant that with such a firm foothold in the East the senatorial party had less need of Octavian. His position became more equivocal day by day; yet he did nothing rash, content to bide his time, and meanwhile improved his oratorical style.

At the end of March, Pansa moved northward in pursuit of Antony, who had now been declared a public enemy. Decimus Brutus, governor of Cisalpine Gaul, had refused to hand over his troops to Antony and had instead shut himself up in Mutina (Modena). He now informed Octavian by carrier-pigeon that his troops were starving and that he must surrender unless relieved. Modena is about equidistant from Parma on the west and Bologna on the east, both of which towns were in Antony's hands. The issue was decided in two ragged battles. Both the consuls were killed, but Antony had been trounced and forced to retreat beyond the Alps all the way to Forum Julii (Fréjus) near Marseilles. The Senate now saw itself victorious and secure; it could drop young Caesar, who in Cicero's phrase would soon find himself "lauded, applauded and discarded." Octavian saw that at all costs he must come to terms with Antony. He knew that Antony would win over the senatorial governors of the northern provinces, Lepidus in Narbonese Gaul, Plancus in Celtic Gaul and Pollio in Spain. Lepidus joined him in May and the other two followed later in the year. Octavian sent a deputation of centurions to Rome asking that, since both consuls were dead, he as their colleague in command should be made consul. The Senate hedged, pleading constitutional objections; whereupon Octavian marched on Rome, the objections were overcome, and on the 19th August Octavian and his uncle Q. Pedius were declared consuls. Octavian had reached Rome's highest office at an age younger even than Pompey, and twenty-four years, not ten, before the legal date. The law confirming his adoption was at last passed by the antique Comitia Curiata: henceforth he was Gaius Julius Caesar Octavianus. The prestige of the name was magical. Yes, the "boy," consul and Caesar, could deal with Antony on equal terms now. Pedius introduced a law outlawing all assassins, after due trial, as a rallying cry for the Caesarians. Then the decrees which had declared first Antony and then Lepidus public enemies were withdrawn. "The collapse of Republicanism in Italy was followed by its collapse in the West": so runs the epitaph of the Cambridge Ancient History on these shabby proceedings. Far shabbier were to follow.

With Lepidus as go-between—"that weathercock of a man" as Decimus Brutus, shortly to meet his death at the hands of a Gaulish chieftain, called him—it was arranged in the autumn of 43 that Octavian, Antony and Lepidus himself should meet on an island in a tributary of the Po between Bologna and Modena. A triple dictatorship was to be established, like that of 60 B.C., only this time it was to be established by law: the three were to be called *tresviri republicae constituendae*, "Triumvirate for constituting the commonwealth"—which was simply a phrase, such as modern statesmen use, for defining the exact opposite: they would tear to shreds what remained of the old republican fabric. The Triumvirs were to retain office for a long period of years, above all other magistrates, with power to make laws and to nominate governors and magistrates. Each was also to have a province, Antony Cisalpine Gaul and Gaul beyond the Alps, Lepidus Narbonese Gaul and Spain, Octavian Africa, Sicily and Sardinia—the hardest of all to administer because Sextus Pompeius, Pompey's son, still held the seas. The soldiers, beneath whose interested eyes the negotiations had been conducted, approved the arrangement: they would far rather assume possession of the good farmland which had been promised to them than carry on with a civil war of which they were sick and tired. They were glad to learn, too, that Octavian was to be betrothed to Claudia, Antony's daughter by the infamous Fulvia, Dolabella's sister. At last the Caesarian front was united. Its unity was to produce one of the most disgusting and shameful transactions in all Roman history.

Before the "avengers," Antony and Octavian, could set out for their campaign against Brutus and Cassius, they needed two things: money and the assurance that no enemy would raise his head in Italy during their absence. Both these ends could be attained by one and the same means, namely selective murder. Sulla's proscriptions had been bad enough, but those of the Triumvirs were worse: the three men sat round the table and swapped lives, even those of relatives and friends, like counters at the gaming-board. Shakespeare has given us the scene:

> *Ant.* These many then shall die; their names are prick'd.
> *Oct.* Your brother too must die; consent you, Lepidus?
> *Lep.* I do consent—
> *Oct.*   Prick him down, Antony.
> *Lep.* Upon condition Publius shall not live,
>   Who is your sister's son, Mark Antony.
> *Ant.* He shall not live; look, with a spot I damn him.
>
> (*Julius Caesar*, IV, 1)

Among those who were condemned to die was Cicero. That Octavian should have acquiesced in the death of his friend and patron, indeed that he should have been a party to the bloody business at all, puzzled ancient commentators. To account for such conduct in the great and good Augustus, as he later became, they postulated a kind of conversion, a change of personality. Augustus could, it is true, be callous, specially in the arranging and breaking up of marriages for political reasons—his treatment of his own sister Octavia is only one of many cases. To him as to most Romans, woman was, in Balsdon's phrase, "a political animal" merely. But only once again would he be a cold, calculating murderer. The plain truth is that in the years 43 and 31 he was the child of one age, and that a vile one, and that in later life he became the father of another, which was to be far better.

Cicero met his end with that mixture of timidity and res-

olution which he had shown throughout his life. It was Antony
who had insisted at the Bononia conference that Cicero should
die. Octavian, it was afterwards said, had stood out against the
demand for the first two days, but gave in on the third: Antony
was determined to kill the man who had humiliated him with
his Philippics. The news of the death sentence—it was one of no
less than two hundred—reached Cicero at his country-house
near Tusculum, the wooded hill above what is now Frascati.

He set out with his brother Quintus for one of his villas down
by the sea, from which they intended to take ship for Macedonia
and so join Brutus; but as they journeyed, Quintus realized that
they had not enough resources to enable both of them to escape
and so, after bidding farewell to his brother, he turned back
home to what he knew would be his death. A few days later he
was betrayed by his servants and killed, together with his son.
Cicero reached the shore and at once embarked. The wind stood
fair; but Cicero as usual faltered. Perhaps after all Octavian
would relent? He landed, travelled twelve miles towards Rome—
and changed his mind again. Back he went to the seashore and
spent a tortured night of indecision. Next morning he bade his
servants carry him by sea to another of his villas farther south. On
reaching it, Cicero entered the house and lay down to rest. His
servants, well knowing the danger he was in, "partly by entreaty,
partly by force" bundled him into his litter and set out once more
for the shore. Too late. The assassins were upon them, led by an
officer whom Cicero had successfully defended against a charge
of murdering his father. Finding the doors shut, they broke them
open, to be met by Cicero's servants, who said they had no idea
of their master's whereabouts—all except one: an emancipated
slave of Quintus Cicero, a Greek to whom Cicero himself had
given a liberal education, told the pursuers that their quarry was
on his way to the shore through a little wood. A centurion called
Herennius with a few soldiers dashed off to intercept the litter
as it came out of the thicket. When Cicero saw him, he
ordered his bearers to set down the litter, "and stroking his chin,
as he used to, with his left hand, he looked steadfastly upon

his murderers, his person covered with dust, his beard and hair untrimmed, and his face worn with his troubles." He stretched his neck out of the litter. Herennius killed him and cut off his head, and by Antony's express order his right hand as well, by which the Philippics had been written. When these relics were brought to him, Antony burst out laughing and had them exposed on the rostra, "a sight which the Roman people shuddered to behold, and they believed they saw there not the face of Cicero, but the image of Antony's own soul." So much for Greek gratitude and Roman decency.

Cicero was in truth the last of the republicans. With all his faults, Cicero embodied the old, steadfast Roman principles. In antiquity, he was compared, as he has been ever since, with Demosthenes, for Demosthenes too fought to the death for a republican idea which had in fact perished while its greatest exponent still lived. But Cicero, if the inferior of Demosthenes in sheer oratorical power (and as a great French critic said, with Cicero you are always conscious of the man, whereas with Demosthenes it is the words themselves that are the live actors), nevertheless achieved something that Demosthenes did not, something indeed that very few men have ever done: he created a language. Latin prose to the very end of the empire and indeed down to our own days is Ciceronian prose. Christian saints modelled themselves on Cicero. Ambrose acknowledged him as his master. Augustine tells us in his *Confessions* that it was a treatise of Cicero's (now, alas, lost) that first turned his thoughts to serious things. His contemporary, Jerome, describes a dream in which he appeared before the Examiner, who asked him what he was. "A Christian," said Jerome. "No," said the Examiner, "You are a Ciceronian." Such was to be the abiding magic of this man. Some years after Cicero's death Augustus, as he had now become, found one of his grandchildren reading a book of Cicero's. The boy tried to hide it. Caesar took it from him and stood for a time silent, turning over the scroll. Then, giving it back to the lad, he said, "My child, this was a learned man, and a lover of his country." The verdict of Cicero's betrayer has been accepted and confirmed by posterity for he had indeed, in Julius' own words, "advanced the boundaries of the Latin genius."

The blood-bath was over; but the Triumvirs were by no means yet secure. Sextus Pompeius, the son of the man who had suppressed piracy, was now the pirate-king, and threatened Rome's food-supply. In the East the menace was equally sharp. Brutus had ingratiated himself with the Athenians and had drawn to his side many of the young Romans then studying there, including Cicero's son and the youthful Horace. Cassius was in control of Asia, and together with Brutus now set about a systematic spoliation of its opulent cities, while their fleet intercepted some treasure-ships bound for Rome. Dolabella had committed suicide. Old Pompeians, homeless since Pharsalus, rallied to their standards. With their control of the sea and of the richest part of the empire the republican leaders reckoned that they could hold the Triumvirs until hunger or disaffection wore them down.

Antony was not thus to be humbled. Crossing the Adriatic in late summer, he assembled the army he intended for his Eastern campaign, twenty legions in all, and sent ahead another eight as an advance-guard. This body advanced along the Via Egnatia, the trunk road to the East which traversed Macedonia and ended at Neapolis, now Kavalla. They had almost reached that port when they came in contact with the republicans, who by a flanking movement forced them to fall back on Amphipolis, themselves occupying the town of Philippi, which lies a few miles west of Neapolis, athwart the Via Egnatia.

The battle of Philippi—or rather battles, for as we shall see there were two—although it was a turning point in the recorded history of man, holds little interest as a feat of arms. Brutus and Cassius had fortified their camp on the rising ground above the lush water-meadows, with an assured supply-line behind them and easy communications with the sea. Their left flank, as they faced Antony and Octavian, was protected by a marsh. The Caesarians had no such advantages: they could be victualled only from Amphipolis, and that by a circuitous and difficult hill road. It was to their interest therefore to force an engagement. During

the first days of October Antony repeatedly tried to bring his
opponents to battle, but without result. He then decided to
outflank them by building a causeway across the marsh. Cassius
started counterworks, and so the battle finally took place almost
by accident. The two sides were evenly matched. Each disposed
of nineteen legions. The Caesarians were better trained, but the
republicans were superior in cavalry. The result of this first clash
was odd: Brutus captured Octavian's camp, and Antony routed
Cassius. Owing to faulty liaison work, Cassius was ignorant of
Brutus' victory and rather than become a prisoner fell on his
sword. Brutus, as soon as he heard of Cassius' defeat, hurried
to his aid; but it was only when he arrived at the little hill
above the camp that he learned of Cassius' death and was confronted by his headless corpse. After saluting him as "the last of
the Romans" he sent the body across to the island of Thasos for
quiet burial. The slaves among his prisoners he massacred, most
of the freemen being released. The winter rains had now begun,
and the Caesarian camp down by the river became water-
logged. Moreover Brutus' fleet had intercepted their reinforcements and supplies: it was therefore essential to bring matters
to a final decision. Unfortunately Brutus' intelligence-échelon
again proved defective, and he was in ignorance of his naval
success, which would have made a second battle unnecessary.
After remaining inactive for three weeks, he yielded to the
pressure of his troops and gave battle on the afternoon of the
23rd October. It was a short, brisk engagement, which resulted
in the rout of Brutus' army, the storming of his camp and the
flight of many of his men. Among those who ran away was
Horace; as he was later to write, he had "thrown away his
shield," a phrase doubly clever: it showed Augustus, whose close
and admired friend the poet had become, that his heart was
not really in the republican cause, and it equated Roman Horace
with the Greek poet Archilochus who had done exactly the same
thing in almost the same place six hundred years earlier. Brutus,
when he too was counselled to fly, replied: "Yes, we must fly,
but not with our feet—with our hands," and killed himself. An-

tony gave him honourable burial and sent his ashes to his mother Servilia.

With Brutus died the republican cause—the republic was already dead. Shakespeare, following Plutarch, has perpetuated the idea of Brutus as "the noblest Roman of them all." This he was very far from being. Avaricious, harsh—he had shown himself to be both. He owed his reputation to two adventitious factors: that he was the descendant of a republican hero whom his contemporaries expected him to emulate, and to the patronage of the man he was to murder, who was in all probability his father, Julius Caesar. Cicero was, as Buchan points out, "in a far truer sense the last Republican."

Both Cicero and Brutus were dead now, and so was the republic. Who was to rule Rome? That question was to take eleven years to answer, and to a brief analysis of it, the last chapter of this study will be devoted.

CHAPTER XIX

THE LAST ROUND

THE fighting was over, but there was as yet no peace. The pirate fleets of Sextus Pompeius and Ahenobarbus, each reinforced by republican refugees, still threatened Rome's supply-routes. The army, swollen to the huge figure of forty-seven legions by the surrendered remnants of Brutus' forces, was in itself a menace. It had to be reduced, and land and bounties found for the disbanded veterans. Money had to be raised. Most immediate task of all, the Triumvirate itself must be readjusted. Lepidus was a failure. He was suspected of collusion with Sextus, and as consul had been the creature of the odious Fulvia. He was, in Shakespeare's phrase, "a slight unmeritable man, meet to be sent on errands." Above all there was the inevitable clash of ambition between Octavian, now twenty-one, and Antony, just twice his age. It was this rivalry which was to mould and dominate the history of the next decade; for all the other difficulties were overcome one by one. First of all came demobilization. Eleven legions, those which were content to remain with the colours, now formed the standing army. Six of them went to Antony, leaving Octavian with five. The provinces were reallocated. Cisalpine Gaul, already enfranchised, now ceased to be a province and became part of the motherland—a step long overdue. Antony was to be master of all Gaul, Celtic as well as Narbonese, transferred from Lepidus. Octavian received Spain, the richest single province of the West, and Africa, plus the nominal possession of Sicily and Sardinia, which were still in the hands of Sextus Pompeius. On the face of it, Antony was the winner, as, on the face of it, he deserved to be. He, not Octavian, was the hero of Philippi. By the Gallic takeover he received yet another great army, no less than twenty-four legions commanded by generals on whom he could count. Then too, he was to hold the gorgeous East in fee, to control its opulence and to use it as the base for his great Parthian campaign, the "grand design" inherited from Julius Caesar. As it turned out, this division apparently so favourable to Antony was to lead to his undoing. In the first place, the process of demobilization and land settlement, which Antony knew must bring Octavian into conflict with great landlords and smallholders alike, was so skillfully conducted that in the end the gratitude of the verterans far outweighed the enmity of the displaced civilians. Hardship there certainly was: of some cases poets have left us their record—Horace found that his father's estate had been liquidated and was forced to support himself as a junior civil servant. Virgil would have lost his little holding near Mantua but for the intervention of powerful friends. Two other poets, Tibullus and Propertius, were reduced to penury. How many more, mute and inglorious, must have suffered the same fate? Nevertheless, in the end, by tact and clemency, Octavian contrived to retain the fidelity of the soldiers without goading the landed interest into overt resistance. (Nor was settlement confined to Italy: Philippi had been constituted a military colony on the morrow of the battle, the first of many such foundations.) Fortunately for Octavian, what might have proved a long and damaging stalemate was brought to an end by the rash stupidity of Fulvia and Antony's brother Lucius. Jealous of Octavian's success, they did all they could to obstruct him, even inducing Antony's officers to prevent Octavian's dispatching soldiers to Spain through Gaul—Antony's domain. Octavian tried persuasion: he was, he pointed out, acting in complete loyalty to the written compact which had been drawn up between him and Antony after Philippi. Let the Senate decide, he urged. Fulvia was for violence, which at once roused Octavian's old soldiers to take up arms in his cause. Fulvia occupied Praeneste (Palestrina) and girded on a sword. Octavian's troops called for a meeting at Gabii, which Fulvia and Lucius denounced as a "jack-boot senate" and declined to attend. Octavian now acted with surprising speed and resolution. He secured Brundisium, to prevent a landing by Ahenobarbus. He cancelled the dispatch of troops

for Spain and gave Agrippa a flying command with which to
bring Lucius to terms. Lucius shut himself up in Perusia
(Perugia). No one came to his rescue, and in the early spring of
the year 40 he was forced to surrender. Octavian proved to be a
gentle victor: he could not openly antagonize Antony. He allowed
Fulvia and Lucius to retire into obscurity; but Perusia was
burned and sacked, and many of the malignants of lesser con-
sequence were put to death. There was one last rebellion in
Campania, led by Tiberius Claudius Nero. Octavian allowed
Nero, his wife Livia and their son Tiberius to escape to Sicily.
Livia was later to be his devoted wife, Tiberius his successor as
Imperator.

Octavian was now the undisputed master of Italy and of Rome.
Antony had neither intended nor foreseen such an outcome. Like
Pompey, like Cassius and Brutus, he had been deluded by the
lure of the East, the *fata morgana* of Roman dynasts. This
miscalculation was Antony's first mistake. His second was Cleopatra.

As with Brutus, so with Cleopatra: the picture drawn by
Shakespeare is not the real original. Cleopatra as "the lass un-
parallel'd," as Antony's "Egyptian dish"—the very embodiment
of sexual seduction, that is the Cleopatra of the popular image.
Cleopatra was not that. Neither was she the "serpent of old
Nile," the new Dido, or the female Hannibal of contemporary
Roman belief. The Romans really did fear Cleopatra, who was
to them the embodiment of the resurgent East and a threat to
Rome so long as she should live. In fact, Cleopatra was neither
a nymphomaniac nor was she an oriental tyrant. She was of pure
Graeco-Macedonian descent, without a drop of Egyptian blood.
"So far from being love's plaything," says Buchan, "she was from
beginning to end the *politique*, pursuing the game of high
ambition with a masterly coolness." Her aim was simple, to restore the kingdom of the Ptolemies to its ancient extent and
grandeur. This she could do only with the aid of Rome, which
meant that she must win over Rome's master. It is possible that
she did love Julius Caesar: he was certainly captivated by her.
Not that she was beautiful. Her portraits show a masterful face,

with a firm chin, a prominent nose and a high forehead. She attracted men by her magnetic charm and held them by her prismatic intellect. She was a brilliant linguist—she had even learned the Egyptian tongue, the first and last of her dynasty to do so. She was amazingly versatile. Plutarch liked neither her nor Antony, his antipathy for Antony being heightened by the fact that the Roman had used Plutarch's great-grandfather as a pack-horse to transport provisions across the Aetolian mountains in the hectic days before Actium. His grandfather had also handed down a good deal of backstairs gossip he had picked up in Alexandria during the hey-day of Antony's enslavement by Cleopatra. Nevertheless, Plutarch's life of Antony is among his most vivid narratives—indeed among the most intimate and glittering productions in the whole range of ancient literature. No doubt that is one of the reasons which induced Shakespeare to use it as the basis for his drama. It so happens that in one passage we can actually, as it were, look over Shakespeare's shoulder and watch him write. He is describing Cleopatra's arrival at Tarsus, whither she had been summoned by Antony in order that she might contribute to his war-chest for the campaign against Parthia. Shakespeare transcribes North almost word for word:

> "The barge she sat in, like a burnish'd throne,
>   Burn'd on the water: the poop was beaten gold;
>   Purple the sails, and so perfumed that
>   The winds were love-sick with them; the oars were silver,
>   Which to the tune of flutes kept stroke and made
>   The water which they beat to follow faster,
>   As amorous of their strokes. For her own person,
>   It beggar'd all description: she did lie
>   In her pavilion, cloth-of-gold of tissue,
>   O'er-picturing that Venus where we see
>   The fancy outwork nature: on each side her
>   Stood pretty dimpled boys, like smiling Cupids,
>   With divers-colour'd fans, whose wind did seem
>   To glow the delicate cheeks which they did cool,
>   And what they undid did."

Antony was captivated. He had known Cleopatra when she was fourteen and he was serving in Egypt with Gabinius; he must often have seen her in Rome when she was living there as Caesar's mistress. But now she was twenty-nine, mature and masterful. Antony was ravished by her. Forgetful of all else, he followed her back to Alexandria. "There in the winter," to quote Buchan, "while Perusia was starving, she played an adroit game. She was a genuine Egyptian patriot and, so far as our evidence goes, showed notable talent in her administration of the land. She was endeared to the native Egyptian people, for she spoke their tongue, was respectful to their gods, and had about herself a divine aura as a reincarnation of Isis. She desired to make her country the richest and most cultivated on earth, and for that she must have the support of the Roman legions. The bait was the conquest of Parthia, which to Antony seemed vital to Rome and for which the wealth of Egypt would provide the funds. Therefore her task was to make herself indispensable to Antony, and during the winter of 41–40 B.C., she wove her enchantments. She was his boon companion, his partner in fantastic adventures, but she did not forget her purpose. She fostered his ambitions but gave him nothing, neither funds from her treasury nor her love, till she was certain that he would pay her price."

Meanwhile back in Italy Octavian was improving his position at Antony's expense. A Parthian invasion had thrown all Syria into chaos, and Antony had been forced to quit Cleopatra temporarily to cope with the Eastern peril, increased by the accession of Roman renegades to the Parthian side. Learning now that Octavian had seized Gaul, and with it the very legions on which Antony was relying for his Parthian campaign, he crossed to Athens, where he was met by his wife Fulvia and his brother Lucius. He decided that he must confront Octavian and sailed for Italy. Neither the Triumvirs nor their troops were in the mood for war. Then most opportunely Fulvia died. It was thus possible in October of 40 to patch up an accommodation at Brundisium. Octavian was to have all the West, except for Lepidus' Africa, and Antony the East, from the Ionian Sea to the Euphrates. The pact was to be sealed by the marriage of Antony to Octavian's sister, Octavia, a saintly and devoted lady, one of the very few attractive characters in the Rome of her day. She had been married to Gaius Marcellus, and their son, Marcus Claudius Marcellus, was later to marry Octavian's daughter Julia and to be regarded as the heir and successor of Augustus. Alas for human hopes! He died at the age of twenty. He was made immortal by Virgil in lines which so moved his mother when the poet recited them to her that she fainted; but fortunately came to in time to give him a nice present. It was this gentle spirit who was now to be yoked with the turbulent Antony. Their friendship thus superficially restored, the two Triumvirs visited Rome together; but their reception was cold, because the citizens were threatened with starvation owing to Sextus' control of the sea. Clearly an end must be made of the pirate-king, or if that were not possible he must be won over. Neither course was easy. After a fruitless meeting at Puteoli, a pact was entered into at Misenum, a promontory at the northern end of the bay of Naples. During the negotiations Sextus gave a grand entertainment on board his flag-ship. In the course of it, when the guests were merry, and jesting about Antony and Cleopatra, Menas, one of Sextus' aides, came behind him and whispered: "Shall I cut the cables, and make you master not only of Sicily and Sardinia, but of the whole Roman empire?" Sextus pondered for a little, and then said: "Menas, you could have done it without telling me. We must be content now: I do not break my word"—a thoroughly Roman attitude in every aspect of it.

The new, pacific outlook was celebrated by Virgil in his Fourth Eclogue, which is a thanksgiving ode to harmony and the prospect of a better age. A child is to be born who will inaugurate a golden age. Of what parentage the child was to spring the poet does not specify, possibly of the union of Octavian and his wife Scribonia, Sextus' wife's aunt. To the Middle Ages, the poem seemed to foretell the birth of the Messiah, and as such entitled Virgil to the near-sanctity he was to enjoy in, for instance, the *Divine Comedy* of Dante. In fact, the treaty of Misenum proved to be a dead letter. Antony overreached Sextus by depriving him of the revenues of the Peloponnese, which was to have been one of his provinces. Sextus was moreover piqued because the Triumvirs refused to recognize him as an equal. He soon reverted to his old ploys, plundering the corn convoys and raiding the Italian coast. There could now be no two ways about it. Reluctant as the young Octavian—he was now twenty-four—might be to take up arms against the son of one of Rome's greatest citizens, a citizen, too, who had fallen a victim to his "father's" ambition, whose very house was now occupied by Antony, yet he could no longer tolerate the menace of this blackmailer, however popular Sextus might be with some of Octavian's opponents. The youthful Caesar appealed for help to Antony. Antony came as far as Brundisium, but finding that Octavian had been delayed, merely left him a message bidding him respect the pact, and then went back to Athens. Octavian must act by himself. New ships were built, bases established at Brundisium and Puteoli. Octavian published the terms of the treaty of Misenum, and with that calculating callousness with which he regarded matrimony, divorced Scribonia on the very day of their daughter's birth.

The divorce was a political proclamation of the severance of all ties between Octavian and Sextus; but it gave him the opportunity of marrying Livia, the daughter of an ardent anti-Caesarian, and currently the wife of Tiberius Claudius Nero. A second divorce was arranged, and Livia became the wife of Octavian. She was to be his friend and guide throughout his long life; and when he died, her son by her first husband would succeed his stepfather as Rome's second Emperor, Tiberius.

Lucky as he had now become in love, Octavian was to continue to be unlucky in war. His campaign against Sextus in 38 was disastrous. He lost half his fleet, leaving Sextus to proclaim himself the son of Neptune as he strutted in his sea-green robes. For the next year's campaign Octavian made better preparations. Agrippa was summoned from Gaul where he was governor. He was also consul-elect and now became commander-in-chief. He brought with him the reputation of a victorious general who, the first since the great Julius himself, had carried Roman arms beyond the Rhine; but with characteristic modesty he refused a triumph while Sextus was still unbeaten and Rome living on short commons. Agrippa was taking no risks; the new campaign was to be organized down to the last detail. The first requirement was a really good harbour, protected from storm and foe alike. We may still admire Agrippa's creation. Near the shore east of Misenum, at the northern end of the bay of Naples, there are two lakes, Lucrinus and Avernus. Agrippa joined them by canals to each other and to the sea. Here the new fleet could be assembled in absolute security. Freed slaves were instructed in oarsmanship for a whole year; and in the manipulation of a new device of Agrippa's whereby grapnels were shot from catapults to facilitate the holding and boarding of an enemy ship. Then in the spring of 37 Antony appeared off Tarentum with three hundred ships. This was not mere good fellowship: for his Parthian campaign Antony needed troops which only Octavian could supply and he hoped to trade his ships for them. With Antony was Octavia, who was able to overcome the not unnatural suspicions of her brother. The Triumvirate was renewed for another five years, *de facto;* but it was really a duovirate, because Lepidus counted for less than nothing now. Antony was to have the East, Octavian the West. Antony was to give his colleague 120 ships, in return for the promise of four legions. In addition, Octavia arranged, as a sort of personal bonus, that her husband should give her brother ten light frigates and receive a thousand picked men from Octavian's bodyguard.

The campaign against Sextus opened on the first of the Julian month, July of 36 B.C. There was to be a triple attack on Sicily, led by Octavian from Puteoli, Statilius Taurus from Tarentum and Lepidus from Africa, with sixteen legions supported by cavalry. Although Sextus was outnumbered he contrived, aided by the weather, to win the first round. On the 3rd of the month, a violent storm sent Taurus back to Tarentum; and Octavian lost half his ships off Sorrento. Lepidus was the only one who succeeded in landing: he blockaded Lilybaeum, on the south coast over against Carthage. This set-back was serious for Octavian: Rome was becoming restive, Sextus reviving the spirits of

the old Pompeians. Maecenas was dispatched to the capital, while
Octavian repaired his shattered squadrons. By mid-August he
was ready to put to sea again. This time it looked as though all
would be well. Agrippa was able to occupy several coast towns,
but once again Octavian failed. He was indeed no soldier. This
moment was the nadir of his fortunes, and he begged a companion to kill him; but they both managed to regain the mainland. Meanwhile Agrippa had effected a junction with Octavian's
lieutenant, and together they closed in on Messana, Sextus' base.
Sextus made a desperate sortie but was defeated off Mylae, on
the north coast of Sicily, on 3rd September. It was the end.
Sextus managed to escape and set out for the East, with the aim
of throwing himself on Antony's mercy; but on the way he
changed his mind and thought it would be more prudent to side
with the Parthians. His intrigues became known to Antony,
whose deputy, after bearing with Sextus for a time, finally had
him executed. Yet such was the reverence which the name of
Pompey still inspired that when that officer later appeared in
the theatre in Rome, he was expelled by the execrations of the
entire audience. Lepidus, to whom Messana had surrendered,
made one last effort to exploit his nuisance value. He demanded
to be awarded Sicily in addition to his province of Africa. But
his troops went over to Octavian, whom he was bound to solicit
as a suppliant. With contemptuous clemency Octavian allowed
him to remain high priest, living in opulent retirement until the
end of his obscure days. (He died in 13 B.C.) Of the legions,
some were disbanded, some rewarded with bounties, others with
grants of land and decorations. Agrippa was given a golden
crown adorned with ships' beaks, which he was to wear on all
triumphal occasions. Ungainly though the bauble must have
been, Agrippa deserved his reward, for it was he who had
organized the victory.

Now surely there would be peace? Octavian was twenty-seven,
and as Buchan points out, he "had attained a power which none
but Alexander and Julius had held before in history." He had been
powerfully aided by his ministers, specially Agrippa; but the final
outcome was due to his own modesty, resolution and foresight.

His return to Rome was a triumphal progress. Gentle and simple alike flocked out of the city to welcome him home, Octavian the bringer of peace. The battle of Mylae was to be commemorated by a yearly festival, a memorial arch was to be erected, a golden statue dedicated with an inscription recording the restoration of peace after the long years of strife. Octavian was to have an official residence next to the plot on which he intended to build his temple of Apollo. Like Julius, he was permitted to wear the laurel wreath and—most important of all—his person was to be sacrosanct. Taxes were remitted, debts cancelled. The poets sang of the joys of security, of happy farms and fruitful fields. The sun shone from an unclouded sky. No, not quite, not yet. There was still a cloud in the East. A struggle between Octavian and Antony was inevitable despite all that Octavia had done, and would do again, to avert it.

For four years Octavian strove to rebuild the West. Carefully and laboriously the whole fabric of the state was overhauled. The frontiers were safeguarded, and Octavian himself, though no strategist, won a reputation for personal bravery in fighting in what is now Croatia. Antony, meanwhile, was declining to his own doom. After three years spent happily with Octavia at Athens, he grew weary of her "too holy, cold and stiff conversation." In the autumn of 37 he summoned Cleopatra (whom he had neglected for nearly four years) to Antioch. He needed her money. He was also in love with her, and for love he was ready to lose half the world. Cleopatra did not love him: she loved no man. She was in love with ambition, and Antony was the man to forward it. Not long after, they were married according to Egyptian rites. In Roman law Antony could neither have two wives at once nor contract a valid marriage with a foreigner. It was thus possible for Octavian for the time being to take no notice of the union: it was mere concubinage, however wounding to Octavia and therefore to himself.

As a wedding-present, Cleopatra simply demanded the restitution of the empire of the Ptolemies as it was in the days of her great predecessor Ptolemy II Philadelphus. Antony handed over all he could: Cyprus, the coasts of Phoenicia and Palestine (except for Tyre and Sidon), central Syria, a slice of Cilicia. Cleopatra wanted Herod's kingdom as well, but here Antony was firm. For one thing Herod was an essential bulwark against Parthia, and for another they were very old friends; so all Cleopatra got was the famous balsam groves down by Jericho and a share of the wealth of Petra. Cleopatra's son by Antony, born in 36, was called Philadelphus to commemorate the re-establishment of the Ptolemaic empire.

Antony pleased the Egyptians. To them he was a god and Cleopatra a goddess, Osiris and Isis, as for the Greeks they were Dionysus and Aphrodite. The twins whom Cleopatra had borne him four years before were now acknowledged and called Alexander the sun and Cleopatra the moon. "Alexander" was to be an augury for Antony's forthcoming conquest of Parthia. That is why he had summoned Cleopatra to meet him at Antioch—where, as at Tarsus in 41, she had at once taken the initiative for her own ends. The conquest of Parthia meant nothing to her. Thus it came about that when Antony did finally mount his Parthian campaign—the dream of so many years—it ended in disaster. The Parthians destroyed part of his troops in battle, his intelligence service broke down, his Armenian allies deserted him. Having lost twenty-two thousand men, Antony managed to bring his tattered remnant back to Syria.

The two lovers, he forty-six and she ten years younger, repaired to Alexandria. They were still to the populace "The Inimitable Livers," the club they had founded six years before; still they revelled and frolicked, by day and by night. In the year 24 Antony roused himself. He invaded Armenia, conquered it and then lost it; for which exploit he celebrated a triumph in Alexandria. This exotic festival, which was presided over by Cleopatra on a golden throne, led men to believe not only that Cleopatra was being glorified as the embodiment of the goddess of Rome, but that Antony actually intended to establish Alexandria as the capital in succession to Rome itself. A yet more fantastic and fatal ceremony was to follow. A huge concourse of people was assembled in the gymnasium, above whom sat Antony and Cleopatra side by side on thrones, Cleopatra being robed

as Isis. Slightly lower, on other thrones sat their three children,
and with them Ptolemy Caesar, known as Caesarion, little Caesar,
Cleopatra's son by Julius. Antony addressed the people. Cleopatra, he said, had been Caesar's wife (à la mode de Macédoine),
Caesarion was Caesar's legitimate son, and he himself was about
to recognize that sacred link. He then proclaimed Cleopatra
Queen of Kings and Ptolemy Caesar King of Kings, joint monarchs of Cyprus and Egypt, and overlords of the kingdoms or
domains of Cleopatra's other children. To Alexander, who was
arrayed in the robes of an Achaemenid sovereign and accompanied by an Armenian bodyguard, Antony gave for his kingdom
Armenia and the overlordship of Parthia and Media, everything,
that is, east of the Euphrates, of none of which did he actually
dispose. Upon Ptolemy, who was apparelled as a Macedonian
with a Macedonian bodyguard, he bestowed the Egyptian possessions in Syria and Cilicia, and the overlordship of all the
client kingdoms "as far as the Hellespont." Cleopatra Selene
received Libya and Cyrenaica. On this strange dream-sequence
(for when it was enacted it was no more than that) the comment
of the Cambridge Ancient History is apt: "It was a glorious house
of cards; whether it could be solidified depended on the answer
to one prosaic question—would the legions fight?"

To find the answer to that question we must return to Rome,
workaday, practical Rome. It had for long been clear to every
political augur in the capital, which meant to every articulate
Roman, that sooner or later Octavian must break with Antony.
The two men were wholly different, in temperament and in
orientation. Octavian had from the outset of his career shown
that his aim was the peaceful development of Rome, of Italy
as the motherland of Rome, and of western Europe as the
patrimony of Rome. Already, in the few years since Philippi, he
had begun the great task to which he was to devote the rest of
his long life. Antony, on the other hand, had spent his days
dawdling and dallying in the East, his private life a travesty of
Roman mores, his public acts a parody of the great Pompey's.
He had, it is true, grievances against Octavian: the legions promised at Tarentum had not been delivered, nor had Antony been

consulted over the demotion of Lepidus and the reappropriation of his province. Octavia had done her utmost to avert the inevitable clash: in the spring of 35 she had even started for the East herself with two thousand legionaries and money as well. Antony accepted the men and the funds, but brusquely ordered Octavia to remain in the West. She stayed on in Athens where she brought up not only her own two daughters by Antony, but Fulvia's children as well.

Antony's grievances, real though they were, were as nothing compared with Antony's transgressions. He still had his followers in Rome, and Octavian knew that he must walk warily against his rival. But the execution of Sextus had caused many to turn against Antony, for Pompey was still "the shadow of the great name"; and now Antony's assumption of oriental sovereignty, joined with an Eastern queen, his "donation" of some of Rome's richest provinces to that queen's children—that must put him out of court.

In 33 B.C. Octavian was consul for the second time. His star was in the ascendant; his solid success on the frontiers and at home had won him the suffrages if not the hearts of the Romans. This year, such was their confidence in his probity, they authorized him to create new patrician families in order to replenish the priesthood. Antony meanwhile was engaged in futile negotiations with the king of Media. He was stationed at Ephesus where Cleopatra had joined him with a treasure of some ten million dollars. He returned abusive answers to Octavian's letters; and the year closed amid their mutual vituperation.

The consuls for the year 32, Sosius and Ahenobarbus, were both supporters of Antony. So out of touch with Roman opinion was the latter that he actually addressed a dispatch to them asking for approval of all his *acta*, including the donations. The consuls suppressed the dispatch: instead of reading it, Sosius delivered a vigorous harangue in Antony's favour, and was only prevented from moving a motion of censure against Octavian by the interposition of a tribune. Both consuls and about a third of the Senate left to join Antony.

Then in May came the news that Antony had divorced Octavia, had been publicly wedded to Cleopatra and had declared Caesarion to be Julius' heir, thereby relegating Octavian to legal bastardy. Clearly the crisis was at hand.

But how was Octavian to bring it to a head? The consuls had withheld the dispatch in which Antony had confessed himself an outlaw and a renegade. How then could the people of Rome be brought to regard him in the same sinister light as Octavian saw him? At this psychological moment a friend arrived from Egypt with the news that Antony had made a will, embodying all his donations, affirming the legitimacy of Caesarion, and requiring, moreover, that if he died in Rome his body, after being paraded through the Forum, should be dispatched to Alexandria for burial with that of Cleopatra. A will! What a godsend! Had not Antony won over the populace after the death of Caesar by reading Julius' will? Now Octavian would undo Antony by the very same means. The will was deposited with the Vestal virgins. They very properly refused to give it up, saying that if Octavian wanted it he must come and fetch it by force. Octavian did not hesitate: the will was soon in his hands. He published it. Not everyone approved of this; it was unfair, they said, to hold a man responsible during his lifetime for what was to be done after his death; but the majority were moved less by legal proprieties than by the actual enormities of the dispositions. The mere fact that he desired to be buried in the mausoleum of the Ptolemies showed, said Octavian, that he intended to transfer the capital from Rome to Alexandria. The Senate—from which most of Antony's supporters had already withdrawn—responded to popular indignation.

Antony was deprived of his *imperium,* and his election to the consulate for the next year, 31, was annulled. In the autumn, Octavian in his priestly capacity, accompanied by the senators, solemnly declared war before the temple of the war-goddess. But only against Cleopatra. Herein he showed characteristic astuteness, if not guile. Having four years before announced the end of civil wars, Octavian did not want to burden himself with the odium of having started them again. By declaring Cleopatra the enemy, he was able to concentrate against her all the anti-foreign fervour of the mob. It was to be not Octavian versus Antony but West against East. In any case what did it matter? Antony now was no longer his own master, but the slave of an alien mistress: he would do just what she told him to do. And that is what he did.

Had Antony been a free agent, it was still possible for him to reach an accommodation with Octavian. His financial resources were, as has been seen, enormous, whereas Octavian could keep his army and fleet in being only by heavy and unpopular taxa-tion: free citizens were required to pay an income-tax at the rate equivalent to twenty-five cents on the dollar—a swingeing sum in those far-off days. Freedmen had to pay half as much. Even in antiquity, critics urged that Antony's great error was not to invade Italy while Octavian was thus embarrassed. It was Cleo-patra who made it impossible. He could not bring her with him, and she refused to let him out of her sight, lest Octavia win him back. It was due to Cleopatra's spite also that by far the ablest of the client-kings, Herod of Judaea, a man of the first ability and an old friend of Antony's, was not present at his head-quarters, where his advice and support would have been in-valuable. Cleopatra hated Herod, and so contrived that instead of bringing his army and fleet to Antony's aid he wasted his strength in a futile war with the Nabataeans of Petra, who, like Herod himself, had actually sent troops to help Antony.

Octavian had great advantages in morale. His soldiers were fighting for their country, they were homogeneous and well-disciplined, they were commanded by Agrippa, the best soldier of the age. Antony had five hundred warships, great men-of-war which an ancient author compared to floating fortresses. His army consisted of over sixty thousand Romans plus about eighty thou-sand Asiatic cavalry and infantry. Against him, Octavian mobil-ized some four hundred ships—of far lighter build—eighty thou-sand foot and twelve thousand horse. Both the armies were very large by ancient standards.

Antony and Cleopatra had spent the winter in Greece, amid revellings and dissipation. Not only had Antony bidden his dependent monarchs to send him supplies and armaments, but all their actors and singers as well. "So that," says Plutarch, "while pretty nearly the whole world was filled with groans and lamentations, this one island [Samos] for some days resounded with piping and harping, theatres filling, and choruses playing." When the festival was over Antony allotted the lovely city of Priene, in Asia Minor, to the exhausted players, and himself went with Cleopatra to Athens. The Egyptian queen was jealous of the reception the Athenians had given to Octavia, of whom they were very fond. She insisted on similar honour for herself, and Antony in his capacity of "Athenian citizen" led the deputation which conferred them on her. In the spring, the doting mallard and his mate removed to Patrae, the port at the western end of the gulf of Corinth. His fleet was strung out along the west coast of Greece, from Corfu in the north to Methone in the far south of the Peloponnese. The reason for this disposition was that the fleet could be supplied only from Egypt, and this line alone could guarantee its communications with Alexandria. The main part of the army was concentrated in the centre of the line, that is to say at Actium, the southern promontory which shelters the Ambracian gulf opposite Prevesa which, not unnaturally, also harboured the greater portion of his fleet. Thus it came about that for the third time in less than twenty years the fate of Rome was decided in Greece.

To confront Antony's mobilization Octavian was compelled to concentrate at Brundisium and Taranto, as a preliminary to crossing to Greece. In order to safeguard his position in Italy during what might be a critical absence, he had taken a bold but effective step. He invited the whole of the West to swear allegiance to him, senators, soldiers, civilians, high and low alike, as their leader against Antony. The oath was to be voluntary, and Bononia (Bologna) as a client-city of Antony's was excluded, but many of Antony's colonists rallied to his rival, so that in later years, Augustus in the great record of his reign (of which a version survives at Ankara) could say: "The whole of Italy of its own accord swore fealty to me." This acknowledgement that to one man, irrespective of legal sanctions, Rome must now commit its fortune and future, is the hairline, as it were, that separates the republic from the empire. Early in 31 Octavian crossed to Greece, unopposed by Antony, who is henceforth more than ever a dream-figure. With him, the young Caesar took all those senators and knights who, despite the oath, might be tempted to make trouble if the course of affairs seemed to favour it. Maecenas was installed in Rome as his deputy. Agrippa, now thirty-two, enabled Octavian to reach Epirus unscathed, by a brilliant naval action. He seized Methone, killing its commander, Bogudes of Mauretania, and immediately after occupied Leucas and Patrae. Antony's lifeline was thus severed: he could count on no more supplies from Egypt. Meanwhile in the north, Octavian's attempt to surprise Antony's base at Actium had failed, and when a cavalry sortie by Antony had proved equally unsuccessful, stalemate set in, but with the odds in favour of Octavian, whose communications were assured and whose troops were encamped in healthy surroundings, whereas those of Antony were suffering from malaria and hunger. Disputes and desertions added to his difficulties. Nor was Cleopatra of the slightest help to him. Plutarch (who it must be remembered is a hostile witness) says that Antony "out of complaisance to his mistress wanted the victory to be gained by sea." The facts are clearly summarized by Buchan. "Cleopatra had as little love for this campaign as she had for the Parthian war, for if Antony defeated Octavian and entered Rome in triumph, he would pass out of her orbit." It was impossible to commit all to a land engagement, with Antony's army in its now demoralized state. "Cleopatra wished to use the fleet and fight a way out; if they succeeded good and well; if not, she and Antony could at least escape to Egypt, refit their armies, and defend the East against Octavian." A deserter informed Octavian of this plan and he took measures to frustrate it. At first he thought of pretending to let the enemy vessels escape, relying on the sight of Antony's scuttling to Egypt to produce large-scale desertions, and then overhauling them; but Agrippa pointed out that, once out of the gulf, Antony's warships would get away intact, because Octavian's lighter ships would be unable to come up with them as they sailed before the wind. An engagement was inevitable. On the 2nd September Antony, having burned such ships as he did not need, embarked about half his army in the remainder and allowed Cleopatra to stow all his treasure-chests in her own squadron. The battle began in the early afternoon, just at the time when the north-west breeze freshens in the summer on those coasts. From the outset Agrippa's fleet had the best of it, harassing Antony's men-of-war much as Drake would one day humble the giants of the Spanish Armada. Antony's ships began to surrender or desert: both his wings were in danger of being outflanked. Both fleets, it must be remembered, were composed of galleys, however they might vary in burthen, that is to say, of ships propelled by oars, whose object was to ram and board, or sink, their opponents. Sail was employed solely for bringing a ship into action or for taking it out of it. When therefore at the height of the battle Cleopatra suddenly hoisted her sails, consternation struck the whole of Antony's host: it could mean only one thing, that Cleopatra had given up the action and was making for Egypt, leaving Octavian as victor. When Antony left his own ship and joined Cleopatra abroad her flag-ship, consternation turned to despair. A few ships reached harbour, the rest hauled down their colours or were sunk, or burnt. The army held out for a little while; but after its commander had fled to Egypt, the remnant surrendered. Some legions were disbanded and sent home to Italy, others were incorporated in Octavian's forces.

It was all over. Octavian was Caesar in deed as well as in name. He was the supreme and undisputed ruler of Rome and of Rome's empire and destiny. But for so great a creation as the republic, it seemed that fate or nature had planned the most splendid and memorable obsequies of which history has record, last rites which Shakespeare has made immortal.

When Antony went on board Cleopatra's ship, he refused to speak to her or to anyone else. For three days he sat in the prow, dejected, silent, with his head in his hands. Only at the first landfall did the women succeed in persuading him to see Cleopatra and once again to eat and sleep with her. When they reached Egypt, Antony resumed his moody seclusion in a sea-girt tower near the Pharos; while Cleopatra busied herself in a scheme for having ships hauled over the isthmus of Suez, so as to sail away to a new life in the outer Orient. When this plan was frustrated by the jealous Nabataeans, who burned the first galleys to reach the Red Sea, Antony rejoined Cleopatra in her palace, and for the last time Alexandria was given up to feast-ing and jollity; only now the revellers called themselves no longer "The Inimitable Livers," but "The Diers Together." They knew the end was near—both of them. They had sent an embassy to Octavian, who was in Asia after wintering in Athens and paying a brief visit to Brundisium. Meanwhile Cleopatra started to in-vestigate the easiest manner of dying. Octavian made no answer to Antony, but he let Cleopatra understand that, provided she got rid of Antony, by death or exile, she herself might hope for generous treatment. Cleopatra solved the problem in a manner in which only a woman, and a Cleopatra at that, could solve it. To kill her lover, to exile her husband—how odious would such treachery make her in the eyes of all men, now and for ever after! No, she would do neither. But suppose he killed himself, for love of her, what then? Would not both of them win immortal renown? Yes, that was the way out—and it was so easy. In July of the year 30, when Octavian's cavalry approached Alexandria, Antony made one desperate sortie against them. It failed. His troops, like his ships, deserted him. At long last he railed against Cleopatra as the author of all his ills. She, ter-rified, retired to her family mausoleum and secured the en-trances with bolts and bars. Then she played her last ace: she sent messengers to Antony to say she was dead. He fell on his sword, mortally wounded. In a last access of passion, he had him-self carried to Cleopatra's tower, into which he was hoisted through an upper window by the queen herself and her women, she bent double with straining at the ropes, he holding up his hands to her, while those on the ground encouraged them. She laid him on her bed, and there he shortly afterwards died, bidding her at the last to make her peace with Octavian and to remember himself only as one who had once been happy and prosperous and was now "A Roman by a Roman, valiantly vanquished."

Hardly had Antony expired, when a Roman officer was announced. It was Proculeius, the one man Antony had bidden Cleopatra trust. Even so she would not admit him, but parleyed with him through the barred gate. She asked that her children might inherit her kingdom. Proculeius merely bade her be of good cheer and put her trust in Caesar. At the same time he had taken careful note of the lay-out of the building; so that when another officer came shortly afterwards as if to continue the negotiations, Proculeius with two men entered unseen through a window and was just in time to prevent Cleopatra killing herself with a dagger. After searching her clothing for concealed poison, he left her under guard. Octavian meanwhile had been told of Antony's death by one of the fallen man's bodyguard, who had taken the fatal sword to bear him witness. On hearing the news and seeing the blood-stained weapon, Octavian behaved in a thoroughly characteristic way. First, he retired into his tent and shed some decent tears over one who had been "allied to him in marriage, his colleague in empire, and companion in so many wars and dangers"—that would look well in the eyes of those who still admired Antony; he then came out, assembled his friends, and read to them the letters he had sent to Antony, as evidence of his own moderation, together with Antony's arrogant replies. That would show people that he had been forced into the opposition which had now ended so fatally. To make absolutely certain that it had ended, Octavian slaughtered little Caesarion and Antony's son by Fulvia, his eldest, Antyllus. There must be no rival heirs, no pretenders. As it happened, although no descendant of Octavian's ever occupied the imperial throne, three of Antony's did; because his surviving six children, brought up by Octavia, became great favourites of Octavian, and two of the daughters married into the imperial family, so that Antony became the ancestor of three later emperors.

Octavian had one interview with Cleopatra, which became a famous "set piece" in Roman annals. She had arranged herself on a sofa, dressed in nothing but one thin garment. About her she had arranged busts and other mementoes of the great Julius. When Octavian came in, she sprang up to welcome him. "Her old charm, and the boldness of her youthful beauty had not wholly left her, and in spite of her present condition, still sparkled from within." From her bosom she produced a sheaf of Julius' letters. She broke down; she cried, she entreated. All to no purpose. Octavian merely answered her point by point, like a lawyer. Cleopatra's steward, perhaps rehearsed for the part, now accused her of keeping back some of her treasure from her conqueror, into whose hands Cleopatra had put what she said was a full inventory of it. Cleopatra flew at the man, until Caesar restrained her. "Is it not hard," she said, "to be accused like this by one of my own servants, when all I have done is to put aside a few trinkets—not for my wretched self, but to give as presents to Livia and Octavia?" Caesar was delighted to hear her talk thus, because he was now persuaded that she meant to live. He was wrong.

One of Octavian's staff, who had a certain liking for Cleopatra, sent her word that she and the children were to be packed off to Rome in three days' time—which meant that she was being preserved to grace the triumph of the man whose great-uncle had made her his consort, and to be haled in chains through the streets of the city in which she had been borne as a queen. With Octavian's permission she made a last pilgrimage to Antony's tomb. Then, having secured herself an asp in an innocent-looking basket of figs, she arrayed herself in all her pomp, as the incarnation of Isis, and sought death by the agency of the peculiar creature of Isis, the asp. Before doing so she had written a letter to Caesar, asking that she might be buried in the same tomb as Antony. At once, on receiving it, he sent messengers to her dwelling. "The messengers came at full speed, and found the guards apprehensive of nothing, but on opening the doors they saw her stone-dead, lying upon a bed of gold, set out in all her royal ornaments."

She was thirty-nine years of age, had been a queen for twenty-two, and Antony's partner for fourteen. Antony was fifty-three. They were buried together, and with them was buried the Roman republic.

AUTHOR'S NOTE

I am grateful to my friend Geoffrey Woodhead, one of the best of our younger classical scholars, for the following valuable information on a confusing aspect of later Republican history.

The situation of Cisalpine Gaul was to some extent anomalous in the early triumviral period. It did become a proconsular province in the Sullan era, notwithstanding that *Cispadane* Gaul seems to have received the franchise at that time. Trans*padane* Gaul got the franchise from Caesar. This meant that between 49 and 42 the proconsular governor with his army was in fact ruling a province full of Roman citizens. After Philippi it seems to have been agreed that *Italia* should extend to the Alps, and although under Augustus generals are found operating there they are not proconsular governors and are in a rather ill-defined situation. They are usually there because of campaigns against intransigeant Alpine tribes.

SOME DATES

133   Destruction of Numantia. Attalus III of Pergamum bequeaths kingdom to Rome: it becomes province of Asia.

         Tiberius Gracchus tribune; attempts reforms; killed in riot.

123–22   Gaius Gracchus twice tribune; numerous reforms; killed in riot.

112–06   War against Jugurtha.

107   Marius opens army to all citizens.

102   Marius defeats Teutones at Aquae Sextiae, (Aix-en-Provence)

101   Marius annihilates Cimbri on Raudian plain.

103–99   Second Servile War in Sicily.

96   Cyrenaica bequeathed to Rome.

92   Iniquitous condemnation of P. Rutilius Rufus.

91   M. Livius Drusus tribune.

91–88   Social War; Italians force Rome to make them Roman citizens.

88   Sulla consul; occupies Rome by military force—the first Roman to do so.

88–84   First Mithradatic War. Sulla takes Athens, 86.

88–82   First civil war.

87   Marius takes Rome and with Cinna starts reign of terror.

86   Seventh consulship of Marius (d. 13 Jan).

83–72   Sertorius maintains Marian cause in Spain.

83   So-called Second Mithradatic War, defeat of Murena—Cappadocia evacuated.

82   Sulla enters Rome (1) in spring (2) after battle of Colline gate on 1st November; proscriptions.

81–79   Sulla's dictatorship; Sullan constitution.

79   Sulla resigns.

78   Death of Sulla.

74–63   Third Mithradatic War. Lucullus in Asia 74–66.

74–67   War against pirates—Pompey victorious.

73–71   Slave War—Spartacus.

66–63   Pompey in the East.

63   Cicero consul; suppresses Catiline's conspiracy; Pompey captures Jerusalem.

60   Pompey, Caesar, Crassus form compact usually called (but with no legal basis) First Triumvirate.

59   Caesar's first consulate. Granted five-year command in Cisalpine Gaul.

58   Clodius tribune; Cicero banished.

58–51   Caesar's conquest of Gaul. Britain twice invaded.

57   Cicero recalled.

56   Conference at Lucca.

55   Caesar's command prolonged for five years; Pompey given Spain, Crassus Syria, for same period.

53   Defeat and death of Crassus at Carrhae, with loss of twenty thousand dead, ten thousand prisoners and eagles of seven legions.

49–45   Second civil war. Caesar crosses Rubicon, Jan 49.

48   Battle of Pharsalus; Pompey defeated by Caesar and Antony; flees to Egypt, where murdered.

47   Caesar defeats Pharnaces at battle of Zela. *"Veni, vidi, vici."*

46   Caesar defeats Pompeians at Thapsus in Africa; Cato commits suicide at Utica. Caesar reforms calendar.

45   Caesar defeats last Pompeian army at Munda in Spain.

44   Caesar assassinated, 15th March. Octavius, Caesar's great-nephew and heir, arrives in Rome; assumes name Octavianus.

43–31   Third civil war.

43   Antony declared public enemy. Reconciliation, followed by Triumvirate of Antony, Octavian and Lepidus for five years. Proscription of two thousand knights and three hundred senators, including Cicero and his brother.

42   Republicans defeated at Philippi. Cassius and Brutus commit suicide.

40   Pact of Brundisium.

39   Conference at Misenum.

38–35   War with Sextus Pompeius.

37   Triumvirate renewed for five years.

36   Lepidus revolts and is discarded by Octavian; henceforth of no account (d. 13 B.C.).

35–33   Antony in the East; Octavian in Pannonia and Dalmatia.

32   Antony divorces Octavia; open breach with Octavian; war declared against Cleopatra.

31   Battle of Actium; total defeat of Antony and Cleopatra.

30   Octavian lands in Egypt; suicides of Antony and Cleopatra. Octavian sole master of Roman world, which he rules as Princeps and Imperator until death in A.D. 14, thus inaugurating Roman empire.

INDEX